Health Care for an Aging Population

Health Care for an Aging Population

Edited by
CHRIS HACKLER

State University of New York Press

"Future of Long-Term Care" by Robert L. Kane is printed with permission of the author.

Published by
State University of New York Press, Albany

© 1994 State University of New York

For information, address State University of New York Press,
State University Plaza, Albany, N.Y. 12246

Production by M. R. Mulholland
Marketing by Bernadette La Manna

Library of Congress Cataloging-in-Publication Data
Health care for an aging population / edited by Chris Hackler.
      p.   cm.
   Includes bibliographical references and index.
   ISBN 0-7914-1999-1 (acid-free).—ISBN 0-7914-2000-0 (acid-free :
pbk.)
      1. Health care reform—United States—Congresses.   2. Medical
care—Utilization—United States—Congresses.   3. Health care
rationing—United States—Congresses.   4. Right to health care-
-United States—Congresses.   5. Aged—Medical care—United States-
-Congresses.   I. Hackler, Chris.
RA395.A3H3957 1994
362.1'0973—dc20   93-37845
                                                                        CIP

10 9 8 7 6 5 4 3 2 1

Contents

Preface   vii

Introduction: Health Care Reform for an Aging Population   1
Chris Hackler

Part I. Aging, Justice, and Scarcity

1. Generational Equity in America: A Cultural Historian's Perspective   19
Thomas R. Cole
2. Between the Generations: Justice and Peace as Alternatives to Age-Based Rationing   33
Stephen G. Post
3. Justice within the Family   43
John R. Hardwig
4. Technological Determinism despite the Reality of Scarcity: A Neglected Element in the Theory of Spending for Medical and Health Care   57
James M. Buchanan

Part II. Rationing according to Age

5. Understanding Callahan   71
Janet A. Coy and Jonathan Schonsheck
6. Justice, Age Rationing, and the Problem of Identifiable Lives   93
Leonard M. Fleck
7. Age Cut-Offs for Health Care Entitlements: The Missing Moral Level   107
Howard Brody
8. Callahan's Medical Rationing Principle: Age or Quality of Life?   115
Sharon E. Sytsma
9. Designing Ethical Alternatives to Age-Based Rationing   121
Nancy S. Jecker and Robert A. Pearlman

Part III. Planning for the Future

10. A Values Framework for Health System Reform   145
Reinhard Priester

11. Limits and Equal Access to Basic Health Care: Suggestions for
    Comprehensive Reform   169
    Robert J. Barnet
12. Just Caring: Lessons from Oregon and Canada   177
    Leonard M. Fleck
13. Future of Long-Term Care   199
    Robert L. Kane
14. Taking the Next Steps: Devising a Good Lifespan for the Elderly   213
    Daniel Callahan

Contributors   225

Index   227

Preface

This collection of essays grew out of a conference held in Little Rock in April of 1989 that was organized around Daniel Callahan's book *Setting Limits: Medical Goals in an Aging Society* (Simon and Schuster, 1987). Most of the conference papers chosen for publication have been revised substantially, and a few additional essays have been solicited to round out the volume. While most of the chapters expressly address Dr. Callahan's book, the others focus more broadly on issues of health care reform.

The conference was organized by the Division of Medical Humanities of the University of Arkansas for Medical Sciences and served as the Spring National Meeting of the Society for Health and Human Values. It was supported by grants from the Morris Foundation, the Arkansas Humanities Council and the National Endowment for the Humanities. Judy Smith, the division's administrative secretary, devoted many hours to planning and running a successful conference and then to preparing the manuscript for publication. I want also to acknowledge the encouragement, skillful guidance, and cheerful patience of Priscilla Ross, my editor at SUNY Press.

I would like to dedicate the book to my parents, who exemplify a good old age; they are devoted to each other and to their family, generous toward the young, intellectually active, and involved in the community.

Introduction: Health Care Reform for an Aging Population

Chris Hackler

The need for change in the system of health care delivery in the United States has finally emerged as a political issue alongside continuing budget deficits, a growing national debt, declining educational outcomes, and decreased competitiveness of American business in the global economy. The two most pressing health care problems at the present time are rapidly increasing costs and lack of access to the system. A more distant but potentially more recalcitrant problem is the aging of our population. Early in the new century the proportion of retired citizens to workers will increase sharply. Soon thereafter the number of frail elderly will burgeon (see fig. 1). The result may be an unprecedented allocation of social resources to the very old. A lasting solution to the present crisis in health care must accommodate these demographic changes, and it must take account not only of the health of individuals but also of the common good and the vitality of society as a whole.

The essays in this volume explore the kinds of changes necessary to meet our long-term health care needs within a just and vibrant society. A focal point is a proposal by Daniel Callahan in his book *Setting Limits: Medical Goals in an Aging Society*[1] to withhold life-prolonging treatment at public expense from the very old. Several of the papers explore Callahan's rich philosophical account of the meaning of aging, the role of the elderly in society, and obligations between generations, as well as his controversial proposal to limit medical spending. Other essays look more broadly at the transformations required to meet both current and future problems and the values that should guide our attempts at comprehensive change. But first a word about the immediate need for health care reform.

The Current Problem

Rising Costs. Health care expenditures have increased over the last two decades an average of 11.6 percent per year, considerably higher than the overall rate of inflation of 8.7 percent.[2] Health care spending in the U.S. for 1992 was $838.5 billion, more than 14 percent of our gross domestic product (GDP). The previous director of the Office of Management and Budget testified before Con-

FIGURE 1

U.S. population aged 85 years or older, 1900 to 2050, in millions
(from the US Bureau of the Census).

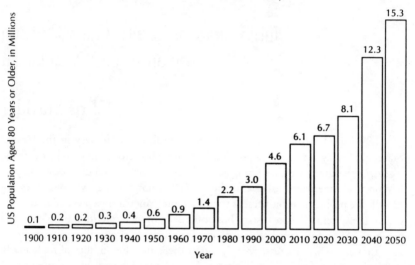

From T. Randall, "Demographers Ponder the Aging of the Aged and Await Unprecedented Looming Elder Boom" *Journal of the American Medical Association,* vol. 269,
p. 2332. Used with permission.

gress that without serious structural changes, health care would account for 17 percent of the GDP by 2000 and 37 percent by 2030.[3] These estimates now appear
conservative. Citizens on fixed incomes are hit hardest by rising costs. Older Americans spent 10.6 percent of their after-tax income for health care in 1961, before
the enactment of Medicare (which provides most of the cost of health care for all
citizens after the age of sixty-five). In 1991, even with the help of Medicare, out-
of-pocket expenses consumed 17.1 percent of their income.[4]

Individual consumers are not the only ones affected by escalating health care
costs. Increased government outlays through Medicare and Medicaid (the federal
health care assistance program for the poor) exacerbate the federal deficit. To control expenditures the government has reduced Medicare benefits, paid only a portion of Medicaid bills, and imposed a prospective payment scheme based on
averages rather than actual costs. The real cost of providing care has not diminished in proportion to the lower levels of reimbursements to physicians and hospitals. Consequently the surplus costs have been shifted from public to private
payers. Such cost shifting has further accelerated the increasing cost of health insurance for individuals and the cost of health coverage for businesses, putting them
at a competitive disadvantage. Chrysler Corporation estimates that health care

costs, including those of its suppliers, added $700 to the cost of each vehicle in 1989, about three times the added cost in Japan ($246) and Canada ($223). Ford Motor Company spends much more for health care than for steel.[5] As more of our money goes to health care, less is available for other critical social needs, such as education and economic investment. (Fig. 2 shows the change in outlay for some of these items.)[6]

There are many reasons for this relentless rise in the cost of health care. Malpractice insurance premiums continue to climb, reflecting increasing litigation and higher awards. Many physicians practice so-called defensive medicine, ordering tests and procedures of negligible benefit only to protect against a potential malpractice suit. A recent study concluded that about $10 billion is spent every year in this manner.[7] Patient education and preventive medicine receive little reward under the current system, which focuses on curing rather than avoiding illness. The cost of care is not addressed in medical education, so that physicians rarely know the cost of a test or procedure they order. This fact reflects a more pervasive attitude. As consumers we expect and demand the highest level of care available, which we equate with the most intensive, extensive, or expensive. We tend to think of medical care as an absolute priority, not subject to the cost-benefit comparisons that usually structure our economic choices (a point James Buchanan makes elegantly in his essay). Moreover, since our bills are usually paid by third parties,

FIGURE 2

Trend of Health Care Costs and Other Sector Expenditures as a Percentage of GNP.

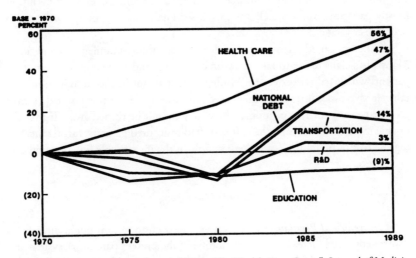

From J. K. Shelton and J. M. Janosi, "Unhealthy Health Care Costs," *Journal of Medicine and Philosophy,* vol. 17, p. 12. Used with permission.

there is little incentive for either consumers or providers to control spending. As a result, our hospitals spend vast amounts building, remodeling, and purchasing the latest technology in competition for patients. There are ten thousand mammogram machines in the United States, while only two thousand would be necessary to meet current demand, and five thousand would screen the entire population.[8] Surely a more rational deployment of resources would significantly reduce total health care outlay.

Limited Access. Americans who can afford it receive the technologically most advanced medical care in the world. Our formidable challenge is to preserve the quality of available care while gaining control over runaway costs and at the same time including all of our citizens in the system. It is clear that the problems of cost and access are related. Most obviously, fewer are able to afford insurance as the cost rises (fig. 3 illustrates this correlation).[9] A recent study by the Agency for Health Care Policy and Research of the Department of Health and Human Services has found that 20 percent of the population of the United States had no health insurance for some or all of 1987. More than twenty four million were uninsured for the entire year, and another twenty three million for part of the year. An estimated fifty million more are underinsured, with policies that provide inadequate coverage (a major illness could produce bankruptcy). Medicaid, the public assistance program for indigent patients, covers only the poorest of the poor in most states. The majority of these people without coverage are the working poor and their dependents. Many small businesses cannot afford to offer health insurance, and several larger and more prosperous companies avoid the expense by hiring mostly part-time workers. Self-employed, seasonal, and temporary workers also may lack coverage.

The uninsured often receive inadequate care under humiliating conditions. Many physicians refuse to take uninsured patients, and some even refuse to take patients with Medicaid coverage.[10] Individuals may not be able to obtain important elective procedures until their needs become acute. At this point they may go to expensive emergency rooms where they cannot be turned away. If they are unable to pay for their care, the cost is shifted to insured patients, further increasing the cost of premiums—another example of the inextricable link between cost and access.

Proposed Solutions

Incremental Revision. A conservative approach to reform might attempt to control costs and increase access by modifying the present patchwork system and encouraging individuals to be more circumspect and parsimonious in their consumption of health care services. To expand access, underwriting practices could be

FIGURE 3

U.S. Health Care Costs and the Uninsured, 1977–1988.

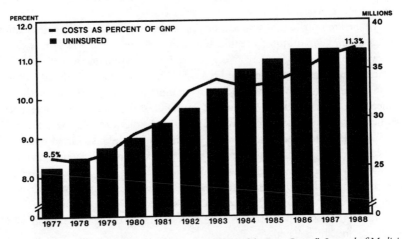

From J. K. Shelton and J. M. Janosi, "Unhealthy Health Care Costs," *Journal of Medicine and Philosophy* vol. 17, p. 10. Used with permission.

regulated so that fewer individuals are denied coverage or thrown into prohibitively expensive risk pools. Medicaid could be extended to cover the "uninsurable" (those who are already in poor health). Managed-care options in the private sector, such as health maintenance organizations or preferred provider arrangements, could be promoted in an effort to control costs. Individuals could be encouraged to accept more modest levels of care rather than demanding the best and most expensive care available. Advance directives could be promoted as a way of controlling wasteful end-of-life expenditures. In addition to the usual language that refuses life-prolonging treatment, clauses could be added to directives authorizing physicians and family to consider the cost of treatment and might explicitly reject expensive procedures that do not have corresponding benefits. Discounts mighteven be offered by insurance companies as an incentive to complete an advance directive.

It is highly doubtful, however, that sufficient savings could be realized from managed care and voluntary restraint to offset the added cost of extending access. Managed care has not had great success thus far in containing health care costs. Increased use of advance directives is unlikely to help significantly; patients who receive sustained intensive care before death account for only about 1 percent of total annual Medicare cost. Volume appears to be much more important than acute intensity of services in determining overall health care costs. Rather than so-called heroic medicine, it is repetition of comparatively "small ticket" items and the needs of chronic illness that are largely responsible for rising expenditures.[11] Concerning medical care in general, it seems naive to expect most Americans to request or voluntarily to accept a lower level of care than their coverage allows. Indeed, it seems unfair to reduce costs by encouraging sacrifice from the altruistic while others continue a more extravagant consumption of resources.

In the long run we must moderate our strong individualist orientation and embrace a more communitarian ethic, but reform of the health care system cannot wait for such a conversion. We must revise the system now so that cost-conscious choices are encouraged and rewarded. This might be attempted within the present market-oriented system by relying more heavily on private health insurance. All citizens would be encouraged through tax incentives to purchase their own health care policies on the private market. Subsidies for those with low incomes would be provided in the form of vouchers or tax credits. Rather than being expanded, Medicaid could be cut back to serve only as a safety net for individuals who cannot obtain private insurance because of a current illness or poor overall health. Cost-conscious consumers would encourage competition among insurers and providers to control costs. Cheaper policies with large deductibles might also help control costs by discouraging overuse of the system and rewarding "healthy behavior."

But it is difficult to see how this consumer choice or market approach could solve the dual problems of access and cost. If the incentives to purchase insurance are large, they will greatly increase the budget deficit, offsetting any savings on Medicaid. If they are small, then many individuals and families will not purchase insurance or will purchase only limited coverage. When they need care it will be provided in the expensive emergency room setting, and the resulting cost shifting will make insurance more expensive. Moreover, a more competitive free-market approach to insurance will intensify risk pooling and the other underwriting practices that place coverage out of reach of the people who need it most, throwing them back on the public sector. A private insurance solution might work if universal coverage could be achieved, but that would entail forcing individuals to purchase insurance and prohibiting discriminatory underwriting practices, neither of which would be attractive to civil libertarians or proponents of free markets. Finally, that competition and enlightened choice would control costs is dubious, since there seems to be little disincentive to develop and use increasingly expensive technology. As we have seen, competition in the health care industry as it is currently structured tends to increase costs rather than diminish them.

Comprehensive Reform. The only effective way to resolve the current crisis in health care is to develop a system that features both universal coverage and budget limits. Universal coverage is necessary, not only because social justice requires it but also because it is the only way to stop cost shifting. Budget limits are likewise necessary to develop and enforce cost-control mechanisms and to maintain a predictable level of spending. The challenge is to design a program that preserves the present system's quality of care, is achievable politically, and is congruent with basic American values of professional autonomy, market economics, and consumer choice. (Reinhard Preister carefully explores these and other basic American values that are likely to shape health care reform.) Socialized medicine, for example, in which physicians are salaried employees of a comprehensive, centrally budgeted and administered system, would provide the most reliable control of costs, but it is neither socially nor politically acceptable at the present time. By general agreement the two most realistic possibilities for attaining universal coverage and budget limits within a largely private system of health care delivery are mandated employment-based coverage and national health insurance.

Mandated Employer Coverage. The politically easiest means to universal coverage is some kind of mandated employer coverage, since it would build on the present system and would preserve the private insurance sector. Most Americans receive their health insurance as an added benefit of employment. We tend to think of workplace coverage as part of the natural order of things, but our system actually took root during World War II, in large part because health benefits were exempt from wartime wage controls and thus could be offered (or demanded) in lieu of a raise in salary. After the war and the lifting of wage controls, the IRS ruled that the cost of health insurance was deductible from taxable income, and the popularity of employment-based coverage was more firmly established.[12]

One basic problem with this arrangement is that it has never covered everyone. Not all businesses offer health insurance, and the unemployed are left with inadequate public programs such as Medicaid. Since it does form our largest base of coverage, however, it seems to many the easiest route to universal coverage. We could simply require every business to provide a minimum level of coverage, with defined benefits, to all its employees. Or we could adopt a so-called play-or-pay system that would require businesses to provide the minimum level of coverage ("play") or pay into a public fund from which the uninsured would be covered. Small firms could pay the same rate at large ones, since the employees of many small firms would be combined to form large pools. The unemployed would still need to be covered, either by extending Medicaid or by including them in the large insurance pools with government subsidy.

The principal organized opposition to mandated coverage comes from small businesses. Among firms with fewer than ten employees, less than half offer health insurance.[13] Many fear that this added cost could not be absorbed, especially at current prices for small-group coverage. For this reason mandated coverage must be accompanied by measures to reduce and control those prices. In addition to pooling of coverage for small-business employees we might do away with current practices of risk rating, that is, varying the cost of coverage according to the health status of the individual, and return to "community rating," that is, basing a single price for a given level of coverage on the average health care costs for an entire community (not just healthy employed people). This would be good for the unemployed as well as for small businesses, since everyone could purchase coverage at the same rates. It would not be good, however, for large business, whose favored rates would rise. More large firms could convert to self-insurance to preserve their advantage, skimming the cream and militating against the concept of community rating.

The most important factor in controlling the cost of health insurance, of course, is controlling the cost of health care. Spending is more difficult to control under a fragmented system of employer-based coverage and private insurance than under a single-payer program of national health insurance. Nevertheless there are some successful models to examine. Hawaii has had a system of em-ployer-based universal coverage for almost two decades. It combines mandated coverage with state subsidies and a state insurance pool for the unemployed. In-surers agreed to return to community ratings, and costs are controlled through annual fee-setting negotiations between insurers and providers. As a result, while everything else is more expensive in this island state, health insurance premiums in Hawaii are the lowest in the country.[14] Germany provides another example of a decentralized system with effective cost control. Most coverage is supplied by a multitude of regional, not-for-profit insurance organizations known as "sickness funds." All employers are required to contribute at rates determined by the vari-ous funds. Fees are negotiated with physicians' associations, and rates are estab-lished with hospitals—the same daily rate for every patient, regardless of diagnosis. Under this system West Germany was able to restrict its growth in health care spending during the 1980s to the overall rate of growth of its gross domestic product.[15]

National Health Insurance. An important element of the cost of health care in the United States is the expense of administering a diverse system of private health insurance. Under our present system insurance is provided by a multitude of companies competing on the private market, each with its own procedures and forms to complete for reimbursement. There are hundreds of kinds of policies and many levels of risk rating. Each company has its own administrative staff, and each provider must have several employees involved in keeping records and filling out various reimbursement forms. Add Medicare and Medicaid regulations and forms, and the result is that too much of our health care spending goes into administra-tion and paperwork and too little into actual patient care. In 1987 the average overhead cost of private insurance carriers was 11.9 percent of premiums, com-pared to administrative costs of 3.2 percent for government programs (primarily Medicare and Medicaid). Administrative costs for public and private programs combined accounted for 5.1 percent of all health care expenditures in the United States. By contrast the cost of administering the public health insurance program in Canada was only 0.9 percent, and the figure for public and private programs was 1.2 percent.[16]

How do the Canadians keep administrative costs so low? They have a single-payer system of national health insurance, covering all citizens equally, administered by the government and financed by taxes in lieu of insurance premiums. Consumers have freedom of choice among private practioners, but as the single payer the government can set budgets and negotiate reasonable fees with providers. Seventy-three percent of all health spending is public (compared to 42 percent in the U.S.). There is a small private-insurance sector, but it is restricted by law to benefits not included in the public program. Out-of-pocket payments are estimated to constitute 20 percent of all health expenditures (about the same as in the U.S.).[17] In addition to universal coverage, administrative efficiency, and budgetary control, a system of national health insurance offers significant advantages. Since health insurance is uncoupled from employment, workers may change jobs without fear of losing their coverage. Dependents will remain insured if they become widowed or divorced from an employed spouse. Differential tax rates correlate coverage with ability to pay, avoiding inefficient and potentially humiliating means-testing for public subsidies. Businesses need no longer purchase insurance in an unpredictable market and administer their own benefit programs.

There are two large problems with instituting a system of national health insurance in the United States: an immediate surge in unemployment and an uncertain "utilization response" to the new system. First, it is obvious that large numbers of insurance company employees (as well as billing clerks in hospitals and doctor's offices) would be out of work. Some, but not all, would find employment with the new public program, since the single-payer system would be more efficient. Most of these skilled workers would find jobs sooner or later, but the immediate effect on an economy just beginning to recover from stagnation could be very serious. For these reasons we might have to phase in the new system, thus producing no effective cost controls for several more years. A new administration pledged to all three goals of economic growth, deficit reduction, and immediate control of health care spending would face obvious political difficulties with a conversion to national health insurance. Although it seems to offer the best opportunity for long-term cost control and overall economic vitality, the short-term damage could be great.

The second serious concern is with the so-called utilization response to the new system: would the response to free care be a surge in demand? If so, savings in administrative efficiency could be more than offset by increased consumption of services. One study estimates that universal access to free care would inflate expenditures by $78.2 billion over 1991 levels while saving only $46.8 billion in administrative costs.[18] This contradicts an earlier calculation that administrative savings would be sufficient to fund care for the uninsured and underinsured.[19] All such predictions are generated from economic models that cannot adequately anticipate the complex behavior of both patients and providers. We simply do not know what level of use to expect. Canada experienced no massive increase when its system was introduced, but as Barer and Evans aptly note, the United States of 1993 is quite different from the Canada of 1967.

A system that is awash with human and physical capacity and technical possibilities, and chafing under utilization constraints that, while ineffective in aggregate, are still onerous and offensive, might very well respond to the extension of coverage with a significant increase in recommended diagnostic and therapeutic interventions. After all, one of the most common arguments for a universal system is to provide "needed" care for those left out at present.[20]

Setting Priorities. Regardless of the direction health reform takes, moving from partial to universal coverage will be highly inflationary at the present rate of consumption. Reductions will be necessary somewhere—in fees, levels of coverage, or availability of services—to offset this inflationary pressure. Oregon has developed a plan for extending coverage to all citizens while holding spending to current levels. It includes a play-or-pay requirement for employers, a high-risk pool funded from public and private sources, and a redistribution of Medicaid funds. The last feature has drawn the most attention. Under the proposed plan Medicaid eligibility would be extended to everyone below the federal poverty level. In order to cover more people with the same amount of money, fewer services will be included in the Medicaid benefit package. A commission was created by the state legislature to develop, in the words of the authorizing legislation, "a list of health services ranked by priority, from the most important to the least important, representing the comparative benefits of each service to the entire population to be served." Services would be included in the package as far down the list as budgeted funds would allow. The state has finally obtained a waiver from the federal government allowing it to use Medicaid funds in the proposed manner.

A national system with universal coverage would obviate the need for Oregon to implement its own program, but its method of distributing scarce financial resources could be an important part of any national plan. While other schemes rely on some combination of fee negotiations, managed care, waiting lists, or triage, Oregon's plan is designed to control costs by explicitly limiting services. Prioritizing services could help determine minimum benefits for nationally standardized insurance policies. Prioritizing could also contribute to a single-payer system, since it would allow periodic adjustment in coverage to enforce limits on spending. In combination with negotiated provider charges and limited deployment of expensive technology, it could be a powerful and flexible tool for both setting and enforcing a global budget. Leonard Fleck's second essay provides a detailed analysis of Oregon's approach and of its possible role in a single-payer system. He also provides a critical account of the managed competition version of employment-based coverage and suggests a hybrid version that would borrow some features from the Canadian model.

Planning for the Future

Our Aging Population. Lurking in the shadows of the debate on health care reform is a problem that threatens eventually to undermine any potential solution. Due in part to the postwar baby boom and subsequent steady decline in the birth rate, the average age of our population is steadily increasing. The trend will slow somewhat during the remainder of this decade, due to the relatively low birth rate during the Great Depression of the 1930s, but it will take a sharp upturn early in the next century. The first wave of the baby boom generation will reach retirement age (and eligibility for Social Security as well as Medicare) about 2011. By 2020, the elderly will account for approximately half of the nation's health care expenditures.[21] By 2040, the average age of the baby-boom generation will be eighty-five. After eighty-five average health costs increase dramatically.[22] Spending on hip fractures, for example, is projected to increase from $1.6 billion in 1987 to as much as $6 billion in 2040 (in constant 1987 dollars). More sobering still is the projection for the cost of care for demented individuals. The prevalence of dementia rises sharply after age eighty-five; those who reach eighty-five have better than a 1 in 4 chance of becoming demented (this estimate may well be too low). In 2040 the cost of caring for demented patients alone is projected to be greater than the current federal deficit.[23]

Hip fractures and dementia are only two of the age-related conditions that require long-term care. Any comprehensive reform, indeed any reform of the health care system that hopes to provide access to basic care and control costs, must include long-term care. There are more residents of nursing homes than patients in hospitals or even available hospital beds.[24] Medicare does not include nursing home coverage, and the small number of private insurance policies available are of uncertain value. Nursing home stays are financed by personal savings and, when those are depleted, by Medicaid. Given current patterns of disability and nursing home use, the cost of long-term care could rise by 2040 to between $84 and $139 billion (in constant 1985 dollars).[25] Long-term care is not synonymous with nursing home care, though currently they are largely the same. Most of the millions of individuals who need long-term care neither want nor need nursing home placement, but their options are limited. We must find ways to make nursing homes more humane and efficient, provide less dispiriting and expensive alternatives to nursing home care, and integrate long-term care—both structurally and financially—into a comprehensive system of health care delivery.

Robert Kane elaborates each of these goals and suggests ways we can assess and assure quality of care.

Even without additional spending on long-term care, the share of the federal budget dedicated to pensions and health care is projected to increase from a current 40 percent to 60 percent by 2040. Without a sizeable tax increase, which seems unlikely, the money to fund entitlement programs for the elderly may be taken from other sectors of the budget, such as education, public works, and public assistance. If taxes were increased to cover such costs, there might be little remaining in the way of private savings to invest in the economy. Thus, a poorly educated, economically stagnant and stratified society could be the consequence of meeting all the health care demands of our aging population.

Age-Based Rationing. One way to deal with increasing expenditures due to the aging of the population is to limit care to the aged. In his book *Setting Limits* Daniel Callahan proposes that life-extending medical treatment not be provided at public expense after a certain age. This policy should be implemented in the context of an enriched understanding of the meaning of aging and of the role of the elderly in society. A special role—as conservators of the past and teachers of youth—ensures that their exclusion from certain benefits does not mean exclusion from the moral community. Furthermore, life-extending care should be rationed only when society commits itself to easing the suffering of old age and improving the quality of life of the elderly. He does not specify an age but suggests that by the late seventies or early eighties we have achieved, or had a opportunity to achieve, life's important goals and rewards and face ever more costly and debilitating medical problems. Rather than prolong lives of increasing incapacity, society should use its resources to see that younger citizens have the same opportunity to live out a "natural life span."

Several of the essays in this volume address the major themes of *Setting Limits.* Thomas Cole examines Callahan's account of the meaning of aging and of fairness between generations from a social historian's perspective. He believes that disputes about generational equity reflect broader social forces, such as the decline of American military and economic power, skepticism about the liberal welfare state, and the loss of a unifying conception of the life cycle. Stephen Post tries to modulate the adversarial tone of the intergenerational equity debate; he develops an image of mutual obligations based on the Judeo-Christian concept of 'covenant' and calls for a communitarian balance of rights with responsibilities. John Hardwig refocuses concerns about generational equity on individual families. Careers or marriages can be threatened by the demands of constant care for frail or demented parents. Savings may be depleted by lengthy hospital or nursing home stays. We currently authorize adult children to make health care decisions for their incapacitated parents but expect them to consider only the interests of the patient, however marginal, and never their own, however great. Hardwig argues for a more balanced approach to such decisions, taking into account everyone's interests and burdens.

The second part of the book is devoted to the difficult and painful issue of age-based rationing of medical care. Callahan's proposal to limit public funding of life-prolonging treatment for the very old prompted immediate and widespread criticism. Janet Coy and Jonathan Schonsheck argue that much of the criticism is based on misunderstanding or a superficial reading of the book. They carefully reconstruct and elaborate Callahan's argument and defend it against some of his leading critics. Leonard Fleck examines the charge that, because lifesaving treatment would be denied to identifiable individuals, Callahan's proposal is not only unethical but also unworkable. As a society we tolerate the sacrifice of "statistical lives" resulting from public policy decisions (e.g., not to fund maternal health clinics or childhood inoculations), but we will spare no expense to save identifiable individuals whose lives are in danger—a trapped coal miner for example. Fleck analyzes the so-called rule of rescue and finds that the rescue analogy does not apply to age-based rationing of medical care. Howard Brody proposes an alternative to a government-imposed age limit, that the elderly consult a "peer network"—a group of respected close associates with whom one's life plan has been developed—to consider whether or not life-extending treatment would be appropriate. Sharon Sytsma agrees with Callahan that rationing medical care will be necessary, but when she examines his position she finds the ultimate basis to be, not age, but quality of life, a criterion she herself finds preferable. Jecker and Pearlman formulate a number of arguments against age-based rationing and then explore some alternative criteria for allocating scarce medical resources. They conclude that basic health care should be available to all and that publicly funded nonbasic services may be allocated according to medical benefit.

The essays in part 3 that have previously been mentioned examine the more general problem of health care reform and explore some further alternatives to setting limits based upon age. The closing paper by Callahan is a response to his critics and a further elaboration of his views on the meaning of old age and its place in allocation decisions. He distinguishes between fixed and flexible categorical standards, assesses the merits of each, and closes with some thoughts about adopting and implementing his proposals in a democratic and pluralistic society.

Notes

A somewhat different version of this introduction was published under the title "Health Care Reform in the United States" in *Health Care Analysis*, vol. 1, no. 1 (1993), pp. 5–13. Used with permission of *Health Care Analysis* (Chichester, England: John Wiley and Sons, Ltd.).

1. D. Callahan, *Setting Limits: Medical Goals in an Aging Society.* (New York: Simon and Schuster, 1987)

2. S. F. Jenks and G. J. Schieber, "Containing U.S. Health Care Costs: What Bullet to Bite?" *Health Care Financing Review* 1991 Annual Supplement, pp. 1–12.

3. S. T. Sonnefeld, R. Waldo, J. A. Lemieu, and D. R. McKusic, "Projections of National Health Expenditures Through the Year 2000," *Health Care Financing Review,* vol. 13, no. 1 (Fall 1991), pp. 1–15.

4. *Health Cost Squeeze on Older Americans: A Report by the Families USA Foundation* (Washington, D.C., 1992).

5. H. Meyer, "Embattled Insurers Fight for Survival," *American Medical News,* Jan. 18, 1992, p. 1.

6. J. K. Shelton and J. M. Janosi, "Unhealthy Health Care Costs," *Journal of Medicine and Philosophy,* vol. 17 (1992), pp. 7–19.

7. B. McCormick, "Study: Defensive Medicine Costs Nearly $10 Billion," *American Medical News,* Feb. 15, 1993.

8. M. L. Brown, L. G. Kessler, and F. G. Rueter, "Is the Supply of Mammography Machines Outstripping Need and Demand? An Economic Analysis," *Annals of Internal Medicine,* vol. 113, (1990), pp. 547–52.

9. Shelton and Janosi, "Unhealthy Health Care Costs."

10. P. Braveman, T. Bennett, C. Lewis, S. Egerter, and J. Showstack, "Access to Prenatal Care Following Major Medicaid Eligibility Expansions," *Journal of the American Medical Association,* vol. 269, (1993), pp. 1285–89.

11. J. R. Webster, Jr., and C. Berdes. "Ethics and Economic Realities," *Archives of Internal Medicine,* vol. 150 (1990), pp. 1795–97.

12. P. Budetti, "Universal Health Care Coverage—Pitfalls and Promise of an Employment-Based Approach," *Journal of Medicine and Philosophy* vol. 17 (1992), pp. 21–32.

13. U.S. General Accounting Office, *Health Insurance: Cost Increases Lead to Coverage Limitations and Cost Shifting,* GAO/HRD 90–68 General Accounting Office, (Washington, D.C:1990).

14. J. C. Lewin and P. A. Sybinsky, "Hawaii's Employer Mandate and Its Contribution to Universal Access," *Journal of American Medical Association,* vol. 269 (1993), pp. 2538–43.

15. J. K. Iglehart, "Germany's Health Care System" (first of two parts), *New England Journal of Medicine,* vol. 324 (1991), pp. 503–8.

16. S. Woolhandler and D. U. Himmelstein, "The Deteriorating Administrative Efficiency of the U.S. Health Care System," *New England Journal of Medicine,* vol. 324 (1991), pp. 1253–58.

17. G. J. Schriber, J. -P. Poullier, and L. M. Greenwald, "U.S. Health Expenditure Performance: An International Comparison and Data Update," *Health Care Financing Review,* vol. 13, no. 4 (Summer 1992), pp. 1–15.

18. J. F. Shields, G. J. Young, and R. J. Rubin, "O Canada: Do We Expect Too Much from Its Health System?" *Health Affairs,* vol. 11, no. 1, (Spring 1992), pp. 7–20.

19. S. Woolhandler and D. U. Himmelstein, "Free Care: a Quantitative Analysis of Health and Cost Effects of a National Health Program for the United States," *International Journal of Health Services,* vol. 18 (1988), pp. 393–99.

20. M. L. Barer and R. G. Evans, "Interpreting Canada: Models, Mind-Sets, and Myths," *Health Affairs,* vol. 11, no. 1 (Spring 1992), pp. 44–61,

21. U.S. Department of Health and Human Services, *Health United States 1984,* Publication PHS 88–1232 (Hyattsville, Md.: U.S. Department of Health and Human Services, 1988).

22. E. Munoz, R. Rosner, D. Chalfin, J. Goldstein, I. Margolis, L. Wise. "Age, Resource Consumption, and Outcome for Medical Patients at an Academic Medical Center," *Archives of Internal Medicine,* vol. 149 (1989), pp. 1946–50.

23. E. L. Schneider and J. M. Guralnik, "The Aging of America: Impact on Health Care Costs," *Journal of the American Medical Association,* vol. 263, (1990), pp. 2335–40.

24. *Hospital Statistics* (Chicago: American Hospital Association, 1987).

25. Schneider and Guralnik, "Aging of America."

I

Aging, Justice, and Scarcity

Generational Equity in America: A Cultural Historian's Perspective

Thomas R. Cole

A specter is haunting America—the specter of old age.[1] Since the 1970s, awareness that America is an aging society has blended silently into fears of nuclear holocaust, environmental deterioration, military and economic decline, social conflict, and cultural decadence. The "first new nation," [2] now a declining empire,[3] no longer seems exempt from Old World destinies. The current mood of pessimism—the loss of faith in a secure and better future—is particularly strong among many who are now reaching middle age. Awakening from a privileged youth spent amidst the unprecedented prosperity that followed World War II, the baby-boom generation (nearly one-third of the total U.S. population) today finds itself the first in American history that cannot count on surpassing its parents' station in life. Prohibitive housing prices, high interest rates, sluggish economic growth, and glutted job markets have turned confident expectations of upward mobility into a gloomy view of the future. This pessimism may not be unfounded: massive trade deficits, the continuing decline of the U.S. manufacturing sector, and the low wages paid to most workers in the growing service sector of the economy cast considerable doubt that today's younger workers will achieve anything like the rising standard of living their parents enjoyed in the 1950s and 1960s.[4]

Beginning in the late 1970s, these frustrations and a growing disenchantment with welfare-state liberalism supplied a new and surprising political color to images of aging and intergenerational relations. Critics of Social Security and Medicare blamed the deteriorating economic condition of children[5] and families on the "graying of the federal budget" (more than half of all federal social spending goes to the elderly) and raised the specter of intergenerational warfare between young and old. Since 1985, these views have been widely publicized by Americans for Generational Equity, an advocacy group that argues that society is displacing current costs onto future generations and ignoring its obligations to children and the unborn. The group trades on the image of a powerful gerontocratic lobby—ruthless in its pursuit of hard-earned tax dollars to buy mink coats, golf carts, and condos.

Until quite recently, the elderly enjoyed a privileged status in welfare-state programs—built on an image of old people as poor, frail, and dependent.[6] But as the generational equity campaign portrays them as politically powerful, selfish, and potentially dangerous, the dynamics of interest-group liberalism are now turning against them. Most of today's retired elderly enjoy generous public entitlements, while younger workers generally pay (directly or indirectly) one dollar in seven to the Social Security system. According to recent polls, surprisingly few young people believe that the system will provide adequately for them when they reach retirement. They have heard forecasts of future "bankruptcy" of Social Security. They know that there will be a smaller ratio of workers to retirees when they leave the labor force. Saddled with a staggering national debt, surprised by the unexpected longevity of their parents, frightened by the rising medical costs of an aging population, many feel as if they were *Born to Pay.*[7]

For the first time in history, most people can expect to live into the "long late afternoon of life." Whereas American life expectancy in 1900 was about forty-nine, today's children will live an average of about seventy-five years (seventy-one for men, seventy-eight for women). This increase represents two-thirds of all the gains in life expectancy achieved since the emergence of the human species! Since 1968, mortality among the elderly has fallen substantially, suggesting that we are not yet reaching the limits of the human life span. While individuals are living longer, they are also having fewer children, creating an older population. In 1920, 4.6 percent of the U.S. population was sixty-five years or older. In 1984, this figure reached 11.8 percent. By 2030, when the baby boom cohort is passing through old age, at least one in every five Americans will be elderly.[8]

Not only are more people living longer; in the American welfare state they are also healthier and more financially secure than ever. Since the 1960s, liberal Social Security benefits have reduced poverty among the elderly from an average of 35 percent to less than 14 percent. Thanks to Medicare and Medicaid, more older people are able to see physicians and to receive long-term care.

Nevertheless, the generational equity campaign's myth of the affluent elderly is seriously flawed; poverty and disease among the very old, women, and minorities remain more recalcitrant than ever.[9] American aging policy does not meet the health or income needs of an important minority of elders.[10] Still, it has been far more successful than programs designed for children and young families, and it has avoided the deep funding cuts that other social programs received during the Reagan era.

Today aging policy faces a series of problems that neither liberal (more professional intervention, more entitlements, more taxes) nor conservative (marketplace solutions: more self-reliance, more savings) perspectives adequately address.[11] Generational equity is only the most visible and widely publicized of these problems, which are rooted in the decline of American military and economic power, the legitimation crisis of the liberal welfare state, and the aging of our population. In addition, the question of justice between the old and the young is also linked to the "spiritual situation of the age"[12]—in particular, our culture's inability to provide convincing answers to deeper existential questions like the quality of life in old age, the unity and integrity of the life cycle, and the meaning of aging.

The current fiscal dilemmas of aging policy originated in the late 1970s, when high inflation (cost-of-living adjustments grew more quickly than anticipated) and slow economic growth rapidly drained Social Security trust funds.[13] Social Security quickly lost its status as an untouchable "sacred cow." Emphasizing that the ratio of beneficiaries to workers had dropped from 1:40 in 1940 to 1:3.3 in 1980, neoconservatives raised the specter of an aging society. Forecasts of intergenerational Armageddon and of Social Security's collapse made alarming headlines.[14] The elderly lost their "favored" ideological status as "deserving poor" and increasingly were portrayed as a threat to the future.

In May 1981, the Reagan administration's first attempts to cut Social Security were soundly rebuffed. In 1982, Reagan appointed a bipartisan National Commission on Social Security Reform. In 1983, its recommendations—delayed cost-of-living increases, taxes on upper-income recipients, and gradual increase of the system's minimum retirement age in the twenty-first century—were adopted. As Achenbaum shows in Social Security: Visions and Revisions,[15] policy makers once again resorted to short-term tinkering with the system rather than face its long-term financial and ideological problems.

The 1983 amendments to the Social Security Act quieted voices of doom, but not for long. Soon after Reagan's reelection came rumblings of the next battle over old-age security: the financing of health care. In the last several years, rising health care costs for the elderly have generated a new sense of alarm. Since 1965, the costs of Medicare and Medicaid have grown so rapidly (and are projected to rise even faster) that observers like Daniel Callahan now fear that the humane programs of medical care for the elderly begun in the 1960s and 1970s will, if continued unabated, become a "new social threat in the late 1980s and 1990s." Total health care costs for people sixty-five and over are expected to grow (in constant dollars) from $50 billion in 1978 to $200 billion in 2000; during these years, the proportion supported by public expenditures will grow from $29 billion to $114 billion.[16]

While epidemiologists disagree about the future health status of the aged, it is clear that longer life has brought with it an increase in chronic disease—a trend that could accelerate in the future.[17] Regardless of which epidemiological forecast one prefers,[18] the sheer growth in the number of older people is staggering. In 1985, the number of people over sixty-five in America exceeded the number under age eighteen; the fastest growing age group today is that of those eighty-five and older, whose numbers will double in the next twenty years. There is little doubt that the elderly's need for health care, especially medical services (outpatient care, hospitalization, home care, hospice care, long-term care) will continue to increase dramatically.

These trends have led to considerable uneasiness (and not only among yuppies and neoconservatives) about the increasingly large share of health care dollars spent on the elderly. Like the "graying" of the federal budget in general, these trends raise questions of intergenerational equity and the social meaning of late life that welfare-state liberals, mainstream gerontologists, and aging advocates have preferred to ignore.

How should we distribute limited health care resources between the old and the young? Is it fair to spend such a large proportion of our health expenditures on the dying elderly? Do these expenditures actually benefit them? Should we be devoting so much of our biomedical research and technology to the diseases of aging? Since none of us live behind the Rawlsian "veil of ignorance" but rather within particular historical and cultural circumstances, questions of distributive justice inevitably lead to questions of social meaning. How do we justify funds spent on a population that is not economically productive? What "good" are old people anyway? What do they contribute to the rest of society? Are there any special virtues or obligations particular to old age? Two moral philosophers have recently taken up these questions from different perspectives but with similar results. Both Daniel Callahan[19] and Norman Daniels[20] construct arguments attempting to justify the provision of a decent minimum of health care for the elderly, health care designed to relieve suffering and improve quality—not quantity—of life. Callahan's book *Setting Limits: Medical Goals in an Aging Society* has sparked a great deal of controversy, primarily for its recommendation that we should set limits to health care costs by withholding certain life-prolonging technology on the basis of chronological age. This is unfortunate, since the most important and enduring aspects of Callahan's book lie elsewhere. Callahan never makes clear how his scheme would save a significant amount of money. His call for relief of suffering and better long-term care could easily be more expensive than life prolongation. And, at bottom, he is interested not only in cost containment but also in philosophizing (in the best sense) about aging and the proper goals of medicine in the face of decline and death.

Callahan's book is fundamentally an attack on the indiscriminate use of biomedical technology to prolong life indefinitely. It is also an attempt to rethink the meaning of old age itself. Echoing several essays in *What Does It Mean to Grow Old?*[21] Callahan deplores the absence of "a coherent, established, and meaningful place" for the elderly in our society. As a communitarian, Callahan thinks we should define the primary purpose of old age as service to the young, rather than individual pursuit of pleasure. He has little patience for the retired couples traveling cross-country with bumper stickers that read, "We are spending our children's inheritance."

Like the old characters in Willa Cather's fiction, Callahan's ideal elders live primarily to benefit their grandchildren. When this communal obligation has been fulfilled, death can be understood as the completion of a natural life span rather than as a failed quest for immortality. This notion of living within the limits of a natural lifespan calls to mind Thomas Jefferson's words. "It is reasonable that we should drop off," he wrote to John Adams in their old age, "and make room for another growth. When we have lived our generation out, we should not wish to encroach upon another."

Once we have lived into our late seventies or early eighties (Callahan allows for variation on individual biographies), society should not use up expensive resources trying to keep us alive. It should, however, guarantee us a decent minimum of palliative care. Callahan contributes two important arguments that are often overlooked in the controversy over his proposal for rationing life-prolonging technology: first, he makes the very un-American claim that old age is a biological limit that we should respect rather than an "endless frontier" for biomedical conquest; second, he decries the impoverished social meaning of aging and calls for public debate about the nature and purposes of late life in the context of a "natural life span."

Norman Daniels is alarmed by the widespread talk of the young and old competing for resources.[22] But he resists the knee-jerk liberal response of blaming the problem on the defense buildup or on attempts to roll back the welfare state. Daniels affirms that generational equity is a genuine moral problem in our aging society, albeit one that is susceptible to political abuse. In *Am I My Parents' Keeper? An Essay on Justice Between the Young and the Old,* he develops a philosophically rigorous argument for meeting the health care needs of all the elderly within a framework that is fair to other age groups.

While Daniels also uses the life span as a central category of analysis, he rejects Callahan's communication assumption that we can prescribe what is "good" or "right" for people at different stages of their lives. Instead, he argues that we should distribute resources to different age groups according to impartial principles that permit individuals to pursue their own opportunities. Daniels calls on us to stop thinking that different age groups must compete for resources in the here and now. Instead, we should realize that over a lifetime, resources are distributed *within stages of life,* rather than *between age groups.*[23] From this perspective, age-based entitlement programs do not take resources from one age group to benefit another; rather, they are a vehicle for "savings" that provides a prudent allocation of resources to different stages of life (in his terms, a "Prudential Lifespan Account").

Like Callahan, Daniels urges us to reduce lavish expenditures designed to prolong the dying of terminally ill patients and to invest in long-term care (medical and mental health care, nursing care, rehabilitative therapy, personal-care services, and social services). He rightly stresses the moral importance of long-term care, which has long been the "neglected step-child" of our health care system.[24] Poor patients in need of skilled care have difficulty finding nursing home placements. Others are prematurely institutionalized because federal policy will not pay for nonmedical home-care services. Nursing home costs and the eligibility requirements for Medicaid drive many spouses into poverty. Families—largely women—providing long-term care receive little support and few services to ease their burden.

It is no accident that both the communitarian Callahan and the liberal-Rawlsian Daniels use the life span (or life cycle or life course) as a fundamental unit of analysis. Like others who have responded to the generational equity movement,[25] Callahan and Daniels turn to this universal category as a way of undercutting the divisiveness enhanced by focusing on age—groups, cohorts, or generations. Daniels's "Prudential Lifespan Account" is particularly effective in disproving the assumption that because the elderly consume a disproportionately large percentage of health care they are receiving more than their "fair share."

In some ways, Daniels's book is really a philosophical and egalitarian version of the liberal ideology that has, until recently legitimated Social Security. Individuals are encouraged to think that they are "saving" or insuring themselves against the vicissitudes of old age and disability. The primary justification for support or care for the elderly derives not from intergenerational obligations but from equal opportunity to pursue one's own life plan at every stage of life. Prudence leads people to support programs, not out of commitment to a common good, but because they have a common stake. And in a society characterized by mass longevity, a life course perspective *can* encourage a kind of solidarity between age groups. Growing up *and* old is both a fate and a privilege that virtually all of us share. The elderly are indeed ourselves or our future selves. Unfortunately, this kind of solidarity is precisely what is threatened by the "specter" of old age.

But the centrality of the life course does not derive only from its abstract universality or its place in legitimating the liberal welfare state. Its unifying power lies in an historical tradition that until recently provided widely shared images of the unity and integrity of the life course. Its social power lies in the chronologically organized institutions built to regulate each individual's journey through the stages of life.

Daniels's account of justice across the life span actually builds on the traditional bourgeois ideal of a society ordered by the natural divisions of human lifetime. The life cycle has long functioned as a legitimating image of this ideal. Born amidst the anxiety and upheaval of the Renaissance and Reformation era, the modern life cycle assumed an almost numinous quality among the European urban middle class struggling for social and religious identity. Its burgeoning iconography played an important role in the emergence of urban individualism. Ministers, artists, and moralists exhorted people to imagine their lives as a series of age-linked roles.

This temporal perspective encouraged the development of individual virtues like self-control, thrift, and long-range planning. It also defused awareness of social inequalities based on class, wealth, gender, or political power. Eighteenth-century republicanism defiantly proclaimed the autonomy and equality of each mature generation. Jefferson's ideas about generational succession derived from his insistence that "the land belongs in usufruct to the living." French revolutionary moralists envisioned an ideal society where individuals would be divided only according to the natural order of ages; every individual could expect to run the course from dependent child to active adult to honored elder.[26]

Set free from the older bonds of status, family, or locality, middle-class individuals over the last 150 years have increasingly viewed their own lives as careers—as sequences of expected positions in school, at work, and in retirement. This pattern of expectations has become both statistically and ideologically normative, constituting what Martin Kohli aptly calls a "moral economy of the life course."[27] By the third quarter of the twentieth century, Western democracies had institutionalized this "moral economy" by providing age-homogeneous schools for youthful preparation, jobs organized according to skills, experience, and seniority for middle-aged productivity, and publicly funded retirement benefits for the aged, who were considered too slow, too frail, or too old-fashioned to be productive.

Hence the power of a life course perspective is not only existential, ideological, or moral—it is also institutional. The course of life today is an essential instrument for the maintenance of social order.[28] Since the late eighteenth century, the structure of the "normal" life course has been created by changes in demography and family life, as well as the growth of age-stratified systems of public rights and duties. Demographically, age-at-death has been transformed from a pattern of relative randomness to one of predictability. Death now strikes primarily in old age, and with much less variance than in the past. Meanwhile, the experience of a "normal" family cycle (including marriage, children, survival of both partners to age fifty-five, "empty nest," and widowhood) became increasingly common and chronologically standardized.

Over the last century, the social transition to adulthood (finishing school, first job, first marriage) has become more abrupt and uniform for a growing segment of the population. At the same time, the spread of universal age-homogeneous public schooling and chronologically triggered public pension systems have divided life into three "boxes": education; work; and retirement. This bureaucratized life course, supported by the state and administered by experts, is now an important means of social regulation. It is also under attack from those who call for an "age irrelevant" society[29] as well as from the generational equity movement. It is also increasingly experienced as a new form of domination and source of alienation.

The moral economy of the life course, then, forms the unspoken historical context of both Daniels's and Callahan's views about justice between the young and the old in an aging society. Both are aware of the need to rethink the moral obligations between age groups and to reformulate the moral economy of the life span in a new demographic context. Yet neither fully appreciates how much has been lost by secularization and modernization of the life course.

Amidst the decline of feudalism, the breakup of the Catholic church, and the emergence of urban commerce, early modern men and women turned to ancient understandings of the life cycle for a sense of stability and order. "Life's course is fixed," wrote Cicero in *De Senectute*. "Nature has only a single path and that path is run but once, and to each stage of existence has been allotted its own appropriate quality." In Ecclesiastes, they were comforted to learn that the natural divisions of a lifetime belong to the divine order of the universe: "To every thing there is a season, and a time to every purpose under heaven." Since the late Middle Ages, much Western medical, philosophical, and religious teaching has been predicated on this notion of the 'seasonableness' or naturalness of the human life cycle. As we have seen, social divisions based on the stages of life have been considered natural and proper. In the late twentieth century, however, we have many doubts about this ancient truism—doubts connected to the growing feeling that old age may be a "season" without a purpose.

The ideal of a society legitimately ordered by the natural divisions of human life-time is now under siege in large part because its view of old age is neither socially nor spiritually adequate and because the social meanings of life's stages are now in great flux. The greatest threat to its legitimacy comes from the demeaning of old age and marginalization of the elderly that emerged during the nineteenth century and became embedded in the bureaucratized life course of the welfare state. Herein lies the key to understanding the contemporary specter of old age.

In our century, vastly improved medical and economic conditions of old age have been accompanied by a loss of *cultural meaning* and vital social roles for older people. The dominant liberal response has attributed these problems to "ageism"— a term that refers to systematic stereotyping of and discrimination against older people, analogous to racism and sexism. Over the last fifteen years, we have witnessed a formidable effort to eliminate negative stereotypes of and prejudice toward older people. Academic gerontologists, humanists, health professionals, social workers, organized elders, and others have attempted to debunk "myths" of old age and to substitute positive images of aging for negative ones. This movement attempts both to redress the social conditions of old age and to reform cultural sensibilities toward aging. The campaign against ageism has done a great deal to free older people from outmoded cultural constraints; at the same time, however, it remains seriously limited. In some quarters, the attack on ageism has so quickly achieved the status of an enlightened prejudice that its limitations have gone unnoticed. Not the least of these limitations is that the attack on ageism, uncritically invoked at the first hint of a negative feeling or idea about old age, is itself part of an historical pattern based on splitting or dichotomizing the "negative" from the "positive" aspects of aging and old age. Appreciating this historical pattern[30] is essential to fashioning a satisfying culture of aging and to rebuilding the moral economy of the life course.

Apart from its class bias and its empirical deficiencies, the attack on ageism perpetuates the existential evasiveness of its Victorian forebears. The currently fashionable positive mythology of old age shows no more tolerance or respect for the intractable vicissitudes of aging than the old negative mythology did. While health and self-control were seen previously as virtues reserved for the young and middle aged, they are now demanded of the old as well. Unable to infuse decay, dependency, and death with moral and spiritual significance, our culture dreams of abolishing biological aging.

While the middle-class elderly have become healthier, more financially secure, and politically potent, they nevertheless suffer from the cultural disenfranchisement imposed on old people in general. "Growing old," says a character in Anthony Powell's *Temporary Kings*, "is like being penalized for a crime you haven't committed." Having satisfied the social requirements of middle age and avoided many previously fatal diseases, older people are often able to live ten or twenty years beyond gainful employment. But then what? Is there something special one is supposed to do? Is old age really the culmination of life? Or is it simply the denouement to be endured until medical science can abolish it?

We must acknowledge that our great progress in the material and physical conditions of life has been achieved at a high spiritual and ethical price. Social security has not enhanced ontological security or dignity in old age. The elderly continue to occupy an inferior status in the moral community—marginalized by an economy and culture committed to the scientific management of growth without limit. For the last sixty years Western observers have sensed this impoverishment of meaning in old age. But only recently have economic and political conditions turned this apparently academic question into an urgent public issue. In rebuilding the moral economy of an extended life course, we not only must attend to questions of justice within and between different stages of life but also must forge a new sense of the meanings and purposes of the last half of life.

This will require a new and integrated appreciation of aging that transcends our historical tendency to split old age into positive and negative poles. Since the early nineteenth century, American culture has characteristically oscillated between attraction to a "good" old age (the healthy culmination of proper middle-class living) and repulsion from a "bad" old age (repudiating the dream of limitless accumulation of health and wealth). We can no longer afford this dualism, which feeds both the false pessimism and the superficial optimism in contemporary discussions in our aging society.

We must also break with our habit of using old age as a metaphor for the success or failure of various political and ideological agendas. This does not mean that our search for more adequate ideals of aging should be "value free"—as if continued scientific research and technology could eliminate all conflict, mystery, and suffering in late life. Rather, we need more social criticism and public dialogue aimed at creating socially just, economically sound, and spiritually satisfying meanings of aging.

We need, for example, to criticize liberal capitalist culture's relentless hostility toward physical decline and its tendency to regard health as a form of secular salvation. A good deal of the pathos that surrounds old age today derives from the instrumental perspective that pervades the scientific management of aging. The one-sided drive to alter, reverse, ameliorate, abolish, retard, or somehow control the biological process of aging intensifies the impoverishment of meaning instead of confronting it. So-called positive aspects of aging often turn out to be disguised forms of the effort to restore youth rather than appreciation of growing old or being old as a fundamental dimension of human existence.

Until quite recently, Western culture emphasized the immutable limits and proper boundaries of the life cycle; it counselled individuals to transform their fate into a journey to self-knowledge and reconciliation with finitude. Contemporary men and women think of themselves not as fated creatures but as active beings who can solve life's problems with science and technology. Yet this is clearly an illusion, since we now receive our fate at the hands of medicine. Our challenge in the future is to find a new synthesis, one in which the ancient submission to natural limits is balanced against the modern drive to find a scientific solution to every problem.

Today there are encouraging signs that the traumatic fear of aging is increasingly offset by awareness of its opportunities for inner growth. The assumption that full intellectual and emotional growth occurs in the middle years has been challenged by the view that human development is not chronologically bounded and that later life can be a time of transformation rather than mere adaptation. In literature and humanistic gerontology,[31] we are seeing a resurgence of the view that old age is a period of unique capacity for wisdom, for understanding the experience of a whole lifetime, and (therefore) for service to the young.

To welcome the elderly back into the moral community, we need more than renewed appreciation for "the gifts of age." We need to understand the obligations and responsibilities as well as the rights and opportunities of old age. We need policies that eliminate the surplus dependency imposed on older people, policies that strengthen their ability to solve their own problems and contribute to their communities. This will require, as Harry R. Moody argues, a life span approach to human development.[32] Just as public investment in the health and education of children is essential to their future productivity, so policies that stimulate self-help, lifelong learning, and social participation among the elderly are essential to maintaining their independence. Human services for and professional intervention with older people need not foster dependency.

Independence among the elderly is not only a matter of human services—it also requires incentives and opportunities for participation and productivity.

Many experienced workers aged fifty to seventy-five leave the work force either because their skills are no longer needed or because they respond to an *employer's* inducements to retire. While these people are generally vigorous, healthy, alert, and capable of making important contributions to the nation's economy and quality of life, their lives are primarily channeled into trivialized leisure and the consumption of professional services. In the year 2010, people aged fifty to seventy-five (which Alan Pifer hopes to popularize as the "third quarter of life") will compose almost one-third of the U.S. population. We clearly cannot afford to continue excluding them from productive life.

Productivity in late life does not necessarily mean the continuation of full-time, paid employment. It means recognizing the contributions—whether in the form of full- or part-time, paid or volunteer work—made to the nation's economy or to its quality of life. Pifer suggests several ways of enhancing the productivity of older Americans.[33] Both industry and government can open up retraining programs to workers over fifty. Public and private pension programs can be changed to allow for partial retirement. The federal government can permit older people to borrow against their Social Security benefits to finance retraining or enroll in new educational programs. As some have already done, colleges and universities can devise special programs to meet the needs of older students. Public-service employment programs for older workers can be expanded, providing modestly paid work to unemployed older workers who want to defer retirement or supplement retirement benefits.

To accommodate an aging society (*and* to continue expanding protection for the poor of all ages), Americans will have to make substantial changes in the welfare state—but not of the sort that either interest-group liberals or neoconservatives envision. A half-century of Social Security history suggests that progressive reform (not abolition or privatization) is both desirable and politically feasible. Despite its limitations, Social Security remains, as Senator Bill Bradley has noted, "the best expression of community that we have in this country today."[34] It rests not only on the principle of social insurance over the individual's course of life but also on an intergenerational compact that must be renegotiated as historical circumstances require.[35]

The "specter of old age" that seems to cloud America's future is actually a reflection of our impoverished ideas about aging and our reluctance to face the real but not insuperable challenges of generational equity. "It can only weaken the vital fiber of the younger generation if the evidence of daily living verifies man's prolonged last phases as a sanctioned period of childishness," Erik Erikson wrote in 1964. "Any span of the cycle lived without vigorous meaning . . . endangers the sense of life and the meaning of death in all whose life stages are intertwined."[36]

The challenges of generational equity, then, involve the distribution of cultural meanings and social roles as well as the distribution of social goods like income and health care. We have clearly entered a period in which the intergenerational compact underlying Social Security is being renegotiated. In this "conversation between the generations,"[37] there is good reason to believe that a new moral economy of the life course can be fashioned. If so, the "abundance of life" in our aging society can yet be channeled toward genuine human development and social well-being.

Notes

Published in *Social Science and Medicine,* vol. 29, no. 3 (1989), pp. 377–383. Reprinted with permission of *Social Science and Medicine* (Oxford, Pergamon Press).

1. H. R. Moody *Abundance of Life: Human Development Policies for an Aging Society* New York: Columbia University Press, (1988), chap. 2.

2. W. A. Achenbaum, "The Aging of 'the first new nation,'" in *Our Aging Society,* ed. A. Pifer, and L. Bronte (New York: Norton, 1986) pp. 15–32.

3. W. R. Mead, *Mortal Splendor: The American Empire in Transition* (Boston: Houghton Mifflin, 1987); P. Kennedy, "The (Relative) Decline of America," *Atlantic Monthly,* Aug. 1987, pp. 29–38.

4. P. Peterson, "The Morning After," *Atlantic Monthly,* Oct. 1987, pp. 43–69.

5. S. H. Preston, "Children and the Elderly in the U.S.," *Scientific American,* vol. 251, no. 6, (1984), pp. 44–49.

6. Moody, *Abundance of Life,* pp. 108–11.

7. P. Longman, *Born to Pay: The New Politics of Aging in America* (Boston: Houghton Mifflin, 1987).

8. J. S. Siegel and C. M. Taeuber, "Demographic Dimensions of an Aging Population," in *Our Aging Society,* ed. A. Pifer and L. Bronte (New York: Norton, 1986), pp. 79–110.

9. M. Minkler, " 'Generational Equity' and the New Victim Blaming: An Emerging Public Policy Issue," *International Journal of Health Services,* vol. 16, no. 4, (1986) pp. 539–51; J. Quadagno, *The Transformation of Old Age Security: Class and Politics in the American Welfare State,* (Chicago: University of Chicago Press, 1988).

10. S. Crystal *America's Old Age Crisis* (New York: Basic Books, 1982).

11. Moody, *Abundance of Life,* chaps. 6, 7.

12. J. Habermas, ed., *Observations on the Spiritual Situation of the Age,* trans. A. Buchwalter (Cambridge: MIT Press, 1984).

13. W. Achenbaum, *Social Security: Visions and Revisions,* (New York: Cambridge University Press, 1986), chap. 3.

14. N. Keyfitz, "Why Social Security Is in Trouble," *The Public Interest*, vol. 58, (1980), pp. 102–119; K. Davis, and P. Van den Oever, "Age Relations and Public Policy in Advanced Industrial Societies," *Population and Development Review*, vol. 7, (March 1981), pp. 1–18.

15. Achenbaum, *Social Security*.

16. D. Callahan, *Setting Limits* (New York: Simon and Schuster, 1987).

17. E. M. Gruenberg, "The Failure of Success," *Milbank Memorial Fund Quarterly*, vol. 55, (1977) pp. 3–24; M Kramer,. "The Rising Pandemic of Mental Disorders and Associated Chronic Diseases and Disabilities," *Acta Psychiatrica Scandinavia* [suppl.], vol. 62 (1980), pp. 382–96; S. J. Olshansky and A. B. Ault, "The Fourth Stage of the Epidemiologic Transition: The Age of Delayed Degenerative Diseases," *Milbank Memorial Fund Quarterly*, vol. 64 (1986), pp. 355–91.

18. K. G. Manton, "Changing Concepts of Morbidity and Mortality in the Elderly Population," *Milbank Memorial Fund Quarterly*, vol. 60, (1982), pp. 183–244; G. Myers and K. Manton, "Morbidity, Disability, and Mortality: The Aging Connection." In *Aging 2000: Our Health Care Destiny*, ed. C. Gaitz, G. Niederehe, and N. Wilson, (New York: Springer-Verlag, 1985), pp. 25–39.

19. Callahan, *Setting Limits*.

20. N. Daniels, *Am I My Parents' Keeper? An Essay on Justice Between the Young and the Old*. (New York: Oxford University Press, 1988).

21. T. R. Cole and S. Gadow, eds. *What Does It Mean To Grow Old?* (Durham: Duke University Press, 1986).

22. Daniels, *Am I My Parents' Keeper?* chap. 1.

23. Daniels, *Am I My Parents' Keeper?* chap. 3.

24. Daniels, *Am I My Parents' Keeper?* chap. 6.

25. E. Kingson, B. A. Hirshorn, and J. M. Cornman, *Ties That Bind: The Interdependence of Generations* (Cabin John, Md.: Seven Locks Press, 1986).

26. D. Troyansky, *Old Age in the Old Regime* (Ithaca: Cornell University Press, 1989).

27. M. Kohli, "Retirement and the Moral Economy: An Historical Interpretation of the German Case" (manuscript 1986).

28. M. Kohli, The World We Have Lost: An Historical Review of the Life Course, in *Later Life: The Social Psychology of Aging*, ed. V. W. Marshall, (Beverley Hills: Sage, 1986), pp. 271–303.

29. B. L. Neugarten and D. A. Neugarten, "Changing Meanings of Age in the Aging Society," in *Our Aging Society*, ed. A. Pifer and L. Bronte, (New York: Norton, 1986), pp. 33–51.

30. T. Cole, "The 'Enlightened' View of Aging," in *What Does It Mean To Grow Old: Reflections from the Humanities,* ed. T. Cole and S. Gadow, (Durham: Duke University Press, 1986) pp. 115–30.

31. D. Polisar et al. *Where Do We Come From? What Are We? Where Are We Going? An Annotated Bibliography of Aging and the Humanities.* (Washington, D.C.: Gerontological Society of America, 1988).

32. Moody, *Abundance of Life,* chap. 12.

33. A. Pifer, "The Public Policy Response," in *Our Aging Society,* ed. A. Pifer and L. Bronte, (New York: Norton, 1986) pp. 391–413.

34. Achenbaum, *Social Security,* p. 8.

35. Achenbaum, *Social Security,* chap. 9.

36. E. Erikson, "Human Strength and the Cycle of Generations," in *Insight and Responsibility* (New York: Norton, 1964), p. 133.

37. P. Laslett, "The Conversation between the Generations," in *Philosophy Politics and Society,* ed. P. Laslett and J. Fishkin, (New Haven: Yale University Press, 1979), pp. 36–56.

2

Between the Generations: Justice and Peace as Alternatives to Age-Based Rationing

Stephen G. Post

The language of intergenerational "conflict" and of justice "between" generations is now common parlance. In 1982 Stephen Crystal pointed out that federal per capita spending on elderly persons exceeded that on children and youth (including educational programs) by a ratio of more than 3:1.[1] Two years later Samuel H. Preston, a University of Pennsylvania sociologist, in "Children and the Elderly in the U.S.," wrote: "Since the early 1960's the well-being of the elderly has improved greatly whereas that of the young has deteriorated."[2] What has emerged from these and other similar observations is a new framework for thinking about justice, namely, "intergenerational equity." Elderly people are blamed for the suffering of the young, who struggle with poverty and second-rate educational facilities.

Unfortunately, those who blame the elderly people for social ills forget that only about 25 percent of the elderly—those with annual incomes greater than $30,000[3]—might be termed "prosperous." The Gerontological Society of America, in a lengthy report critical of the conflictual interpretation of intergenerational relations, acknowledges that the financial and social challenge of caring for growing numbers of elderly persons is substantial and that inevitably this challenge raises questions about the "quantity and quality of opportunities available to younger generations."[4] But it appropriately emphasizes that the elderly are not all well off, citing 1984 data that puts 21.2 percent of elderly persons (5.6 million people) below near-poverty thresholds of $6,224 for an elderly single individual and $7,853 for an elderly couple.[5] Programs such as Social Security, the report adds, benefit all generations, because they relieve the family of providing financial support for the elderly and are thus not one one-way flows of resources. But what is most impressive about the report is its emphasis on providing for the young. The trends that are described by Preston and others "should be very alarming to advocates for the elderly," it states.[6] Elderly persons, it is argued, have a great stake in the well-being of the young, since a vital economy requires a capable workforce. Moreover, the elderly have a stake in a government responsive to the needs of all its people, since limited responsiveness to the young suggests that the vulnerable of all ages are in jeopardy. The conclusion of the report advises that "those concerned with responding to the challenge of an aging society understand the power of various frameworks to define the terms of the debate, and therefore give careful consideration to the various ways this debate can be framed and to the implications these approaches to policy-making can have for persons of all ages."[7]

The intent of this chapter is to develop an image of mutual obligations between the young and the old that can serve to deflect the adversarial tone of the emerging intergenerational equity debate. Necessary duties of both the young and the old that contribute to intergenerational harmony are emphasized. Without a renewed commitment to these duties, gradations of conflict will disrupt sacred reciprocities. The challenges of an aging society are viewed as opportunities for a renewed covenant between the young and the old. From a discussion of the duties of the elderly, and then of the young, this perspective is developed. I write as a humanist, not as an expert in public policy or the empirical data that are readily available elsewhere.

But before criticizing the adversarial framework in which much debate about the young and the old is now unfortunately framed, I will briefly summarize my arguments against the categorical age-based rationing of life-saving health care, since proponents of this doctrine fuel the fires of adversity by placing elderly people on the defensive.

Against the Age-Based Rationing of Health Care

Age-based rationing carries substantial moral and social costs. To my knowledge, no proponent of such rationing has seriously considered these costs. Proponents, in response to the criticisms I pose here, must do more than acknowledge that all systems of rationing are inevitably painful for someone. Obviously, some approaches to cost containment are less painful than others. Few could be more disruptive of essential social harmonies than age-based systems.

First, age-based rationing threatens to fragment the covenant between young and old, since it builds on an adversarial construct of intergenerational relations. Instead of pursuing justice for all vulnerable people regardless of age, our attention is diverted to a fabricated war between the generations, as though resources made available to the young must be stripped away from the aged. Respect for elderly people is needlessly threatened as the final stage of their lives becomes dispensable. I can think of no policy that would more powerfully spell a "broken covenant" between younger generations and elderly people than categorical age-based rationing.

Second, such rationing weakens the fragile veneer of human equality. As Amitai Etzioni argues, "Like all allocations, bans, or prohibitions based on irrelevant criterion—be it race, religion, gender, or age—rationing health care to the elderly is clearly discriminatory."[8] Elderly people are segregated into a separate category on the false assumption that they have lived out their best years. Equal-regard would then apply only to those under some arbitrary age cutoff. Some proponents of age-based rationing suggest that equality would not be threatened, because rationing would apply to everyone, so it is unlike discrimination on the basis of race, religion, and gender. However, a universal application of a reprehensible practice does not make it just. Age-based rationing is clearly discriminatory and ageist.

Third, such rationing is a threat to human freedom, an essential feature of any common good. Elderly people are heterogeneous, and a just society will respect their reasonable choices regarding medical treatment. Before the point of medical futility is reached, or of low probabilities of success for costly interventions, each individual should be free to make his or her own personal decision that life has run its course, that it is time to throw in the towel. To impose an age-based cutoff is to lose ground for personal conscience and reflects an undue pessimism about the ability of older people to make good decisions. I know of no ethical theory so compelling and uncontroversial as to justify, for reasons of so-called justice, the imposition of an obligation to die before one personally thinks that "the flame is no longer worth the candle."

Fourth, through age-based rationing, the contributions of elderly people would be lost to society. So many older people have made their greatest contributions to society, family, and friends in old age. Proponents of age-based rationing seem to assume that this "extra time" is dispensable. But regardless of our culture's "cult of youth," human beings are often at their generative best artistically, culturally, and socially, in life's final stage.[9]

Fifth, age-based rationing proposals are likely to encourage preemptive suicide among elderly people.[10] No longer allowed access to interventions that would restore them to a reasonable quality of life, they would be condemned to an avoidable and unnecessary downward course that makes assisted suicide or even mercy killing attractive. Abstract theories tend to obscure the brute fact: it is this person who, simply because he or she is old, must face needless relegation to hospice-like care and death.

Sixth, because women outlive men on the average, age-based cutoffs immediately raise questions about justice between men and women. It is particularly interesting that the proponents of age-based cutoffs are men. As I have pointed out elsewhere, it has been estimated that by the year 2000, there will be 37.2 men for every 100 women aged eighty-five and older.[11] Thus, when we consider the population most affected by age-based rationing, clearly women are largely the vulnerable ones. To my knowledge, the philosophical proponents of age-based rationing, such as Norman Daniels and Daniel Callahan, have been men who have not given much attention to feminist literature. They are not antifeminist, but they are clearly nonfeminist and uninterested in gender studies. My own position is that women, who spend so many of their years fulfilling the needs of others through direct caregiving, deserve to have their final years of sisterhood or solitude respected as recompense.[12]

Having made these arguments in a general way, I hasten to suggest that proponents of age-based rationing turn their idealism toward measures to curb health care costs that are more respectful of persons. Age-neutral definitions of medical futility, or of poor quality outcome specific to particular disease conditions, would be worth considering. But setting limits on the basis of age alone takes the wrong approach. As C. Everett Koop warns in the Foreward to *Too Old for Health Care?*, "I offer one closing admonition: Be careful! Your decisions about someone else's life might affect your own sooner than you think."[13]

But the scope of this chapter is wider than age-based rationing, for I intend to broadly construct a framework for thinking about intergenerational relations that goes beyond adversarial assumptions. It is to this task that I now turn, although the rationing debate will emerge again.

The Wider Context of Adversity

Critics of current policy claim that elderly persons receive too much of the economic pie through rises in Social Security payments, the post–World War II expansion in pension systems, and the advent of Medicare. The phrase "welfare for the rich" was coined to designate the portion of Social Security that goes to households with annual incomes greater than $30,000. A typical cover story entitled "Grays on the Go" fuels the stereotype that the elderly are all staging one grand retirement party.[14] It is easy to think that in the United States we take from the poor and the young to give to the prosperous elderly.

Reasonable critics will ask why the elderly are exempted from the screenings that other recipients of federal assistance must endure in order to be designated as truly needy. Several decades ago it was mistakenly assumed that all older people were in need of governmental support.[15] This gave rise to public entitlements based on age rather than need. Such a policy may have been necessary at the time, but the economic standing of the elderly has improved over the last two decades, so that some combination of age and need is a better criterion for public assistance. Of course as many as ten million elderly persons, by some estimates, now remain at or very near the current poverty line. Blacks and women, who generally do not receive much Social Security because they often lack the long history of employment that issues in substantive annual payments into this system, constitute the bulk of the poor elderly. Apart from age, and on a needs-basis alone, a claim could be made that these elderly are deserving.

With one third of the United States population over 60, and with those over 85 the fastest growing age-group, caring for the truly needy elderly places a heavy burden on the shoulders of society. In 1900, the life span for men was 47 years, for women 49 years; now, it is 71.5 years and 78.8 years respectively.[16] This demographic transition to an aging society is a source for serious concern, and society should not support extravagance on the part of those elderly persons who are in fact prosperous.

Again, though, many of the elderly are not rising at noon only to bask in the sun at the Phoenix country clubs. As Binstock warns, the new myth that the elderly are all relatively well-off has "provided the foundation for the emergence of the aged as scapegoat in American society."[17] Poverty among the elderly has certainly not been eliminated. Furthermore, adds Binstock, we must be on guard to prevent any backlash against the elderly in times of economic decline, when lack of resources should really be attributed to factors such as the balance of trade and the national debt.

A Covenantal Response

Mutual duties in the traditions of Judaism and Christianity are described through the covenant metaphor. The term *covenant* has been thoughtfully defined by James F. Childress: " 'Covenant' suggests a reciprocal relationship in which there is receiving and giving. But it is not reducible to a contract with a specific quid pro quo, for it also contains an element of the gratuitous which cannot be specified."[18] Participants in a covenant must be at least as other-regarding as they are self-regarding. This ethic does not require radical self-abnegation or rejection of all reasonable self-concern. However, it does require transcendence over egocentric behavior. Regarding the ideal of intergenerational harmony, the mutual interdependence of the covenant relationship has much to offer.

Duties of Elderly People

Somewhat paradoxically, through serving the young the elderly help secure their own well-being. In a classic of modern anthropology, Leo W. Simmons examined the moral status of the elderly in primitive societies and found that they are highly regarded where they contribute most to the lives of the young: "Perhaps the simplest and most effective way of eliciting the support of others has been to render essential—if possible, indispensable—services to them."[19] The fact is that the roles of the elderly have in the past "hardly ever been passive" at any stage in the cycle of life.[20] Moreover, their activities have done much to influence their security. Regarding the ancient Hebrews, Simmons writes: "Their security has been more often an achievement than an endowment—an achievement in which favorable opportunities have been matched with active personal accomplishments."[21]

However much one might question Daniel Callahan's controversial age-based rationing proposals, he can be commended for developing the thesis that the old, so long as they are able, have significant duties to the young. His discussion of the meaning of old age is too extreme in its rejection of legitimate self-regard: "If the young are to flourish," he writes, "then the old should step aside in an active way, working until the very end to do what they can to leave behind them a world hopeful for the young and worthy of bequest."[22]

Narcissism should always be discouraged, but it would also be wrong to place a greater burden on the elderly than on others—for example, by denying them clearly beneficial medical treatment simply on the basis of age. True, as Callahan argues, the old "cannot claim a right to self-absorption or an exemption from civic duties."[23] Nevertheless, covenant duties to the common good do not require radical self-abnegation, and they do not hold obvious trump over the remaining years of the aged. Callahan's contention that the elderly have "already" lived their lives, and therefore must even sacrifice potentially prosperous years on the basis of a categorical age-based cutoff of medical technologies, takes the ideal of reasonable self-denial much too far.[24]

The proposition underscored thus far is this: those elderly persons who can do so should, to a reasonable extent, devote energies to caring for the young (in addition to caring for other elderly persons). This is both a moral end in itself, and a means of encouraging degrees of reciprocity from the young. Without intending to encourage any negative stereotypes of the elderly, William F. May warns against an inclination to "clutch at possessions" the "closer one gets to the final dispossession of death."[25] May emphasizes the need for virtuous behavior. He comments that in the late Middle Ages avarice was identified as the "chief besetting sin of the aged." The problem of narcissism and self-centeredness pervades American society in all age groups and must be reversed insofar as this is possible.

One manifestation of covenant obligations to the young would be a reluctance on the part of the old to waste scarce resources. Extravagance will not make the mortal immortal. As the elderly become more numerous in the decades ahead, utilization of resources when the struggle against death becomes futile is to be avoided, as is extravagance generally. At least with regard to medical technology, some elderly persons need to be liberated from the view that death is "wrong."

Duties of the Young

With regard to the young, their commitment to the intergenerational covenant must be as firm as that of the old. The young are often narcissistic. A genuine commitment to others is an essential beginning of covenantal relations. That I have considered the elderly first in this essay is not meant to imply that they have missed the mark more than the young, although as teachers of the young they may have a special duty to set an example of virtue.

Norman Daniels makes a creative effort to persuade the young to support benefits for the elderly. Aware of the perceived competition between the young and the old for scarce resources, Daniels is convinced that tensions could mount as the number of older persons rises. His solution is this: we must "stop thinking of the old and the young as distinct groups."[26] The young, after all, age and become the old; thus "The key to solving the problem of justice between age groups is acknowledging the humbling fact that we age."[27] Prudence dictates that the young allow redistribution of resources to the old, because eventually the currently young will themselves benefit from those same redistribution policies. An appeal to prudence operates on the assumption that the younger person paying into social programs for the elderly will ultimately benefit.

Prudence and enlightened self-interest might convince the young that they have obligations to themselves grown old, but they do not encourage compassion for those now elderly and in need. Moreover, people have a tendency to identify with their age-group, with its symbols and ideals, its struggles and its disputes. The sense of being in an age-group, and the tendency to advocate for it, will not be easily swept aside by prudential "life span" arguments. The problem of overcoming adversarial attitudes of "our" interests as distinct from "their" interests requires attention to mutual duties between the young and the old based on transcendence of narrow self-interest.

The young need to develop other-regarding virtues, but there are obstacles. First, there is a problem of self-centeredness, for this erodes the covenant between generations. Daniels tries to solve the problem of intergenerational relations by building on a theory of self-interest that is ultimately inconsistent with self-sacrifice in its basic philosophy of the human self and that can contribute to the very problem it is intended to solve. The young must become people of virtue who value community as much as self and who understand community as essential rather than derivative. First, then, the young must learn the meaning of communitarianism vis-à-vis individualism.

Second, the young must overcome ageism in order to extend neighbor-love to persons as such, regardless of age. Our culture creates negative images of the elderly in part because we overvalue youth. Nearly every novel, television advertisement, and film idealizes youth and physical vitality, so the old begin to look abnormal. Butler may be right to suggest that even beyond culture there is the problem of "a deep and profound prejudice against the elderly which is found to some degree in all of us."[28] Elderly people remind the young of mortality, of loss of beauty, vitality, memory, and the like. A fundamental fear of age is something accentuated in a culture with a passion for youth. In what has been characterized as a "death-denying society," the old are easily scorned. The young must be vigilantly on guard against ageism, for otherwise an entire social group is categorically denied respect and care.

The achievement of other-regard and the demise of ageism are hindered by the eclipse of tradition that characterizes modernity. Karl Barth underlined that importance of the "teaching function" associated with the elderly, whose insights into traditions both religious and moral give them value in the eyes of the young.[29]

And in relation to their own children, writes Barth, "they do not merely represent their own knowledge and experience but that conveyed to them by their own predecessors."[30] In modernity, the loss of tradition means that the elderly have limited opportunity to function as teachers; correlatively, the young find no valuable information in what the old convey. It is more difficult for the old to be viewed positively by the young. Ours is, for the most part, a forward-looking culture, and a source of valued knowledge is more likely to be the latest computer software than a wise old man or woman. But this is no excuse for ageism.

A Communitarian Ideal

The possible horizon of intergenerational adversity is disconcerting. One way to mitigate such conflict is to move away from the language of "rights" toward one of mutual duties and responsibilities, for the emphasis on rights diverts attention from the real challenge at hand, that is, the enhancement of social harmonies through intergenerational reciprocities.

There are many potential morally rich alternatives to the conflict between young and old that has of late made its way into the halls of Congress. Young people, for example, could work with various elder-care projects that would involve participants in the everyday care of elderly citizens in their communities. Perhaps we need large private or public programs aimed at the mobilization of younger persons for elder care. Older persons in addition to caring for one another, have traditionally cared for grandchildren. But in a society as mobile and uprooted as ours, sometimes the opportunity for ties between grandparents and grandchildren is small. Perhaps, though, the elderly could work in child care programs and schools and with recreation programs for children. These are just some preliminary suggestions of ways to make intergenerational interdependence and community central to the American culture within the context of the life cycle. Other creative ways to encourage intergenerational harmonies are easy to envision.

The aging society is a challenge that could contribute to the moral fabric of society if persons both young and old can be properly responsive to it. Indeed, it provides an opportunity for a renewed commitment to community, and for the repudiation of conflictual frameworks. I do not think that the proper response to the aging society is found in age-based cutoff of life-saving medical care.

Notes

1. S. Crystal, *America's Old Age Crisis: Public Policy and the Two Worlds of Aging* (New York: Basic Books, 1982), p. 5.

2. S. H. Preston, "Children and the Elderly in the U.S.," *Scientific American*, vol. 251, no. 6 (1984), p. 44.

3. E. R. Kingson, et al. *Ties That Bind: The Interdependence of Generations.* A report of the Gerontological Society of America. (Washington, D.C.: Seven Locks Press, 1986) p. 3.

4. Kingson, *Ties That Bind,* p. 2.

5. Kingson, *Ties That Bind,* p. 3.

6. Kingson, *Ties That Bind,* p. 120.

7. Kingson, *Ties That Bind,* p. 165.

8. A. Etzioni, "Health Care Rationing: A Critical Evaluation," *Health Affairs,* vol. 10, no. 2 (Summer 1991), p. 94.

9. T. P. McDonnell, "America's Obsession with Youth—Some Literary Origins," *This World: A Journal of Religion and Public Life,* vol. 16 (Winter 1987), pp. 105–9.

10. C. G. Prado, *The Last Choice: Preemptive Suicide in Advanced Age* (New York: Greenwood Press, 1990).

11. S. G. Post, "Justice for Elderly People in Jewish and Christian Thought," in *Too Old for Health Care? Controversies in Medicine, Law, Economics, and Ethics,* ed, R. H. Binstock and S. G. Post, with a Foreward by C. E. Koop (Baltimore: Johns Hopkins University Press, 1991), p. 124.

12. See S. G. Post, "Women and Elderly Parents: Moral Controversy in an Aging Society," *Hypatia: A Journal of Feminist Philosophy,* vol. 5, no. 1 (Spring 1990), pp. 83–89.

13. Koop, Forward to *Too Old For Health Care?* p. x.

14. N. R. Gibbs, "Grays on the Go," *Time,* vol. 131, no. 8 (1988) pp. 66–75.

15. Robert H. Binstock, "The Aged as Scapegoat," Gerontologist, vol. 23 (1983), pp. 136–43.

16. Kingson, *Ties That Bind,* p. 1.

17. Binstock, "Aged as Scapegoat," p. 136.

18. J. F. Childress, *Who Should Decide: Paternalism in Health Care* (New York: Oxford University Press, 1982), p. 42.

19. Leo W. Simmons, *The Role of the Aged in Primitive Society* (New Haven: Yale University Press, 1945), p. 82.

20. Simmons, *Role of the Aged,* p. 42.

21. Simmons, *Role of the Aged,* p. 82.

22. D. Callahan, *Setting Limits: Medical Goals in an Aging Society* (New York: Simon and Schuster, 1987), p. 43.

23. Callahan, *Setting Limits,* p. 49.

24. Callahan repeats his call for age-based rationing in a later book, *What Kind of Life: The Limits of Medical Progress* (New York: Simon and Schuster, 1990), pp. 151–54,

25. William F. May, "Who Cares For the Elderly?" *Hastings Center Report,* vol. 12 (Dec. 1982), p. 36.

26. N. Daniels, *Am I My Parents' Keeper? An Essay on Justice between the Young and the Old* (New York: Oxford University Press, 1988), p. 18.

27. Daniels, *Am I My Parents' Keeper?* p. 40.

28. R. N. Butler, *Why Survive: Growing Old in America* (New York: Harper and Row, 1975), p. 11.

29. K. Barth, *Church Dogmatics,* vol. 3, no. 4, trans. A. T. Mackay (Edinburgh: T. and T. Clark, 1961) pp. 244–45.

30. Barth, *Church Dogmatics,* p. 243.

3

Justice within the Family

John R. Hardwig

A seventy-eight-year-old married woman with progressive Alzheimer's disease was admitted to a local hospital with pneumonia and other medical problems. She recognized no one and had been incontinent for about a year. Despite aggressive treatment, the pneumonia failed to resolve and it seemed increasingly likely that this admission was to be for terminal care. The patient's husband (who had been taking care of her in their home) began requesting that the doctors be less aggressive in her treatment and, as the days wore on, he became more and more insistent that they scale back their aggressive care. The physicians were reluctant to do so, due to the small but real chance that the patient could survive to discharge. But her husband was her only remaining family, so he was the logical proxy decisionmaker. Multiple conferences ensued, and finally a conference with a social worker revealed that the husband had recently proposed marriage to the couple's housekeeper and she had accepted.

People are attached to other people—through marriages, friendships, and families. We must not forget this fact when we think about the health care implications of an aging population. We must not think only of our "health care system" and the citizens who must pay for it. For many of the burdens of an aging population are borne *privately*, by spouses, relatives and friends. We must not—as too often happens—discuss issues of access to health care or of intergenerational justice as if the members of the older generation were more or less uniformly attached to the members of the younger generation. The burdens of the old fall very unevenly, both among families and within families. In this paper, I will consider only one of many problems confronting families with aging members—the problem of proxy decisions for incompetent patients.

Of course, the connection between proxy decisions and an aging population is not a simple, straightforward one. Many old people are quite competent and in no need of anyone to make proxy decisions; many proxy decisions are made on behalf of children or of adults who are not old. Nonetheless, one consequence of an aging population is a large increase in the number of proxy decisions that must be made, as more and more people live long enough to become incompetent. Because it is technically easier to sustain life than it is to keep people competent, it seems likely that further technological developments will only increase this trend toward a larger and larger number of proxy decisions.

Proxy decisions will always strike us as ethically troubling: patient autonomy is the cornerstone of our medical ethics, and it is always more difficult to ensure that the wishes of the patient are embodied in treatment decisions when someone else must speak for the patient. And proxy decisions are especially disturbing when we fear that the proxy's judgment is tainted by his own interests, so that the proxy is covertly requesting the treatment *he* wants the patient to have, rather than the treatment the *patient* would have wanted.

This problem of interested proxies is exacerbated by the fact that we usually select "the next of kin" as proxies—people who often turn out to have strong interests in the treatment of the patient. We do this for two reasons: (1) those who care deeply for the patient are more likely than others to really want the best for the patient and (2) those who are close to the patient are generally most knowledgeable about what the patient would have wanted. This familiarity allows us to apply the "substituted judgment" standard of proxy decision, and given a commitment to autonomy, substituted judgment is an ethically better basis for proxy decision making than the "reasonable person" or "best interest" standard.

The apparent alternative would be to have proxy decisions made by outsiders—physicians, court-appointed guardians, or ethics committees. We must learn to recognize that such outsiders also have interests of their own and that their proxy decisions may also be influenced by these interests. But the more common worry about outsiders is that they rarely know the patient as well as members of the patient's family and that their concern about the individual patient does not run nearly as deep. Proxies who are members of the patient's family have a difficult time ignoring their own interests in treatment decisions precisely because they, unlike outsiders, are so intimately involved with the patient and have so much at stake.

Our increasing technological capability compounds the problem of interested proxies: as the time between incompetence and death increases, proxies will usually have more and more at stake in medical-treatment decisions. Thus, it seems that our theory of proxy decisions has boxed us into a Catch-22 situation. Knowledgeable about patient wishes usually means close, but close almost always means having interests of one's own in the case. Disinterested usually means distant, and distance usually brings with it less real concern, as well as lack of the intimate knowledge required to render a reliable substituted judgment.

However, I will urge that the reservations we have about the proxy decisions of interested family members are partly of our own making. The theory of proxy decisions that is endorsed by the courts, almost all medical ethicists, and most physicians is deeply flawed and must be recast. Although medical practice is some-times better than the conventional theories of proxy decision making, some of our deepest worries about proxy decision makers grow out of the morally inappropri-ate instructions they are often given.

If the current theory about proxy decisions for incompetent patients is mis-taken, the accepted view of decisions by *competent* patients will have to be modi-fied as well. However, I will be able to discuss decisions by competent patients only very briefly at the end of this paper.

The husband in this case seems a perfect scoundrel. The physicians involved in the case all believed that he should be disqualified as a proxy decision maker, due to his obvious conflict of interest and his patent inability to ignore his own in-terests in making decisions about his wife's care. There was no reason to believe that the patient would have wanted to limit her treatment, so the conclusion seemed inescapable that the husband was not faithfully discharging his role as proxy decider.

Both traditional codes and contemporary theories of medical ethics hold that physicians are obligated to deliver treatment that reflects the wishes or the best interests of the patient and that the incompetence of the patient does nothing to alter this obligation.[1] There is similar unanimity about the responsibilities of a proxy decision maker: proxy decision makers are to make the treatment decisions that most faithfully reflect the patient's wishes or, if those wishes cannot be known, the best interests of the patient. If the proxy does not do so, commentators almost uniformly recommend that physicians reject the proxy's requests and have re-course to an ethics committee or to the courts.

Despite this impressive consensus of both traditional codes and contempo-rary theories of medical ethics, I was intrigued by this case and pressed the attend-ing physician for more details. "Why is the husband in such a hurry? Perhaps he hopes that his wife will die, but she is dying anyway. Is he afraid that she might not die?" "No," the attending physician responded, "his worries are primarily financial. He is afraid that he'll lose his house and all his savings to medical bills before she dies. Since the housekeeper has no assets, they will then be left poverty stricken."

To some, this seems even worse: the husband has not only allowed his own interests to override considerations of what is best for his wife but also has become concerned with crass financial considerations, and he has let those kinds of con-siderations predominate. If his decision is not altogether self-centered, it is only because he is concerned about his fiancée's future as well as his own. But married men are not supposed to have fiancées.

I do not necessarily want to argue that the husband made the correct decision. And I don't know enough about him to be able to judge his character. But I do think his decision should not be rejected out of hand as being patently inappropriate.

First, I don't think that we can just assume that the presence of another woman means that he was insensitive to his wife's interests. I certainly know couples who have gotten divorced without losing the ability to genuinely care about each other and each other's interests. Second, while choosing to divorce a long-standing wife simply because she is now demented is difficult—"How can I abandon her at a time when she is so vulnerable?"—remaining married to a woman with Alzheimer's—an increasingly unreachable, foreign wife—is difficult, too. His wife's dementia undoubtedly meant increasing isolation for him as well as for her. And given that, his search for companionship does not seem unreasonable or morally objectionable. Third, the husband also had been the patient's primary caregiver for *years* without any prospect of relief for himself or improvement for his wife. He probably longed for a chance to spend his few remaining years free of the burdens of such care. And, finally, supposing the husband to be an adherent of traditional values, he would not be able to bring himself to simply "live with" the housekeeper, or consider himself no longer married while his wife was still alive, or yet accept medical care with no intention of trying to pay for it. Perhaps more "liberal" attitudes toward marriage and the payment of debts would have served his wife better. But we cannot be sure about that.

I have no doubt that the husband's proxy decisions were influenced by his own interests. Given the reasonableness and magnitude of the interests he had at stake, it is hard to see how he could ignore them. How can *we* ignore his interests? I wondered. And how can we reasonably ask him to ignore them? I don't think we can.

The attending physician and I didn't get further on this case than my suggestion that the husband's concern about his financial future was an appropriate consideration in deciding on a course of treatment for the patient. The physician was shocked that I thought this kind of consideration was relevant.

Nevertheless, we limit treatment all the time in an effort to save money for the government or an HMO. We develop theories of rationing and "costworthy" medicine to justify such decisions.[2] We regularly deinstitutionalize people, partly to limit the cost of the care we as a society must provide. We limit the number of nursing-home beds available for this man's wife and other Alzheimer's victims for the same reason. We thus force the burden of long-term care onto the families of the ill. And then we tell them that they must not consider their own burdens in making treatment decisions. I cannot make ethical sense of this.

We consider *our* pocketbooks, so how can we in good conscience tell proxies that they must ignore the much, much greater impact of aggressive treatment on their personal financial futures? I would insist that financial considerations for a seventy-five-year-old person with limited means are never trivial. We must recognize that, for him, nothing less is at stake than the quality of the rest of his life, including, quite likely, the quality of his future health care.

If we find it morally repugnant that proxies decide to limit treatment due to the burdens of long-term care on the family, then it is incumbent upon us to devise an alternative to our present system under which families deliver 75 percent of the long-term care. And until we have such an alternative in place, we dare not direct the husband that he must ignore the impact of treatment decisions on his own life. For *we* do not ignore the impact of such decisions on our lives. Moreover, the burdens of his wife's treatment to him may well outweigh any benefits we might be able to provide for her.

There are, of course, many, many cases like this, ones in which optimal care for a patient will result in diminished quality of life for those close to the patient. This care can impose a crushing financial burden, depriving other family members of many different goods and opportunities. But the burdens are by no means only financial: caring for an aging parent with decreasing mental capabilities or a severely retarded child with multiple medical problems can easily become the social and emotional center of a family's existence, draining away time and energy from all other facets of life. What are we to say about such cases?

I submit that we must acknowledge that many treatment decisions inevitably and dramatically affect the quality of more lives than one. This is true for a variety of very different reasons. First, people get emotionally involved with one another, and whatever affects those I love affects me, too. Second, people live together, and important changes in one member of a living unit will usually have ramifications for all the others, as well. Third, the family is still a financial unit in our culture, and treatment decisions often carry important financial implications that can radically limit the life plans of the rest of the family. Fourth, relationships of marriage and the family are also legal relationships, and one's legal status hinges on the life or death of other members of the family.

Fifth, treatment decisions have an important impact on the lives of others because we are still, to some extent, loyal to one another. Most of us still do not believe that family and friendships are to be dissolved whenever their continued existence threatens one's quality of life. I know of a man who left his wife the day after she learned that she had cancer, because living with a cancer-stricken woman was no part of his vision of the good life. But most of us are unable or unwilling to disentangle ourselves and our lives from others as soon as continuing involvement threatens the quality of our own lives.

This loyalty is undoubtedly a good thing: without it we would have alliances for better but not for worse, in health but not in sickness, until death appears on the horizon. It is a good thing, even though it sometimes brings about one of the really poignant ironies of human existence: sometimes it is precisely this loyalty that gives rise to insoluble and very basic conflicts of interest, as measures to promote the quality of one life undermine the quality of others. If the husband in the case we have been considering had simply divorced his wife when she was diagnosed as having Alzheimer's, she would have died utterly alone. As such, only her own interests would have been relevant to her treatment. Her husband's loyalty—impure though it may have been—has undoubtedly made her life with Alzheimer's much better for her. But it also makes her treatment not simply her own.

Now, if medical treatment decisions will often dramatically affect the lives of more than one, I submit that we cannot morally disregard the impact of those decisions on all lives except the patient's. Nor can we justify making the interests of the patient predominant by claiming that medical interests should always take precedence over other interests. Life and health are important goods in the lives of almost everyone. Consequently, health-related considerations are often important enough to override the interests of family members in treatment decisions. But not always. Even life or death is not always the most important consideration. Thus, although persons become "patients" in medical settings, and medical settings are organized around issues of life and health, we must still bear in mind that these are not always the most important considerations. We must beware the power of the medical context to subordinate all other interests to medical interests, for nonmedical interests of nonpatients sometimes morally ought to take precedence over medical interests of patients.

Because medical treatment decisions often deeply affect more lives than one, proxy decision makers must consider the ramifications of treatment decisions on all those who will be importantly affected. Including themselves. Everyone with important interests at stake has a morally legitimate claim to consideration; no one's interests can be ignored or left out of consideration. And this means nothing less than that the morally best treatment in many cases will not be the treatment that is best for the patient.

An exclusively patient-centered ethics must be abandoned. It must be abandoned, not only—as is now often acknowledged—because of scarce medical resources and society's limited ability to meet virtually unlimited demands for medical treatment. It must be abandoned, as well, because it is patently unfair to the families of patients. And if this is correct, the current theory of proxy decisions must be rejected in favor of an ethics that attempts to harmonize and balance the interests of friends and family whose lives will be deeply affected by the patient's treatment.[3]

There is a second, related point. Arguably, there is a presumption that substituted judgment is the morally appropriate standard for a proxy decision maker. But this can be no more than a *presumption,* and it can be overridden whenever various treatment options will affect the lives of the patient's family. In fact, substituted judgment is the appropriate standard for proxy decision making in only two special (though not uncommon) situations: (1) when the treatment decision will affect only the patient or (2) when the patient's judgment would have duly reflected the interests of others whose lives will be affected. In other situations, proxy deciders should make decisions that may be *at odds with* the known wishes of a formerly competent patient.

Consider again the case with which this paper began. I didn't know the patient, and I have no idea what kind of a person she used to be. Let us, then, consider two rather extreme hypotheses about her character. On one hand, suppose that the patient had been a very selfish, domineering woman who, throughout their marriage, had always been willing to sacrifice her husband's interests to her own. If so, we can reliably infer that she would now have ignored her husband's interests again, perhaps even ridden roughshod over them, if she could have gotten something she wanted by doing so. Therefore, we can conclude that she would have demanded all the medical treatment available, regardless of costs to him. We can even imagine that she would have relished her continuing power over him and her ability to continue to extract sacrifices from him. Obviously, her husband would know these facts about her. The substituted judgment standard of proxy decisions would have us conclude that if that is the kind of woman she was, this would *increase* her husband's obligation to make additional sacrifices of his interests to hers.

Suppose, on the other hand, that this woman had always been a generous, considerate, unselfish woman; deeply sensitive to the interests of her husband and always ready to put his needs before her own. If that's the kind of woman she was, the theory of substituted judgment allows—strictly speaking, even *obligates*—her husband to sacrifice her interests once again by now demanding minimal care for her. After all, he knows that that's what she'd have done, had she been competent to make the decision. Even if he wanted to give her the very best treatment as an expression of love or gratitude for her concern for him throughout their lives, substituted judgment would require that he ignore those desires. That's what *he* wants for her, not what she would have chosen for herself.

But surely that is exactly wrong. The theory of substituted judgment has it backwards. Loving, giving, generous people deserve to be generously cared for when they can no longer make decisions for themselves, even if they would not have been generous with themselves. And what do selfish, domineering, tyrannical people deserve? The answer to that question depends on your ethical theory. Perhaps neglect, maybe even retribution, is justified or at least excusable. Perhaps tyrannical behavior releases the family from any *special* obligation to care for the now incompetent tyrant. But unless you believe that good people should not be rewarded for their virtues, you will agree that caring, giving individuals deserve better care than domineering, self-centered individuals.

Where did we go wrong? What led us to widespread acceptance of the theory of substituted judgment? The major mistake was the one we have been considering—the mistake of believing that medical treatment affects only the life of the patient or that its impact on other lives should be ignored. If the patient's interests are the only ones that ought to shape treatment decisions, those interests are best defined by the patient's point of view. Proxy deciders are, then, obligated to replicate that point of view insofar as possible. But most decisions we make affect the lives of others—that's the main reason why there is ethics in the first place. And the present incompetence of a patient should not obligate others to perpetuate the patient's former selfish ways.

It would, of course, be possible to modify and defend the doctrine of substituted judgment by reinterpreting the concept of autonomy.[4] Patient autonomy is, after all, the main reason we embrace substituted judgment, and we usually define patient autonomy as "what the patient would have wanted." But if we were to work instead with a truly Kantian notion of autonomy, we would arrive at a very different theory of substituted judgment. For Kant would insist that a domineering, selfish person would acknowledge that she deserves less generous care when she becomes incompetent than a more caring, giving person deserves. While she might not actually elect to receive less generous care if she were able to choose for herself, the moral judge within her would recognize that she deserves less care from others due to the way she has treated them.

On Kant's view, then, the treatment she would choose for herself is not the appropriate standard of autonomy. Rather, her judgment about what is fair or what she now deserves would be the true meaning of autonomy. Kant would insist that the selfish, domineering ways of an individual are all heteronomous, despite the fact that the person consistently chose them. He would further insist that a request for medical care that requires inordinate sacrifices from one's family is also heteronomous, even if the patient would have wanted that. This interpretation of autonomy and substituted judgment are clearly very different from the standard interpretation in medical ethics.

Barring a radical rethinking of the very concepts of autonomy and substituted judgment, the doctrine of substituted judgment must be rejected. At the very least, our standard view of substituted judgment must be replaced with a theory in which the interests of the incompetent are constrained by what is morally appropriate, *whether or not* the patient would have so constrained herself. Often, the patient would have been sensitive to the interests of the rest of the family. But not always. In any case, the interests of other members of the family are not relevant to proxy decisions *because* the patient would have considered them as part of her own interests; they are relevant *whether or not* the patient would have considered them.[5] It is simply not the regard of the patient for the interests of her family that give those interests moral standing. No patient, competent or incompetent, deserves more than a fair, equitable consideration of the interests of all concerned would grant. Fairness to all includes, I would add, fairness to the patient herself in light of the life she has lived and especially the way she has treated the members of her family.

The theory of proxy decision making must be rebuilt. While proxy deciders must guard against *undue* consideration of their own interests, undue consideration of the *patient's* interests is likewise to be avoided. Proxy deciders have been given the wrong instructions. Instead of telling them that they must attempt to put themselves into the shoes of the incompetent patient and decide as she would have decided, we must tell them that the incompetent patient's wishes are the best way to define *her* interests, but what she would have wanted for herself must be balanced against considerations of fairness to all members of the family.

Fundamental changes in the theory of proxy decisions will need to be created and defended. And a view such as mine faces a host of important questions. I cannot develop an alternative theory in this paper; indeed I cannot even fully answer the most pressing questions about an alternative. Here, I can only provide suggestions about the way I would try to approach four of the most immediate questions about the theory of proxy decisions I would advocate.

First, proxy deciders must, as I have said, avoid *undue* consideration of either their own interests or the interests of the patient. But how is "undue consideration" to be defined? A full answer to this question would require an account of the family and of the ethics of the family. We can begin, however, by noting that, prima facie, equal interests deserve equal consideration. But what defines equal interest? Norman Daniels had developed the concept of a 'normal opportunity range' for the purpose of allocating resources to different individuals and different age groups.[6] Perhaps this concept could be extended to problems of fairness *within* families by asking how different treatment options will affect the "opportunity range" of the various members of the family. If so, "undue consideration" could be partially defined as a bias in favor of an interest that affects someone's opportunity range in a smaller way over an interest that affects another's opportunity range in a greater way.

But even if this suggestion about the "opportunity range" could be worked out, it would represent only one dimension of an adequate account of undue consideration. Another dimension would be fairness to competent and formerly competent members of the family in light of the way they have lived and treated each other.

Second, whose interests are to be considered? For example, what about the interests of family members who do not care for the patient or who have long been hostile to the patient? Lack of concern for the patient and even hostility toward the patient do not, on my view, exclude family members from consideration. Such family members still may have important interests at stake; moreover, we must not assume that the neglect or hostility is not merited. Neglect or hostility toward the patient would, however, diminish what fair consideration of their interests would amount to.

What of the interests of close friends or companions who are not members of the family? 'Family' as I intend this concept is not restricted to blood or marital relationships. Close friends, companions, unmarried lovers—all of these relationships may entitle persons to consideration in treatment decisions. Those who are distant—neither emotionally involved with the patient nor related by blood or marriage—will almost never have strong enough interests in the treatment of a patient to warrant consideration. (Health care professionals may have strong interests, but they have special professional obligations to ignore their own interests and are usually well compensated for doing so.) I see no principled way to exclude consideration of anyone whose interests will be importantly affected by a treatment decision.

Third, wouldn't any theory like the one I propose result in unfair treatment of incompetent patients? After all, we do not require that competent patients consider the interests of their families when making treatment decisions. And if competent patients can ignore their families, doesn't fairness require that we permit incompetent patients to do so, as well? I have argued elsewhere that if we want to insist on patient autonomy, we must insist that patients have *responsibilities* and *obligations,* as well.[7] In many cases, it is irresponsible and wrong for competent patients to make self-centered or exclusively self-regarding treatment decisions. It is often wrong for a competent patient to consider only which treatment she wants for herself. We must, then, start trying to figure out what to do when patients abuse their autonomy—when they disregard the impact of their treatment decisions on the lives of others. Sometimes, no doubt, we should seek to find ways to prevent patients from abusing their autonomy at too great a cost to their families.

Still, competent patients are almost always permitted to ignore the interests of their family members, even if it is wrong to ignore them. We do not force them to consider the impacts of their decisions on others, nor do we disallow their decisions if they fail to do so. How, then, can it be fair to incompetent patients to develop a theory of proxy decisions that will, in effect, hold them to a more stringent moral standard by requiring them to accept treatment decisions made in light of their families' interests? The answer to this question is, I think, that there are many things that we are at liberty to do, but only so long as we do not need an agent to help us accomplish them. If we can file our own taxes, we may be able to cheat in ways that a responsible tax advisor will refuse to. We may get away with shoddy deals that an ethical lawyer would not be a party to. Thus, the greater freedom of competent patients is only a special case of the generally greater freedom of action when no assistance of an agent is required.

Fourth, what about the legal difficulties of an alternative view of proxy decision making? They are considerable: it is presently *illegal* to make proxy decisions in the way I think is morally appropriate. The courts that have become involved in proxy decisions have almost all opted for exclusively patient-centered standards. I do not have the expertise needed to really address the legal issues my view raises. My purpose here can only be to try to challenge the faulty moral foundations that undergird present legal practice.

However, it is possible that family law could provide a model for a revised legal standard of proxy decision making. Family law recognizes the legitimacy of proxy decisions—for children, for example—that are not always in the best interest of the person represented by the proxy. It *has* to, if only because there are many cases in which the interests of one child will conflict with those of others. Nor does family law require parents to ignore their own interests in deciding for a child; instead, it defines standards of minimum acceptable care, with the hope that most families will do better than these minimum standards. Perhaps we should similarly separate the legal from the moral standard for proxy decisions. If no abuse or neglect is involved, the legal standard is met, though that may be less than morality requires of a proxy decision maker.

All these issues—about undue consideration, about eligible interests, about fairness between competent and incompetent patients, about the law of proxy decisions—may seem very complex. I can say only that I do not believe they are unnecessarily complicated. Many important decisions within families are very complicated. In medical ethics, we have simplified our task by working with an artificially over-simplified vision of the interests and decisions of families in medical treatment. So, if my critique of the present theory of proxy decisions is correct, we all—medical ethicists, reflective health care practitioners, legal theorists, lawyers—have a lot of hard work to do. The change I propose is basic, so the revisions required will be substantial.

I close now with a word of caution and a word of encouragement. The word of caution: we must recognize that even the necessary revisions in our moral and legal theories of proxy decisions would not resolve all the problems of proxy decisions. Proxy deciders with interests that conflict with those of the patient do face serious moral difficulties and very real temptations to give undue weight to their own interests. Although both notions of 'overtreatment' and 'undertreatment' will have to be redefined in light of the considerations I have been advancing, pressures from proxies for inappropriate treatment will remain. I do not wish to minimize these difficulties in any way.

But we should not give proxies the morally erroneous belief that their own interests are irrelevant and then censure them for allowing their interests to "creep in" to their decisions. Instead, we must deal forthrightly with the very real difficulties arising from interested proxy decisions, by making these interests conscious, explicit, and legitimate. Then we must provide guidance and support for those caught in the moral crucible of proxy decisions. This approach would not only be more ethically sounder but also, I believe, decrease the number of inappropriate proxy decisions.

Finally, an encouraging word. The Alzheimer's case that I've cited notwithstanding, the practice of medicine is often better than our ethical theories have been. It has generally not been so insensitive to the interests of family members as our theories would ask that it be. Indeed, much of what now goes on in intensive-care nurseries, pediatrician's offices, critical-care units, and long-term care facilities makes ethical sense *only* on the assumption that fairness to the interests of the other members of the family is morally required. To mention only the most obvious kind of case, I have never seen a discussion about institutional versus home care for an incompetent patient that did not attempt to address the interests of those who would have to care for the patient as well as the interests of the patient.

Current ethical theory and traditional codes of medical ethics can neither help nor support health care professionals and proxies struggling to balance the patient's interests with those of the proxy and other family members. Indeed, our present ethical theory can only condemn as unethical any attempt to weigh in the interests of the family. Thus, our ethical theory forces us to misdescribe decisions about institutionalization in terms of what is physically or psychologically *possible* for the family, rather than in terms of what is or is not too much to *ask* of them.

If we were to acknowledge the moral relevance and legitimacy of the family's interests, we would be able to understand why many treatment decisions now being made make sense and are not unethical. And then we would be in a position to develop an ethical theory that would guide health care providers and proxies in the throes of excruciating moral decisions. As our society struggles to provide health care for an aging population and individual families struggle to provide care for their own aging relatives, the need for this improved ethical theory will become more and more urgent.

Notes

This essay is a slightly revised version of "The Problems of Proxies with Interests of their Own," published in the *Journal of Clinical Ethics*, vol. 4, no. 1 (1993). Copyright 1993, *Journal of Clinical Ethics*, used with permission.

1. L. Edelstein, "The Hippocratic Oath: Text, Translation and Interpretation," *Bulletin of the History of Medicine*, suppl. 1 (1943):p. 3; World Medical Association, "Declaration of Geneva," *World Medical Journal*, vol. 3, suppl. (1956), pp. 10–12; World Medical Association, "International Code of Medical Ethics," *World Medical Association Bulletin*, vol. 1 (1949), 109–11; Beauchamp, T. L., and Childress, J. F., *Principles of Biomedical Ethics*, 2d ed. (New York: Oxford University Press, 1983); Buchanan, A. E., and Brock, D. W., *Deciding for Others: The Ethics of Surrogate Decision Making* (New York: Cambridge University Press, 1989); Childress, J. F. *Who Should Decide? Paternalism in Health Care* (New York: Oxford University Press, 1982); Hastings Center, *Guidelines on the Termination of Life-Sustaining Treatment and the Care of the Dying* (Bloomington: Indiana University Press, 1987); Pellegrino, E. D., and Thomasma, D. C., *For the Patient's Good* (New York: Oxford University Press, 1988); President's Commission for the Study of Ethical Problems in Medicine and biomedical and Behavioral Research, *Making Health Care Decisions: The Ethical and Legal Implications of Informed Consent in the Patient-Physician Relationship*, vol. 1 (Washington, D.C.: Government Printing Office, 1982); Veatch, R. M., *A Theory of Medical Ethics* (New York: Basic Books, 1981).

2. See, e.g., the following: Callahan, D. *Setting Limits: Medical Goals in an Aging Society* (New York: Simon and Schuster, 1987); Daniels, N. *Just Health Care* (New York: Cambridge University Press, 1985); Evans, R. W., "Health Care Technology and the In-

evitability of Resource Allocation and Rationing Decisions," *Journal of the American Medical Association*, vol. 249 (1983), pp. 2208–19; Morreim, E. H., "Fiscal Scarcity and the Inevitability of Bedside Budget Balancing," *Archives of Internal Medicine*, vol. 149 (1989), pp. 1012–15; Veatch, R. M., "Justice and the Economics of Terminal Illness," *Hastings Center Report*, vol. 18 (Aug.–Sept. 1988), pp. 34–40. Thurow, L. C., "Learning to Say 'No,'" *New England Journal of Medicine*, vol. 311 (1984), pp. 1569–72.

3. There are a few scattered references that acknowledge that the interests of the patient's family may be considered. At one point, the president's commission states that "the impact of a decision on an incapacitated patient's loved ones may be taken into account." President's Commission for the Study of Ethical Problems in Medicine and Biomedical and Behavioral Research, *Deciding to forego Life-Sustaining Treatment: Ethical, Medical and legal Issues in Treatment Decisions* (Washington, D.C.: U.S. Government Printing Office, 1983), pp. 135–36. The Hastings Center *Guidelines* counsels consideration of the benefits and burdens to "the patient's family and concerned friends," but only in the special case of patients with irreversible loss of consciousness (p. 29). Buchanan and Brock devote one page of their impressive work, *Deciding for Others* to the "limits on the burdens it is reasonable to expect family members to bear" (p. 208). But these are only isolated passages in large, systematic works, and they do not inform the overall theory developed in these works. The discussion of neonatal care is the only place I know where the interests of members of the patient's family have received systematic attention. (A good example is C. Strong, "The Neonatologist's Duty to Patients and Parents," *Hastings Center Report*, vol. 14 [Aug. 1984], pp 10–16.) The fact that many ethicists seem willing to consider family interests in the case of newborns but not in the case of older patients suggests that we may not really consider newborns to be full-fledged persons.

4. I owe this point to an anonymous reviewer.

5. Thus, I am in substantial disagreement with even that one paragraph from the president's commission's report that goes furthest toward something like the position I embrace. For the president's commission would allow proxies to consider the interests of family members only if there is substantial evidence that the patient would have considered their interests. But on my view this is not the reason that the interests of the members of the patient's family are relevant. If the patient was a selfish, inconsiderate person, this does not mean that the interests of her family somehow become morally illegitimate or irrelevant.

6. Daniels, *Just Health Care*.

7. Hardwig, J. R., "What About the Family? The Role of Family Interests in Medical Treatment Decisions," *Hastings Center Report*, vol. 20 (Mar.–Apr. 1990), pp. 5–10.

4

Technological Determinism despite the Reality of Scarcity: A Neglected Element in the Theory of Spending for Medical and Health Care

James M. Buchanan

Introduction

In the United States, a large and ever-increasing share of total economic value is directed toward outlay on medical or health care services. This end-use of value, along with its rate of growth, is of major concern to anyone who understands the elementary reality of scarcity. The finitude of the resource base, the labor force and its complement of accumulated and natural capital, guarantees that the share of total value directed into medical services cannot continue to grow without limit.

It has proven to be very hard, however, to get analytical "handles" on the fundamental issues here, "handles" that will allow us to sort out just where the problem is and to begin to identify ways and means of dealing with some central elements. I propose to make yet another effort, this time from the perspective of a constitutional political economist who is not an expert in the economics, the technology, or the ethics of health or medicine. I want to suggest that perhaps, just perhaps, the listing of causal sources has been incomplete. In particular, I want to suggest that the central problems may not be those that emerge directly from the institutional structure described by the mix of public (governmental) and private financing, may not be those that emerge directly from the moral hazard that accompanies any large-scale insurance arrangement, may not be primarily because of the explosion in medical-malpractice litigation, and may not be those that emerge directly from the organization of the supplying industry. These familiar problems may, themselves, become apparent sources of concern only in the presence of a more fundamental relationship. I want to suggest that an ultimate causal source of difficulty emerges from the singular nature of the "demand" for medical services, at least for some major portion of these services, and that economists who analyze this "demand" as if it were analogous to other final or consumption service end-uses of economic value may have confused the whole policy discussion.

Let me qualify my argument by acknowledging that I am offering one insight or perspective; I do not claim all-inclusive explanatory power.

I shall clarify the discussion first by analyzing the "demand" for medical services in terms of elementary economic principles. In this early part of this discussion, I shall resort to highly abstracted and admittedly partial models of the medical-health characteristics of the population. The analysis is designed to demonstrate why the advancing technology of medical-service delivery tends to drive the whole "machine," thereby "exploiting" peculiar features of the "demand." In this sense, my title is accurately descriptive; my analysis explains why resource outlay in medical services tends to be technologically deterministic, despite the elementary reality of scarcity.

Once having gotten the elementary economics out of the way, I shall then turn to the ethical issues that necessarily emerge. I shall address these issues from a constitutionalist perspective that will allow us to establish a forum for dialogue, even if the perspective remains silent on the ultimate normative choices that we must make, either directly or indirectly.

Utility and All That

Presumably, individuals produce value in order to spend it on final end-uses or consumption. And the professional economist models the rational choice behavior of individuals as utility maximization. Individuals spend or use their scarce resources so as to maximize the flow of utility or satisfaction that they can achieve. From this simple model of choice behavior, an important principle emerges. The scarce resource yields a maximum flow of utility only if it is allocated among uses in such fashion that a unit of that resource yields the same return in all of the uses to which it is put. Applied to the individual who considers spending alternatives that are possible under given income or wealth constraints, this principle suggests that a dollar spent must yield the same utility return in all uses. If this result is not present, then clearly it would be rational to shift spending from use that yields less to the use that yields more, again as measured in increments of utility or satisfaction.

This elementary model of choice behavior, which is part and parcel of any economist's tool kit, suggests that rational choice requires spending on any valued end-use be made at the margin, in terms of "more or less" rather than in terms of comparative total outlay. From this emphasis on the calculus of margins, which is itself consequent upon the maximization framework, there follows the implication that, in the economic sense, there is no differentiation to be made among the separate potential end-uses of value. A dollar is a dollar is a dollar, and the dollar spent for medical services, at the margin, yields a return equal to the dollar spent on popsicles. From this elementary model of choice behavior, the generalized principle of consumers' sovereignty in a market economy emerges. The preferences of consumers ultimately determine the mix of valued end-items produced by an economy's scarce resources.

Technological development affects this mix only as it may modify relative costs of goods that may be produced and, through such changes in costs, relative prices confronted by consumers, and, hence, relative quantities of differing goods purchased.

I want to suggest here that this elementary model may become a source of misunderstanding at the point where it conflates all potential outlays as withdrawals from an exogenously determined income or wealth constraint. I want to suggest that the economist's categorical distinction between the constraint set and preferences may be misguided and that the dividing line here may be endogenous in itself to the choice calculus of the individual. That is to say, there may exist categories of spending that are treated by individuals to be withdrawals from income or wealth *prior to* the standard calculus of utility maximization. I shall describe this phenomenon by saying that the demands for any such potentially valued items are *lexicographically* related to other end-uses.

I suggest, specifically, that the preferences for or the demand for medical and health care services tend to fit this classification, at least in important respects. No one would spend willingly on medical services if it were not that one feels it necessary. I make an exception for hypochondriacs who literally enjoy trips to the clinic. The individual purchases medical services, directly or indirectly, in order to be able to restore, or preserve, that level of well-being attainable by a rationally selected outlay on nonmedical goods and services. In this sense, medical services are categorically distinct from other end-uses of value, with the partial exceptions of services such as emergency plumbing, hurricane or earthquake damage repairs, automotive towing, and a few others. In a very real sense, outlay on medical services does not compete with other outlays constrained within an exogenously determined budget; medical service outlay comes "off the top," so to speak, and becomes a determinant of rather than determined by the budget constraint. The difference here is recognized indirectly by the presence of medical outlay deductions under general income taxes.

When we pose the question of how much is to be spent on medical and health care services, whether this question be put to the individual who spends privately in the market or to the public chooser (voter, legislator, or bureaucrat) who spends publicly in the governmental sector, the answer is: "Whatever is necessary."

By comparison and contrast, consider how this answer would sound if asked in the context of spending on food, clothing, entertainment, travel, or housing. Suppose we ask an individual how much should be spent on clothing. If he or she responds by saying, "whatever is necessary," we should dismiss the response as meaningless. By contrast, there tends to be a target level of "well-offness" that outlay on medical services purports to restore, before consideration of other outlays.[1]

The Attenuation of Consumer Sovereignty

The elementary fact that we demand and purchase medical and health care services (or, at least, a substantial share of these services), either privately or publicly, lexicographically before the exercise of choices among other valued end-uses, tends to reduce the user's interest in the process and manner of delivery of the services relative to that exercised in the purchase of other goods and services. Because the objective sought is "whatever is necessary to keep one healthy"—so that, once in such a state, we can get on with life—we tend to be much less concerned about just how the required services are supplied. The individual, as final user, tends to abrogate his choice-making role and to allow the suppliers themselves to select among alterative means of delivery. Analogues are present in these situations noted above; when our car breaks down, we tell the mechanic to "fix it," and we rarely inquire specifically and directly into the means through which the repairs actually are to be carried out.

With medical-service delivery, this feature often is discussed in terms of an asymmetry of information between the final user and the supplier; we defer to the doctor because we accept that he knows better than we do just what services are needed to restore or preserve our "well-offness." I am not questioning the empirical reality of some differential in information here. My analysis does suggest, however, that the apparent acquiescence of the final user in the alleged "expertise" of the supplier stems, at least in part, from the absence of the user's direct interest in the consumption flow of services, as such. The combined unwillingness and inability of final consumers-users of medical services to monitor suppliers may produce results that are value wasting rather than value economizing. Again, and as with the alleged informational asymmetry, the fundamental causal element may be the peculiar nature of the demand for medical services rather than the incentive structure.

Technological Dictatorship

So long as the resource requirements dictated by the current technology are severely limited relative to the total potential value generated in the economy, the lexicographic character of the demand for medical services may be accommodated without serious concern. Persons in varying decision capacities can continue to treat medical services outlay lexically before other end-uses of economic value without calling necessary attention to the ultimate contradiction between such an ordering and the finitude of the resources base.

Suppose, however, that advance in technology expands the public's definition and conception of "well-offness." Suppose there arise prospects for a reduction in the probability of premature death from disease and for an extension in longevity. Suppose further, however, that these prospects can be realized only by commitment of significantly large increments in resource cost. The continuing public response that medical care supply be extended to meet the demand described as "whatever is necessary" becomes an engine through which relatively enormous demands on resources can be mobilized. And this technologically driven allocative result will tend to emerge under almost any arrangement for the organization and financing of the medical-service delivery, although these aspects, of course, may retain secondary relevance.

Let me clarify the discussion by introducing a highly simplified example, which is in no way intended to be descriptive but is constructed exclusively to convey the principle at work. For all ages, there were 315 thousand broken arms reported in the United States in 1978, presumably resulting from a variety of causes. Each person so injured demanded restorative treatment, and, within limits, each person presumably was provided with basically the same essential services, as determined by the then-available technology. For illustration, let us say that, on average, an arm fracture required a resource outlay of $300. Recall the data are from 1978, not 1994.

This demand was lexicographic, by which I mean that this total outlay on repairing broken arms was largely independent of the potential demands for non-medical services and of the costs of treatment. The outlay on repairing broken arms depended on the number of fractures, which was stochastically predictable, and on the available technology. And, so long as this technology was such as to keep the overall resource requirements within tolerable bounds, there need have been no conscious awareness of the conflict with overall availability of resource.

Now, however, let us assume, strictly for purposes of making the argument here, that a new and totally different technology of bone repair had become available, a technology that almost miraculously would have repaired a broken arm quickly, so that full usage was restored after only one day. Assume further, however, that this new technique involved a resource cost one thousand times that of the old technology, $300,000 in this illustration.

If the same set of user-consumer attitudes should have carried over, attitudes that required the outlay that was "necessary," given the technology available, there would have resulted a threshold shift in total resource commitment to arm repairs. And this result would have emerged under almost any organization of the delivery system. If we assume that all members of the population were insured fully through private or public schemes against broken arms in 1978, and that the outlay per fracture under the old technology was $300, each person would have faced, on average, an insurance premium (ignoring administrative costs of the insurance system) of roughly $0.42. This premium now would increase to $420, under the introduction of the new technology, for insurance against broken arms alone.

The example indicates that, as technological advance is generalized over all categories of medical care, the resource commitment may become extremely large relative to the size of the economy, and note also that the resource commitment depends strictly on the technology. It is important to recognize that the causal influence runs from the technology directly to the resource use, without the intervening "filter" through expressed preferences, as would be the case with resource usage on ordinary goods and services. To the extent that the demand for medical services, in the aggregate, is lexicographic, the total resource outlay depends strictly on the rate of technological advance. And the self-interest of suppliers acts both to accelerate technological change and to promote uniform rates of adoption of new technology over all sectors and regions of medical service delivery. The socio-institutional "engine" seems capable of generating levels of outlay that are far beyond those already attained. It becomes relatively easy to think of a share of one-quarter of the total value produced in the economy being devoted to medical and health care services by the century's turn.

Efficiency Considerations

Economists have tended to concentrate attention on changes or reforms that will insure that the medical services supplied in response to demand are delivered efficiently. Their focus has been on the perverse incentives faced by suppliers in the face of informational asymmetry, on the moral hazard present under any large-scale insurance scheme, on the free-rider behavior of users under public financing arrangements, on the cost-increasing results of effective cartelization of delivery systems. The reforms advanced by medical economists take the form of suggestions for increasing the competitiveness among suppliers, both among separate "firms" and among separate professional practitioners across the industrial group, for requiring copayment by users under insurance systems, whether these be governmental or private, and for regulatory political-bureaucratic intervention when organizational rearrangements fail to produce desired results.

As an economist, I do not challenge the arguments advanced by those of my colleagues who concern themselves with the efficiency gains promised on successful implementation of those and other possible reforms. My emphasis is, however, quite different, in that I suggest that even in the ideal-utopian world where each and every one of the economists' recommendations is adopted, where medical service delivery is ideally efficient, the lexicographic nature of demand insures that the central allocative issue will remain. As a society, we will still be devoting what appears to be an excessively large share of total value produced in the economy to outlay on the medical and health care sector.

The Ethics of Lexicographic Preferences

I have reached the end of my tether as an economist when I have explained the results that we observe, speculated a bit about alternative futures, and advanced or supported proposals for reform designed to increase efficiency in ical service delivery. If I am to go further and criticize the allocative results that I predict to occur, I must shift to more controversial subject matter. If there is no efficiency-based criterion to be mounted, and if the results still seem to "appear to embody an excessively large commitment of resources to medical services," I must examine the basis for such an intuition. The "ethics of lexicographic preferences" cannot be avoided.

Let me clarify again the meaning of lexicographic preferences, especially in application to medical services. I have suggested that as an empirical generalization, persons demand the outlay on medical services that is "necessary to maximize survival and longevity" and that such a target level of medical care comes to be determined technologically, relatively independently of the manner in which the delivery system is financed or organized. If we are to question this working out of lexicographic preferences on ethical grounds, we must isolate and identify just who is damaged or harmed; in some comparative sense, who suffers as a result of lexicography in preferences for medical services?

I do not want to concentrate on distributional differences that may violate canons of simple justice when all persons do not share the preferences in question. If those with lexicographic preferences for medical services make up a dominant majority coalition, and if the industry wholly or partially is organized and financed publicly, those persons who do not share these extreme preferences may be coerced into financing and ultimately consuming medical services beyond the level they prefer. In this case, claims that the system is unjust or unfair may become ethically legitimate.

However, I want to concentrate on the more difficult question that may arise when *all* persons in the society share lexicographic preferences for medical services. If the delivery system is tolerably efficient, and if participants know the relationship between total resource commitment and the state of technology, can there then be any objection raised to the allocative results, even if very large shares in total value seem precommitted to the medical sector of the economy?

This question becomes especially difficult for an individualist-cum-contractarian, as I often classify myself in all such discussions as this. The individualist cannot invoke the existence of some external source of value that would produce criteria with which to evaluate alterative sets of individual preference patterns. By adopting the individualist philosophical stance, one is thereby committed to a denial that such external sources of evaluation exist. Any criticism of individual preference patterns must be derived, therefore, from the evaluation of some individuals themselves. But if we presume that all persons in a society hold lexicographic preferences for medical services, how can there possibly be any ethical grounds for criticism?

One intellectual ploy that might be suggested is to adopt the familiar contractarian procedure and examine the choice calculus that might emerge from behind an appropriately drawn veil of ignorance and/or uncertainty. This procedure does allow some escape from the constraints imposed by identifiable self-interest while it preserves the individualistic character of the choice setting without invoking external evaluation, as such. This exercise is helpful in forcing some further clarification in the meaning of lexicographic preferences for medical services.

In his private, individually identified capacity as a present or future consumer-user of medical services, the individual may exhibit strict lexicographic preferences. That is, for himself or herself, as an identified user-consumer-patient, the individual may demand that which is "necessary to maximize survival and longevity." At the same time, the same individual, if placed behind the appropriately drawn veil of ignorance and/or uncertainty, may not have such extreme preferences. In this latter setting, the person is forced, essentially, to choose that supply of medical services that is to be made available to anyone (everyone) in the relevant group of participants. And it is surely plausible to suggest that no inconsistency arises between the presence of lexicographic preference in the private-individualized setting and the absence of such preferences in the veil-of-ignorance setting. The presumed differences between choices made in the two settings are directionally predictable. Clearly, the working out of privately identified lexicographic preferences for medical services may generate a larger commitment of resources to the medical sector than the commitment that would be generated under institutions that, directly or indirectly, force persons into some veil-of-ignorance stance. There arises, in this case, an interesting argument for governmental or socialized decision making, one that is almost counter to those that were advanced traditionally. Governmental or collectivized decision making, in something that resembles veil-of-ignorance settings, becomes a way to *limit* overall resource commitments to the supply of services to meet demands that are lexicographic when exercised privately.

The above discussion of the possibility that preferences tend to be lexicographic if exercised privately but nonlexicographic if exercised and expressed publicly or through collective decision structures is, in one sense, a digression from my main argument, because my presupposition is that lexicographic preferences are present in the demand for medical services, regardless of the institutional-structural setting within which individuals exercise demand choices. This empirical presupposition that lexicographic preferences for medical services exist in the veil-of-ignorance choice setting as well as in the privately identifiable choice setting should be tested, of course. And the existence of differences in the basic preferences in the private and the collectivized setting may explain, in part, the relatively smaller resource commitment for medical services in fully socialized systems than in quasi-privatized systems.[2] But casual empiricism also suggests that, even in collectivized structures, preferences tend to be lexicographic. It seems plausible to suggest that the resource commitments in the collectivized delivery systems are as dependent on the rate of technological advance as are the commitments in quasi-privatized systems.

In any case, for purposes of my argument here, I want to presume that lexicographic preferences characterize choices as to medical services demands in all settings. That is to say, whether persons purchase their own medical services, either directly or through voluntarily chosen insurance schemes, or whether persons participate, directly or indirectly, in collective decisions as to the collective demands for medical services, the lexicographic character of the demand is presumed to be descriptive. This presumption allows me to return to the central ethical question in its strongest form. If persons in a society share the lexicographic preferences for medical services, how can there be anything "wrong" with whatever result that emerges, regardless of the size of the resource commitment that the exercise of such preferences may involve?

As noted earlier, the working out of the lexicographic preferences for medical services becomes equivalent to the taking of a share of total value (income) "off the top," so to speak, with this share itself being determined by the state of current technology. The effect is as if the income available for disposition over all utility-enhancing uses is reduced as medical technology advances. There is presumably no clear relationship between the potential supply of work effort and disposable income. But because saving is itself one use of income that is available for disposition after the "necessary" outlay on medical services, we can predict that there will be an inverse relationship between the rate of technological change in medicine and the absolute level of saving and, through this, of capital formation in the economy.

It is plausible, therefore, to envisage an economy in which an ever-increasing outlay, both in absolute amount and relative to total product value, is devoted to the health care industry while the rate of saving and capital formation falls, again both in absolute amount and relative to total value of product. In the limiting case, we can imagine society with a low income level but with most of the income produced devoted to the medical-service industry.

If we invoke an intergenerational veil-of-ignorance construction, we may suggest that such a society will be less preferred than one in which the total outlay on medicine and health care is restricted through the use of some intergenerational rule. An intergenerational veil-of-ignorance construction has the following property: an individual is presumed to be unable to locate himself or herself generationally. That is, the individual cannot know whether, in actuality, he or she will be born in 1990, 2010, 2030, 2050, or some generation thereafter. Suppose, however, that behind such a veil, the individual is allowed to choose between (1) a regime that would leave the working out of lexicographic preferences undisturbed and (2) a regime that incorporates some explicitly chosen limit to the total outlay. It seems plausible to suggest that the individual in such a choice setting may prefer the second of these regimes, which would predictably involve a higher level of income in later periods, but at the expense of some restriction on the full satisfaction of the lexicographic preferences for medical services in earlier periods. The actual choice here would depend, of course, on the predicted rate of advance in medical technology as well as on the cost and other characteristics of this technology over the extended number of periods.

If we shift out of the strict individualist-contractarian normative framework and adopt a more evolutionary perspective that places an independent value on the viability of a complex socioeconomic-political interaction through time, an argument in support of collectively imposed constraints on the total resource commitment to medical care might be developed. The regime that allows for a higher rate of capital formation would have survival value relative to the regime that devotes its potential for saving to outlay for currently used medical services.

Summary and Conclusion

I deliberately have confined the discussion in this lecture to the implications of a single element in the economics of medical services, an element that may not have received sufficient critical attention from economists. I have suggested that preferences for medical and health care services tend to be lexicographic, in the sense that the full satisfaction of these preferences takes priority over other possible end-uses to which economic value might be put. This feature or characteristic of the demand for medical services creates a direct linkage between the rate of advance in medical service technology and the total resource commitment made by society in meeting this demand.

My concentration on this single relationship should not be taken to represent any relegation to secondary importance of those other features of the complex institutional structure for delivery that have been stressed by others who have examined the basic economics of the medical industry. I have suggested, however, that these complementary features tend to be made more serious in their impact by the existence of the underlying lexicographic preferences. Further, I have suggested that, even if these familiar complementary features of the complex structure of medical care delivery should be adjusted or reformed in full compliance with economists' dictates, the technology-dependent resource commitment implied by the lexicographic preferences would remain problematic.

The derivation of an ethical criticism of the exercise of lexicographic preferences, if such do indeed exist, is not, however, an easy task, especially for the individualist-contractarian, even if there arises some strongly felt intuitive sense that something may be "wrong" with such preferences, as exhibited. In order to mount any ethical criticism that seems at all defensible, it becomes necessary to introduce an intergenerational perspective. In this very long range view of things, a regime that collectively adopts some rule that effectively places restrictions on the size of the overall resource commitment to medical services, and perhaps especially the share of the aggregate commitment that involves maintenance and extension of nonproductive lives, may well be preferred to the regime that incorporates no such rule among its complexity of institutional arrangements.

Critics of my thesis may attack me as a Cassandra who raises unnecessary fears about prospects for excessively large resource commitments to the medical and health-care industry. They may bring this charge on either one of two separate arguments. There may be critics, especially economists, who remain wedded to the rational-choice models of the formal analysis in the textbooks, models that implicitly deny the possible existence of lexicographic preferences, especially as applied over large potential changes in resource commitments. Persons will reduce, or so it may be argued, the outlay on medical services in the face of technology-driven quality improvement as costs accelerate beyond certain limits. Hence, so long as the delivery system is financed and organized so as to incorporate incentives that are broadly compatible with the furtherance of standard efficiency norms, there is little cause for worry.

A second, and perhaps less effective, criticism may be mounted that acknowledges the possible existence of lexicographic preferences but suggests that the technological advances to be expected will increase quality of care greatly, relative to the accompanying increases in cost. This criticism, which is likely to emerge from participants in the medical care industry itself, implies that ultimate users-consumers indeed will get "value for money" and, therefore, need not express concern for any comparative wastage of value through overextension of resource outlay.

Of course, no one can predict the rate of technological development in the medical-care or any other industry, but the dramatic research successes over the whole area of related research programs in genetics, molecular biology, biochemistry, and related areas in applied medicine offer little evidence that mitigates against the widely shared concerns about overextendibility, especially in the face of observed dramatic increases in outlays over recent decades.

I conclude, therefore, with this question: how much can we as a body politic "afford" to spend on medical and health care? The laissez-faire response emergent from the mixed private-public delivery system now in place does not offer, for me, a satisfying resolution to this question. But these unsatisfactory results under the mixed system of delivery are surely no basis for any argument to the effect that a more collectivized structure, under lexicographic preferences, would accomplish net improvement.

"The fault, dear Brutus . . ."

Notes

This lecture was delivered at the annual Philosophy of Science Lecture Series of the University of Arkansas for Medical Sciences, April 24, 1990, and published by the University of Arkansas Board of Trustees, which holds the copyright. Used with permission.

1. As noted, economists' concentration on utility maximization subject to exogenously determined constraints has neglected the possibility that some potential outlays

themselves may affect the constraint set. By contrast and comparison, psychologists, who do not work within the economists' model of choice behavior, have examined the problems involved in ordering potential demands hierarchically. Economists reject all such attempts in terms of failure to understand marginal adjustments. My argument here is that, for a limited subset of potential uses of outlay, the approach taken by psychologists may yield helpful insights that the economist's model tends to leave out.

I remain almost a total illiterate in psychology, but the discussion of motivation by Abraham Maslow has been helpful here. See A. Maslow, "Motivation and Personality" (New York: Harper and Row, 1954).

2. See J. M. Buchanan, *The Inconsistencies of the National Health Service*, Occasional Paper no. 7 (London: Institute of Economic Affairs, 1965).

II

Rationing according to Age

5

Understanding Callahan

Janet A. Coy and Jonathan Schonsheck

The relevance of philosophy to public policy issues—especially the moral evaluation of public policy alternatives—is being more widely acknowledged by legislators and other public officials as well as by philosophers.[1] In this article, we discuss some of the general criteria for sound philosophy and public policy. We then apply those criteria to a particular policy debate: the controversy that swirls about the policy proposals advanced by Daniel Callahan in *Setting Limits: Medical Goals in an Aging Society.*[2]

The Methodology of Philosophy and Public Policy

It sometimes happens, in our moral lives, that we have to "make the best of a bad lot," we have to "choose the lesser of two evils." Having surveyed all the available alternatives, and determined the "moral credits" and "moral debits" that accrue to each, we conclude that *every* alternative has a net balance of moral debit over moral credit. For the consequentialist, this means that every alternative will result in a balance of disutility over utility (however utility is specified); for the nonconsequentialist, every alternative requires the violation of one or more moral principles.

Given the possibility of such moral quandaries, it is clearly inadequate to "isolate" an individual alternative, assess its moral credits and debits, and reject it solely upon the determination that the moral debits exceed the credits. For all one knows at this point, every alternative action is morally *worse:* every alternative would create an even greater balance of hardship and suffering or would a entail more serious violation of justice or individual rights. Singling out alternative actions for isolated moral assessment is a methodological error; to determine the morally optimal course of action, one must undertake a moral *comparison* of the various alternatives.

Precisely the same is true when doing philosophy and public policy. *Policy* alternatives generate moral debits and moral credits; it sometimes happens that every policy option would generate a balance of moral debits over moral credits. Given the possibility of such policy quandaries, one ought not to "isolate" an individual policy proposal, assess its moral credits and debits, and reject it solely upon the determination that the moral debits exceed the credits. For all one knows at this point, every policy alternative is morally worse. To determine the morally optimal public policy, one must undertake a moral comparison of the various policy alternatives.[3] (Indeed, this sort of quandary is more likely to arise in policy than in individual morality; for an individual, there is often the alternative of "quietism," of doing nothing; a state's "doing nothing" is very often *itself* correctly considered to be the state's "policy.") Thus, while the "isolated assessment" of a policy option is a *component* of a sound moral decision-procedure for public policy—indeed, a *vital* component—it is *only* a component. *Rejecting* a proposal on account of its moral debits (whether or not they exceed its moral credits), without a moral assessment of alternatives to that policy, is at best premature. And if the alternatives are all morally inferior, it is precisely wrong.

There is a corollary of the methodological mistake of thinking isolated assessment is sufficient for rejecting policy alternatives: the presumption in favor of the current policy. This mistake is made when one subjects a novel policy proposal to moral scrutiny but leaves existing arrangements unscrutinized. The new proposal is assumed to be morally suspect; the current policy is assumed to be morally acceptable. The correct methodology is, of course, a moral *comparison* of the two policy options, the novel and the extant.

It should go without saying—but unfortunately it doesn't—that the very first steps in the moral evaluation of public-policy issues is getting clear on precisely *what* is being proposed and *why* it is being proposed: getting clear on the policy proposal itself and its supporting argument. To the extent that the policy itself is not understood, the moral evaluation will be inaccurate; to the extent that the supporting argument is not understood, the strength of the support will not be determined.

This article is an examination of a specific case: Daniel Callahan's *Setting Limits: Medical Goals in an Aging Society.* Callahan's book addresses an urgent policy matter: the allocation of social resources to health care for the elderly. Callahan's proposals—or what some readers have taken to be his proposals— have been widely rejected; some of those rejections have been vicious.[4] In virtually all of them, however, one encounters instances of the methodological mistakes we have discussed: a failure to understand the policy proposal itself or its supporting argument; the rejection of the proposal "in isolation," that is, without making a moral comparison with alternative policies; the presumption in favor of the present, absent a moral investigation of current policies. So as we turn now to the controversy swirling about *Setting Limits* it is with a dual purpose: to advance the public debate about the allocation of social resources for health care for the elderly and to illustrate crucial methodological requirements of sound philosophy and public policy.

Getting Clear on the Policy Proposal and Supporting Argument

Daniel Callahan, in writing *Setting Limits*, hoped "to stimulate a public discussion of the future of health care for the aged" (p. 23). In this, he cannot be disappointed: at conferences, and in the professional and popular literature, Callahan's proposal is the subject of discussion and debate. Or, more accurately, controversy swirls about what various people *claim* is Callahan's position. We find much of this debate disappointing and philosophically unproductive; neither Callahan's policy proposal itself nor its supporting argumentation is well understood. At conferences and in the critical literature, we have witnessed no small amount of "Callahan bashing."

Why is it that Callahan is so often misunderstood? Broadly, there are four reasons. First, at the beginning of the book, Callahan does *not* discuss in detail the policy he advocates. Rather, he provides a series of *preliminary glosses* of that policy proposal (as indicators of where the overall argument is heading) and then argues particular portions of his case. The various arguments are marshalled, and the refined and qualified policy proposal formulated, only late in the book. The consequence: critics have fastened upon various of the preliminary glosses, incorrectly focusing their critical work on these early formulations. Second, Callahan does not carefully discuss the *relationship* between the two quite different elements of the policy proposal's justification. The consequence: critics tend to address one or the other, but not the two simultaneously; Callahan's justification seems much weaker than in fact it is, and the burden of the critic seems much lighter than in fact it is. Third, the title of the book is misleading. This is a book about establishing priorities in the allocation of social resources; it would have been more aptly named *Setting Priorities*. In titling the work *Setting Limits*, Callahan has directed attention to the most controversial part of his policy proposal. The consequence: critics have severed that part from the overall justifactory framework, attacking it with great passion—and not addressing the more fundamental public policy issues. Fourth, Callahan needed to coin a term to facilitate part of the discussion; most unfortunately, he choose "tolerable death." Despite the fact that this concept bears no philosophical weight in Callahan's justification, critics have treated it as the linchpin of his position. The consequence: substantial critical energy has been devoted—pointlessly—to the issue of what constitutes a "tolerable death."

Despite these faults, Daniel Callahan's *Setting Limits* is an important work that addresses pressing social issues. The aging of the population, the escalating costs of medical care, the growing national debt, and the annual budget deficit combine to create serious problems in urgent need of solution. But because of these faults, some time must be devoted to relating the policy proposal and reconstructing the supporting argument.

Callahan's Social Resource Allocation Policy Proposal

The expository strategy that Callahan selected is to discuss at length various reasons favoring his Social Resource Allocation Policy Proposal (often hereafter SRAPP)—a proposal not fully specified until late in the book. However, he needs to *refer to* the proposal that is the point of marshalling all those considerations—and this he does in a variety of rough formulations. Unfortunately, critics have gravitated to these allusions and attacked them as if they were the proposal itself. However, "the proposal" is that which can (and *must*) be gleaned from a careful reading of the entire work, with all its qualifications and elaborations and specified exceptions. The most concise statement of the proposal is as follows.

1. Government has a duty, based on our collective social obligations, to help people live out a natural life span, but not actively to help extend life medically beyond that point.

    By life-extending treatment, I will mean any medical intervention, technology procedure, or medication whose ordinary effect is to forestall the moment of death, whether or not the treatment affects the underlying life-threatening disease or biological processes.
2. Government is obliged to develop, employ, and pay for only that kind and degree of life-extending technology necessary for medicine to achieve and serve the end of a natural life span; the question is not whether a technology is available that can save a life, but whether there is an obligation to use the technology.
3. Beyond the point of a natural life span, government should provide only the means necessary for the relief of suffering, not life-extending technology. (pp. 137–38)

It is vital to look more closely at some of the clarifications, qualifications, and exceptions offered by Callahan at various points in the text. First, the focus of Callahan's argumentation is not the cessation of medical care per se but of *government funding* for certain kinds of medical procedures; recall in the three principles specified above the prominent reference to "government." Additionally, Callahan frequently notes that his policy proposal concerns the allocation of *social* resources. Second and third: it is *life-extending* care that should not be funded by government—and that only in *some cases*. All three of these points figure prominently when Callahan refers to "my proposal that life-extending medical care be denied to some elderly people under some circumstances as part of government health-care policy" (p. 197). But as regards physically frail, mentally alert patients: "If they have lived a full life, however, extended intensive care and advanced life support would be unwarranted at public expense, an unjustified effort (unless necessary to reduce suffering) to extend life" (pp. 183–84). Fourth, palliative care—in contrast to life-extending care—*ought* to be provided at government expense—as is indicated in the third principle (quoted above). Fifth, it might be the case that the medical procedure that most efficiently relieves suffering has the effect of extending life; it should *not* for that reason be denied. As Callahan writes, "under no circumstance would it be acceptable to fail to relieve suffering because of the possibility of life extension" (p. 173).[5] Sixth, the cutoff of government funds would not apply to the vigorous very old—at least, not until one's second crisis. According to Callahan, "The care of the *physically vigorous elderly person* poses the fewest problems. All levels of care appear appropriate, at least through the first round of illness and disease" (p. 184; emphasis in original).

To summarize Callahan's social resource allocation policy proposal: life-extending medical procedures ought not be provided at public expense to those who have lived a full life span if they are no longer physically vigorous or mentally competent. Everyone is free to purchase, from personal resources, whatever medical care one wishes. Palliative care ought to be provided at government expense; even if palliative care has the effect of extending life, it ought nonetheless be provided.

The Synergism of Elements Supporting Callahan's Proposal

Resource Scarcity. If social resources were sufficient to satisfy every request, there would be no economic need to establish priorities. However, it is not fiscally possible to provide, drawing on social resources, every medically possible procedure for every citizen: "Medicine cannot give every person what he or she may desire" (p. 59).[6] As a consequence, some individuals will receive certain medical treatment, and some will not. We then confront the issue: do we want to decide this on the basis of ad hoc procedures—publicity, proximity to services, interest of the medical community, and so forth—or to establish priorities on the basis of principle? Callahan, of course, argues for the latter. We must *rank* the various claims on the public treasury—realizing that in truth there is no such thing as the "public treasury," but only tax revenues and a growing national debt. The essence of Callahan's argument here is that, in an era of dwindling resources, life-extending medical procedures for those who have lived a full life span, who are no longer physically vigorous, who are in their second (or subsequent) crisis, ought not rank as high as other types of care—for example, life-extending care for those who have not achieved a "natural life span" and palliative care for the elderly themselves.

The upshot of the argument from resource scarcity (often hereafter RS) is *not* that, by adopting Callahan's policy proposal, resources will be saved. Indeed, Callahan acknowledges that adopting his policy might well cost more than the current policy (pp. 147–53). The relevance of the argument from resource scarcity is that, since we cannot do all that we might wish, we need to *establish priorities.* As previously mentioned, *Setting Limits* would be more aptly titled *Setting Priorities;* setting limits is one consequence (albeit an important and controversial consequence) of setting priorities. Callahan writes, "We must try, then, to establish a consensus on the health needs of different age groups, especially the elderly, and establish priorities to meet them" (p. 135).[7]

Philosophical Conception of Aging and Death. The second synergizing element supporting Callahan's social resource allocation policy proposal is a carefully developed philosophical conception of aging and death (hereafter often "PCAD"), one that includes specific implications for understanding the proper "ends of medicine" (p. 22). Callahan argues that because we currently lack any collective, community-based conception of aging, death, or "a whole life," (p. 40) individuals are left to struggle on their own to make sense of the decline associated with aging and to struggle with death itself. (That this task is left to the individual is not surprising, given our individualistic, rights-based traditions.) When combined with what Callahan calls the "modernization of aging"—the "belief that the physical process of aging should be aggressively resisted" (p. 26)—the result is the denial that there is any purpose or value in the aging process. In particular, we see no *social* value; hence, there is no "community among the generations" (p. 30).

Callahan believes that both the young *and* the old would be better served if we, as a society, were to actively seek a collective sense of the "meaning and significance of aging and death." "Meaning" here refers to "the interior perception . . . that one's life is purposive and coherent in its way of relating the inner self and the outer world" (p. 33); "significance" is "the social attribution of value to old age, that it has a sturdy and cherished place in the structure of society and politics, and provides a coherence among the generations that is understood to be important, if not indispensable" (p. 33). Although Callahan acknowledges that some individuals do find limited meaning to their aging and death—via their individual family lives (p. 44)—without a *social* purpose for the aged, the aged will not find "larger meaning" or significance of a kind that is "equal in value" (p. 49) to the meaning and significance their lives had at earlier stages. Currently, all the old can seek is "more of the same"—more of what they had when they were younger—with no special purpose or goals for the late stages of life. Further, lacking the broader social significance and community among the generations, it is difficult or impossible to justly allocate resources to the elderly (p. 32); there is no rationale for the protection of the elderly, except "sentimental beneficence" (p. 32).

Callahan argues that we need to work toward such a collective sense of meaning and significance; it would enhance the psychological well-being of aging individuals and also help ensure that the elderly receive proper respect and, thus, proper care. However, in order to achieve this, certain limits on the human condition need to be *accepted*. These include the realities that life has "relatively fixed stages" (p. 40), and that "old age, of necessity, is marked by decline and thus requires a unique set of meanings to take account of that fact" (p. 40). Accepting these limits allows one to understand "the wholeness of a human life" (p. 64) and "the idea of a 'natural life span' " (p. 64).

In order to more fully discuss these concepts, Callahan needs a term for labeling death at the end of a "natural life span," a term that contrasts with "premature death"—death that occurs before one has lived a "natural life span." Callahan writes: "I will first propose a definition of a tolerable death. If we could agree on that, we would then have, in effect, the basis for a correlative idea of a natural life span and thus, perhaps, the foundation for an appropriate goal for medicine in its approach to aging" (p. 66). However, the *role* of "tolerable death" in Callahan's overall argument is quite *minor*—its function is merely to help define the (vastly) more important term, "natural life span," which bears all the philosophical weight. Callahan proposes (in *part*, duly modified and qualified) that social resources not be allocated to life-extending measures for those who have lived a "natural life span." "Tolerable death" bears *no* philosophical weight. There is no argument in Callahan that has "tolerable death" per se as its premise and "withholding of social resources" as its conclusion. Callahan does not argue that social resources should not be devoted to life-extending care for those who have lived a "natural life span" because their deaths would be "tolerable"; rather, he argues that other demands—for example, palliative care for those very individuals and life-extending measures for those who have not yet lived a "natural life span"—have a higher priority. Indeed, Callahan does not even hold that a "tolerable death," as he defines it stipulatively, is in *any* broader sense "tolerable."[8]

Once the limits of aging and death are accepted and in one sense, embraced, one can not only make sense of this "natural life span" but also begin to articulate the unique role of elderly in society: The elderly are best positioned (1) to "integrate the past with the present" (p. 42), (2) to serve as valuable role models, because they can "appreciate what it means to live in the present," (p.42) and (3) to provide the perspective of the cycle of generations, because only they "can know what it means to go from past through present to future" (p. 43). Indeed, not only are the elderly the only ones who can fulfill such roles, it is their obligation to do so (p. 46).

Such a *social* understanding of the role of the elderly not only provides individuals with the means for understanding the meaning and significance of their own aging but also provides the basis for understanding society's obligations to the elderly. It explains why we, as a society, owe them respect and care. But what respect and care entail is not *more* life (once the elderly have achieved a "natural life span") but *better* life. What we owe them is care, not cure. The focus on cure, on seeking merely *more* life, fosters the tendency to not accept the inevitable limit on life and to not seek a collective sense of aging and death. Care, in contrast, fosters respect while accepting the inevitable decline and death of the individual. These are powerful reasons for accepting Callahan's philosophical conception of aging and death in place of the "modernization of aging."

The Synergism of Elements

What, precisely, is the relationship between the philosophical conception of aging and death and the evidence of resource scarcity—the two elements that *somehow* support Callahan's social resource allocation policy proposal? Throughout the work, we find the two elements inextricably linked. We believe that it does not rest alternatively on one, or the other, nor on their mere conjunction. Our central exegetical thesis concerning *Setting Limits* is this: Callahan's social resource allocation policy proposal rests on the "synergism" between his philosophical conception of aging and death and his argument from resource scarcity. Callahan's philosophical conception of aging and death, considered alone, lacks urgency. Concerns about resource scarcity supply urgency. But those concerns about resource scarcity seem harsh. The philosophical conception of aging and death softens that harshness. There is a *synergism* between these two elements of the justification, because each ameliorates that which is disquieting about the other. And the justification of Callahan's social resource allocation policy proposal is to be found in that synergism.

One *could* argue for a specific (re-)allocation proposal solely from resource scarcity—but that is not Callahan's argument. Furthermore, such a defense lacks compassion. One *could* argue for a specific (re-)allocation proposal solely on the basis of a philosophical conception of aging and death—but that is not Callahan's argument. Furthermore, such a defense lacks urgency. An argument based on the synergism between PCAD and RS—Callahan's defense—lacks *neither;* it is simultaneously sensitive and pressing. Economic realities preclude government funding of all procedures for all people. Social justice requires that the determination of who shall and who shall not receive social resources be *principled,* rather than arbitrary. According to Callahan's PCAD, seeking life-extending procedures for those who have lived a full life is misguided, and thus ranks lower than many other pressing social needs—especially life-extending medical procedures for those who have *not* lived a full life span and palliative care for the elderly themselves. Resource scarcity is the hard reality; a new concept of aging and death would not only be healthier, independent of resource scarcity, but also in the context of scarcity, temper the brittleness of Callahan's proposal.[9]

At three distinct points, Callahan discusses a relationship between PCAD and RS by making a counterfactual claim; while there are minor differences, it is best to read this as a single claim, stated several different times. As this counterfactual claim has been the source of much misunderstanding of Callahan's position, it warrants discussion. Callahan writes,

> While the question of resource allocation provides an occasion to inquire into the relationship between the goals of medicine and the future of aging

(see Chapter 5), I do not intend to rest my case on that basis, even though it provides some collateral support. I want to lay the foundation for a more austere thesis: that even with relatively ample resources, there will be better ways in the future to spend our money than on indefinitely extending the life of the elderly. That is neither a wise social goal nor one the aged should want, however compellingly it will attract them. (p. 53)[10]

Callahan articulates a particular philosophical conception of aging and death. He recommends it to us. He believes that we would be psychically healthier, as individuals and as a society, were we to subscribe to it; it would give meaning and significance to aging and death. *If* we subscribed to it, we would not merely accept, we would *embrace,* a certain pattern of social resource allocation as regards health care—in particular, we would not allocate social resources to life-extending measures for those who had already lived a natural life span. If we subscribed to Callahan's PCAD, we would devote more resources to ensuring a natural life span to younger people and to palliative care for the very old. And we would do this even if we had ample resources and, indeed, even if we had infinite resources. But Callahan does *not* argue simply that, since his PCAD is superior to the modernization of aging, social resources should not be devoted to life-extending measures for the very old (provided other conditions are met). That is, Callahan does *not* (attempt to) justify his SRAPP on the basis of his PCAD alone (even though he urges us to subscribe to his PCAD, and, if we did, we would re-allocate social resources as per his SRAPP).

Were we to adopt Callahan's PCAD, we would embrace limits even if we had ample resources, even if we had infinite resources. However, the United States does not have infinite resources or even ample resources. Indeed, social resources are scarce. Since it is not possible to devote social resources to all possible medical treatment for all persons, we must establish priorities. The life-extending needs of those who have *not* yet lived a natural life span have a higher priority than the life-extending needs of those who *have already* lived a natural life span. Thus, it is incorrect to read Callahan as attempting to justify his SRAPP "independent of" the fact of resource scarcity (though he does urge adoption of the PCAD independent of resource scarcity). The justification Callahan offers for his social resource allocation policy proposal is the synergism of resource scarcity and his philosophical conception of aging and death.

Callahan and Critics

The critics of Callahan have tended to inaccurately synopsize his social resource allocation policy proposal—and the version they offer is more vulnerable to attack. Several have *rejected* (what they take to be) the policy proposal after making a moral assessment in isolation from alternatives—that is, have urged its rejection on moral grounds without determining whether the moral debits of alternative policies exceed the moral debits of Callahan's SRAPP. And we find a strong presumption in favor of the status quo, the unargued (and unwarranted) presumption that existing arrangements are morally superior to the policy proposal offered by Callahan. Additionally, the "justification" attributed to Callahan is often simply mistaken, or omits an essential element, or fails to grasp the relationship between RS and PCAD—these too make the position easier to attack.

Let us take a careful look at the work of four philosophers who have written critical reviews of *Setting Limits*.

Nancy S. Jecker

The SRAPP and its Justification. Among the first to offer critiques of *Setting Limits* was Nancy S. Jecker, who published critiques in companion pieces that appeared in *QQ* and *Public Affairs Quarterly*.[11] These articles seem designed to arouse the passions against Callahan, rather than to contribute to cool philosophical inquiry. Their titles are inflammatory: "Excluding the Elderly: A Reply to Callahan" (Jecker 1987) and "Disenfranchising the Elderly from Life-Extending Medical Care." (Jecker 1988). Her characterization of Callahan early in the latter article casts a dark shadow: "limits to life must be set" (Jecker 1988, p. 52). Of course Callahan believes that a limit to life—death—must be *accepted:* that's an essential element of his PCAD. And of course Callahan proposes that limits to government-financed, life-extending medical procedures (under specified conditions) ought to be *set.* But neither of these is equivalent to, or has the tone of, "limits to life must be set."

In attempting to relate Callahan's SRAPP, Jecker refers to "Callahan's argument for the moral acceptability of restricting access to geriatric medical care" (Jecker 1988, p. 57). This is doubly misleading. First, Callahan does not propose "restricting access" to care per se; he argues for limits on the allocation of social resources (under specified conditions), not for preventing the elderly from receiving care. Second, Callahan argues for limits to the allocation of social resources (under specified conditions) to *life-extending measures,* not to "geriatric medical care" generally. Indeed, Callahan's SRAPP calls for increased spending on certain sorts of geriatric medical care, for example, the relief of suffering.

Such are the inadequacies of Jecker's account of Callahan's SRAPP—what of her account of Callahan's justification? According to Jecker, what "serves to distinguish Callahan's views" from others "is that Callahan attempts to support age rationing independent of social justice arguments that appeal to the fact that rationed goods are scarce" (Jecker 1988 pp. 51–52) And later she claims that "Callahan's argument . . . does not depend upon the assumption that the means to extending persons lives are in short supply" (Jecker 1988, p. 57). On what does Jecker base this startling claim? On a misunderstanding of the counterfactual discussed above.

In the early chapters of his book, Callahan makes this clear: "I want to lay the foundation for a more austere thesis: that even with relatively ample resources there will be better ways in the future to spend our money than on indefinitely extending the life of the elderly. He adds that "even if we had unlimited resources, we would still be wise to establish boundaries." (Jecker 1988, p. 57)

Jecker interprets the counterfactual as the position that Callahan's social resource allocation policy proposal rests upon his philosophical conception of aging and death *alone*. For this interpretation to have any plausibility, Jecker must hold as irrelevant the *extensive* portions of the book that are devoted to the matter of resource scarcity.[12] Jecker seems to be reading the counterfactual as though it said, Although we have relatively ample resources, there will be better ways in the future to spend our money. But we find no textual support for this interpretation.

Callahan does indeed urge adoption of his PCAD. And it is true that if we *were* to adopt his PCAD, we would embrace his SRAPP. However, we have not (yet) adopted his PCAD. And social resources are scarce—and will become even more scarce in the future. We believe—and believe the textual evidence conclusive—that Jecker is precisely wrong in claiming that "Callahan attempts to support age rationing independent of social justice arguments that appeal to the fact that rationed goods are scarce" (Jecker 1988 pp. 51–52). Callahan *is indeed* offering a social-justice argument, an argument that explicitly acknowledges resource scarcity. Or more precisely: one of the two elements whose synergism supports Callahan's proposal is resource scarcity.

Additionally, Jecker attempts a "reconstruction" of Callahan's argument, a reconstruction whose central philosophical concept is 'tolerable'; she moves from "tolerable death" to its being "tolerable for the government to refuse to pay for life-extending treatment for old persons" (Jecker 1988, p. 57). This is misguided; as we have shown, "tolerable death" is merely a stipulative definition. Callahan does not hold that "tolerable deaths" are, in any broad sense, *tolerable,* nor does he speak of government actions as "tolerable." Callahan's SRAPP does not rest on that which is "tolerable"; it rests upon the synergism between resource scarcity and his philosophical conception of aging and death.

Purported Counterexamples. Jecker also seeks to reject Callahan's SRAPP by constructing a counterexample. She offers us the case of Sue:

Suppose Sue is a widow who enjoys good physical health and is mentally alert. She takes tremendous pleasure in a painting hobby, in visits from great-grandchildren, and in watching afternoon television shows. Suppose further that Sue is eighty-two, and that she depends upon Medicare and Medicaid to cover her health expenses. On Callahan's proposal for age rationing, if Sue suffers a cardiac arrest, then the fact that she has had a long life history should militate against government financing of rescue measures designed to extend her life—e.g., cardiac pulmonary resuscitation, coronary bypass surgery to replace clogged arteries, or various medications. (Jecker 1987, p. 14)

The case of Sue, however, is not even a prima facie counterexample to Callahan's proposal—she does not satisfy all the conditions for exclusion from government-financed treatment. Jecker has specified that Sue "enjoys good physical health and is mentally alert"; as regards the "physically vigorous person," Callahan states that "all levels of care appear appropriate, at least through the first round of illness and disease" (p. 184). So Sue is saved—at government expense. (While Sue is a counterexample to the early allusion to Callahan's proposal, she is not a counterexample to Callahan's SRAPP.)

Now let's alter the case so that it does constitute a prima facie counterexample. Imagine that Sue has *already* had a heart attack and has received a coronary bypass at public expense, but she no longer enjoys good health or is not mentally alert. Surely the argument for Sue's receiving additional expensive treatment at public expense is weakened. Nonetheless, there's still an impulse to assent to further treatment—strengthened by Jecker's next words: "It is useful to imagine as vividly as possible what implementing Callahan's proposal would involve. Suppose Sue's attack begins while she is at home" (Jecker 1987, p. 14). If we approach the issue in this way—we limit the issue to whether a particular individual will or will not receive treatment—then everyone with even a glimmer of hope for "recovery" (and some without even a glimmer of hope) arouses our sympathies—and gets treatment. However, it is possible to limit the issue to yes or no for particular patients, without a nanosecond's thought to the consequences of assenting to government-financed treatment, only by refusing to view the issue as the allocation of scarce resources—precisely what Jecker has done. But saying yes to Sue entails saying no to someone else: that's the essence of the allocation predicament. Sue can be saved, but that means someone else will die. Well, not exactly—it might be only that another will receive lesser treatment. But it might also be the case— if Sue's treatment is quite expensive—that *several* others will be denied treatment and thus will die. While there is no one-to-one mapping of lives to lives, there *is* a one-to-one mapping of dollars to dollars: every dollar devoted to Sue is a dollar *not* devoted to some other person in need of medical care or to other social purposes. Perhaps funds should be transferred to Sue from some other area of the federal budget; perhaps taxes ought to be raised to pay for Sue's care. Perhaps so. All such proposals should be evaluated as matters of social justice. But it is unfair to play on our emotions about Sue while systematically ignoring the consequences for other people of saying yes to Sue. It's not enough to construct a prima facie counterexample and then show us the patient, asking us whether we want the person to die. No one does. We want everyone to live. Forever.[13] But of course this is not possible. Some people will receive government-financed treatment, and some will not. And unless the selection is to be totally arbitrary, we need a principled way of determining precisely who will benefit. Callahan offers such a proposal; Jecker urges rejection of it but offers no alternative proposal. The essence of philosophy and public policy, as we have argued, is the moral assessment of *competing* policies—for example, a policy by which Sue receives social resources versus a policy by which Sue does not. To determine the morally superior *policy*, one must investigate the *entirety* of the proposal, not just its implications for one, individual case.[14]

Nora K. Bell

Writing in *Hypatia*, Nora K. Bell[15] devotes little space to the specifics of Callahan's proposal for the allocation of social resources for health care. Tone and nuance are omitted, and the text that *does* appear is misleading. Bell interprets Callahan as

> proposing "a different way of providing care than is commonly considered: that of using age as a specific criterion for the allocation and limitation of health care" . . .
> In this section of his book Callahan "reconstructs the ends of aging" and advances his thesis that age should be a limiting factor in the provision of health services; that upon reaching the end of a "natural life span" further medical intervention should be acknowledged as inappropriate. (Bell, p. 170)

As we have argued, Callahan's "proposal" is that which he formulates late in the book, where he supplies accompanying qualifications, clarifications, and noted exceptions. Here Bell quotes from a *very* early gloss of the proposal, one that merely *hints at* that which Callahan ultimately proposes. Furthermore, "limiting the *provision* of health services" is ambiguous; it can mean (*i*) not providing *social resources* for health services, and (*ii*) *denying access* to health services. Callahan proposes a species of the former (duly explicated), but not of the latter. Finally, Callahan proposes that social resources not be devoted to *life-extending* measures for those who have lived a "natural life span"; he does *not* hold that "further medical intervention should be acknowledged as inappropriate." Indeed—as we have noted—Callahan believes that resources should be *diverted* from life-extending treatment to life-enhancing measures.

As regards Callahan's "justification" of his SRAPP, Bell writes "Callahan's argument seems to rest on the presumption that there is little value in providing certain health services to persons who have reached the end of full and natural lives" (Bell, p. 176). However, in text that Bell quotes, Callahan explicitly denies this: "My principle of age-based rationing is not founded on the demeaning idea

of measuring 'productivity' in the elderly" (Bell p. 140). When set against Callahan's long and sensitive discussion of the meaning and significance of aging and
death, this attribution is not merely wrong, but genuinely unkind. Also concerning "justification," Bell claims that "what Callahan wants the reader to adopt is
captured in his distinction between tragedy, outrage and sadness"; this is followed by quotation of a passage from *Setting Limits* in which Callahan draws
these distinctions. (Bell, p. 172). Bell offers no reason, however, for thinking that
the rather literary passage—rather than the carefully crafted policy proposal itself,
with its accompanying clarifications, qualifications, and so on—is the *essence* of
Callahan's position. This tripartite distinction among tragedy, outrage, and sadness cannot function as a policy proposal—but then, that is not its intended
function.

   Most of Bell's review essay is devoted to challenging Callahan's definition
of a "tolerable death." Bell's strategy is to "note . . . the differences in the biographies of men and women" (Bell, p. 173) and then argue that the death of many
women, when the death fits Callahan's definition, "will be a tragedy and an outrage" (Bell, p. 176). As we have shown, this strategy is misguided. Callahan does
not hold that "tolerable deaths" are tolerable in any ordinary sense. Callahan's argument is *not* simply that social resources ought not be devoted to life-extending
measures for people who have lived a natural life span. Rather, he holds that
given the constraints of resource scarcity (in synergism with his PCAD), such
measures for such individuals ought to have a lower priority than other demands
on social resources. Methodologically, Bell's strategy is very similar to Jecker's attempt to construct counterexamples; the burden of proof is similar too. It's not
enough to argue that deaths that fit Callahan's definition of "tolerable death"
might not be tolerable but even be tragic—Callahan has already acknowledged
that. To reject Callahan in this way, one must argue about *priorities*—that devoting social resources to life-extending measures for those who have already lived a
natural life span is so important that resources ought to be diverted from other
goals (within health care or from other areas of the budget) to that goal or that
it is so important that additional resources ought to be raised. This Bell has
not done.

   Finally, Bell's central thesis is that Callahan's proposal for allocating social
resources for health care would work to the serious detriment of women and thus
should be rejected.[16] If accurate, this is a very serious objection. Bell claims that
"nowhere in the final chapters of *Setting Limits* does Callahan take note of the implications of his thesis for women, or of the special plight of women among the
aged . . . Nowhere does he discuss the fact that the limits he suggests imposing may
have tragic consequences for women" (Bell, pp. 172–73).

   This isn't right. Callahan is indeed aware of the special plight of women; his
discussion of the implications of his SRAPP on women is to be found in the context of comparing his proposal with current policies.[17]

We have noted that, in synopsizing Callahan's proposal, Bell has not distinguished between "life-extending measures" and "palliative measures." Nor has Bell related the fact that, while Callahan advocates not devoting social resources for the former (in specified cases), he advocates *increasing* the social resources devoted to the latter.

Does the limitation on social resources for life-extending procedures work to the disadvantage of women? In light of the fact that women tend to live longer than men, there is a temptation to hastily conclude that it does. But this needs to be *argued;* one is not entitled to *presuppose* that it is in the interests of the very old (regardless of gender) to receive life-extending measures. When the social context of such measures is the "modernization of aging," the preoccupation with life-extending treatment robs aging of meaning and significance. Or so argues Callahan; holding to the contrary requires arguing against Callahan's philosophical conception of aging and death.

Nonetheless, let us assume arguendo that limiting social resources for life extension does work to the disadvantage of women. One must now ask: will any portion of the SRAPP work to the differential *benefit* of women? The answer, clearly, is yes. Given the fact that women generally outlive men, and disproportionately live in poverty (there is no disagreement between Callahan and Bell on this[18]), women will be specially *advantaged* by the diversion of social resources from life-extending procedures to life-enhancing care. *Even if* the portion of Callahan's SRAPP regarding life-extending measures works to the disadvantage of women, whether the policy *on the whole* works to the disadvantage of women cannot be determined without factoring in the special benefits that would accrue to women from the palliative-care portion of the policy proposal—and this Bell has not done.

It is perfectly respectable to argue that, all things considered, Callahan's SRAPP would work to the disadvantage of women. But one must consider all things—not only the portions of his proposal that might appear to work to the disadvantage of women but also those portions that clearly work to the advantage of women.

Dan W. Brock

Quite recently, Brock published a joint review of *Setting Limits* and Norman Daniels's *Am I My Parents' Keeper? An Essay on Justice between the Young and the Old.*[19] Discussing the support Callahan gives to his SRAPP, Brock writes:

Callahan in fact displays considerable ambivalence about the relation of scarcity, and an increased awareness of scarcity, to his proposal. On the one hand, he notes the familiar data on the expanding numbers and proportion of the elderly in society, as well as their disproportionate and rapidly growing use of health care resources, and comments more than once that we cannot continue to pour resources into extending life and postponing death (C, pp. 21, 137; appendix).

On the other hand, he also repeatedly notes that his motivation is *not* simply to reduce health care expenditures, but instead to provide a revised view of aging and old age that will be a benefit to and improve the lives of the elderly as much as the young (C. pp. 53, 116). (Brock, p. 307)

Here Brock correctly cites Callahan's philosophical conception of aging and death and the argument from resource scarcity. But where he sees "ambivalence," and thus an undeveloped and weak justification of Callahan's SRAPP, we see the two elements whose synergism provides strong support for Callahan's proposal. (It's a case not of "on one hand . . . on the other hand" but of the hands locked together.) Later in the essay, Brock claims that the "missing consensus" about Callahan's PCAD is Callahan's "only justification" (Brock, p. 309); this too is incorrect, vastly underassessing the justifactory power of resource scarcity in synergism with the PCAD.

As discussed above, Nancy S. Jeckers attempts to construct several counterexamples to (what she takes to be) Callahan's SRAPP. We find in Brock's review essay a very curious philosophical move. In the body of the article, Brock tells the story of an elderly writer who develops pneumonia; she could easily be saved with short-term hospitalization and antibiotics. It *seems* that Brock is attempting to construct a counterexample to Callahan. However, Brock acknowledges in a footnote that this case does not meet all the conditions for exclusion from government-funded treatment (Brock, p. 311, n. 6) What Brock is doing, it turns out, is questioning one of Callahan's stated exceptions. Brock's criticism is well taken; insisting upon a principled justification for an exception to a policy is methodologically sound philosophy and public policy. However, this is something Brock could have done in a straightforward way. One wonders just why it is raised in a footnote to a passage that *appears* to be offered as a counterexample but is acknowledged not to *be* a counterexample. Predictably, our hearts go out to the eighty-two-year-old writer—and harden against Callahan. By the time one realizes that saving the writer does not entail rejecting Callahan's proposals, damage has been done.

Larry R. Churchill

Churchill has also published a joint review essay of Callahan and Daniels.[20] He places the work of Callahan and Daniels in the historical context of moral psychology and the long debate about the relationship between private interest and public interest. This is most helpful. An unhappy consequence, however, is that there is little space left for discussing the particulars of the two works. Churchill's synopsis of Callahan's SRAPP is incomplete and misleading. And while Churchill does not criticize Callahan on the basis of this inadequate synopsis, promulgating it is counterproductive all the same: "Callahan couches his argument in a sense of finitude about the goals of medicine—to help people achieve a natural life span (which he defines as life through the late seventies or early eighties) and, beyond that, to relieve suffering. Deliberately life-extending health care after the achievement of a natural life span is to be avoided, and such things as mechanical ventilation and artificial resuscitation are not to be initiated" (Churchill, p. 173). What Callahan argues we should "avoid" is not simply medical procedures per se, but devoting social resources to various procedures, under specified conditions (although if we accepted his PCAD, patients themselves would avoid certain procedures). And Churchill omits important conditions here; it is not Callahan's position that social resources *never* be allocated to "mechanical ventilating and artificial resuscitation" to anyone who has already lived a natural life span. For the "physically vigorous elderly person," Callahan claims that "all levels of care appear appropriate, at least through the first round of illness and disease, and even for those who have lived a natural life span if there is a solid prospect of a few (say, four or five) more years of good life" (p. 184). (Artificial resuscitation is included in "all levels of care" [p. 181].) Furthermore, the "sense of finitude about the goals of medicine" includes two distinct elements: the acceptance of aging and death (of Callahan's PCAD) and the finitude of social resources. Both synergizing elements need to be specified in order to capture both the compassion and the urgency of Callahan's position. Additionally, Churchill's account of the role of resource scarcity in Callahan's argument is inconsistent. He writes, "For both Daniels and Callahan, the overriding assumption which animates the discussion is the combination of scarce health care resources and near-infinite needs" (Churchill, p. 171). In our judgment, Churchill *under*estimates the role of resource scarcity in one context, and *over*estimates it in another. He *over*estimates the importance of scarcity—at least with respect to Callahan—when he claims that "neither book makes sense devoid of the assumption of scarcity" (Churchill, p. 171). As we have argued, Callahan urges the adoption of a new understanding of the meaning and significance of aging and death—his PCAD—*independent of* resource scarcity. While the justification of the books' central policy recommendation requires invocation of resource scarcity, reflecting on the meaning and significance of aging and death would make perfect sense—indeed would be a vital social task—even in the *absence* of scarcity, even if resources were abundant.[21] And in reconstructing Callahan's argument, Churchill *under*estimates the importance of resource scarcity. Indeed, it does not appear. He writes, "Callahan's real argument rests on two major claims, one about the ends of medicine and the other about the meaning of old age" (Churchill, p. 173). As we have argued, these are two pieces of the philosophical conception of aging and death, a conception that is itself one of the two synergizing elements of the justification. Despite his earlier claim that what "animates" Callahan's discussion is resource scarcity, Churchill does not include that in his account of Callahan's justification of the social resource allocation-policy proposal. Its omission renders that justification weaker than in fact it is.

Finally, we disagree with Churchill about the general enterprise of Callahan. Churchill claims that, "In all fairness, I think that Callahan wants to signal the need for more wholesale changes in health priorities, but he does not address this in detail" (Churchill, p. 175). We believe that virtually the entire book addresses in detail the need for wholesale changes in health priorities; again, the book might have been more aptly titled *Setting Priorities*.

The Presumption in Favor of the Present

While critics have been quick to tally the moral debits of Callahan's social resource allocation policy proposal (or what they take to be his SRAPP), existing arrangements have not received the same sort of moral scrutiny. As we have argued, this is a serious methodological failure in doing philosophy and public policy. Little attention is being paid to the urgency of the issues or the moral quirks of current public policy.

Although only 5 percent of the elderly are living in an institutional setting at any given time, it is estimated that "one in two persons aged 65 and older will spend some time in a nursing home during their lives, and one in four will spend a year or more."[22] According to the Long Term Care Campaign, it is estimated that 7.1 million elderly Americans needed long-term care in 1989 (Fact Sheet, (p.1). The average annual cost of nursing home stay exceeds twenty-five thousand dollars (Fact Sheet, p. 1). Yet Medicare and private insurance policies cover the cost of nursing home and home care only in the form of short-term critical nursing care and rehabilitation after the patient has experienced an acute illness or injury. Custodial and maintenance care are *not covered*. In fact, Medicare covers less that 2 percent of long-term care costs; private insurance, only 1.4 percent (Fact Sheet,p. 1). Families and patients paid 51 percent of the $41.6 billion spent on nursing-home care for the elderly in 1987, up from 44 percent of such costs in 1980 (Fact Sheet, p. 3). Nearly five out of ten elderly people living alone will spend down their income and assets to the poverty level after only thirteen weeks in a nursing home; more than two-thirds do so in a year (Fact Sheet, p. 3). Even if the catastrophic health care bill had not been repealed, general custodial care would not have been covered by Medicare either in the nursing-home setting or the home-care setting.

These statistics highlight the problems facing elderly Americans in financing their health care. They point to the facts that the current system does not cover significant health care needs of the elderly and that one form of rationing of health care services is already occurring. We concur with Callahan's judgment that "the form that rationing is taking, which is simply to make the elderly pay for an increasing share of their care, is neither fair, open, nor forward-looking. Rationing by age is not desirable in many respects, but it is far more desirable than any other solution that has been offered. But, then, no long-term solutions have been offered" (p. 200).

All this makes clear that, as a society, we confront numerous problems of distributive justice in the allocation of social resources for health care. The alternative to confronting these issues is the continuation of the extant arrangement of haphazard allocation based upon no principles of distributive justice—and that is an option that truly is "intolerable."

Criteria for Criticizing Callahan

We conclude by reviewing the requirements of sound philosophy and public policy as applied to the Callahan controversy—that is, the conditions that must be met to philosophically advance the discussion of these vital issues.

The critic of Callahan employing the method of counterexample must first construct a prima facie counterexample, that is, a case that satisfies all of Callahan's conditions for exclusion from government-financed treatment. But this is not enough; it is not enough merely to arouse our sympathies about hypothetical (or even actual) individuals. The critic must then argue that allocating social resources to providing life-extending treatment to such persons (persons who fit all the other criteria for exclusion) is of higher priority than other pressing social needs, for example, providing life-extending care to those who have not lived a natural life span or palliative care for the elderly themselves—or education for children, or reducing the deficit, and so on.

Ultimately, *Setting Limits* is a book about setting *priorities;* ultimately, the critic who *rejects* Callahan's social resource allocation policy proposal must offer and defend a different set of social priorities. Whether or not one employs the method of counterexample, one must confront the issues of priority.

Now the critic might first address the expenditure side of the budget—arguing for reallocation of health care dollars or reallocation from other areas of the budget. But this must be *argued*—precisely *why* devoting resources to life-extending measures for those who have already lived a natural life span is more important than devoting those resources to competing social needs. Alternatively, the critic might first address the revenue side of the budget, arguing that revenues ought to be raised (i.e., taxes increased) in order to obtain the resources needed for these medical procedures. But this *too* must be argued—precisely why it is more important to procure such treatment than to maintain (or even reduce) taxes. But in the final analysis, the critic who *rejects* Callahan's proposal must address both sides of the budget; the complete social justice argument would specify both revenues and ranked expenditures.

Finally, the critic must argue that devoting social resources to these life-extending measures is consistent with a conception of aging and death that gives meaning and significance to the elderly. Or, alternatively, the critic must argue that providing meaning and significance is not as important as Callahan argues that it is.

Notes

Reprinted with the permission of University Publications of America, from *BioLaw: A Legal and Ethical Reporter on Medicine, Health Care, and Bioengineering.*

1. Several journals devoted to these matters have recently appeared: *Journal of Applied Philosophy, International Journal of Applied Philosophy, Public Affairs Quarterly,* and *BioLaw.* Furthermore, established journals continue to exert influence: *Ethics, Philosophy and Public Affairs,* and the *Hastings Center Report.*

2. D. Callahan, *Setting Limits: Medical Goals in an Aging Society* (New York: Simon and Schuster, 1987). Henceforth, references to this book will appear in the main text.

3. For an example of this as regards nuclear weapons policies, cf. Jonathan Schonsheck, "Wrongful Threats, Wrongful Intentions, and Moral Judgements about Nuclear Weapons Policies," *Monist,* vol. 70, no. 3 (July 1987), pp. 330–56.

4. Dr. Christine K. Cassel writes, "It is one thing to let people die because their lives have become an inconvenience to them; it is quite another to let them die because their lives are an inconvenience to us" (*American Medical News,* Feb. 19, 1988, p. 58.) And C. Everett Koop, M.D., is quoted as saying, "I tend to think that when Callahan looks at a group of people who are a problem, he tends to think about how you can get rid of the people, rather than, how do you address the problem?" (*Northern California Medicine,* Mar. 1990, p. 8). We provide a careful account of Callahan's policy proposal, and its supporting argument, in the text; neither of these comments is worth dignifying with a formal response.

5. Cf. also Callahan, *Setting Limits,* pp. 183–84.

6. Cf. also Callahan, *Setting Limits,* pp. 20–24 and Appendix.

7. Cf. also Callahan, *Setting Limits,* p. 141.

8. Indeed, Callahan himself talks of people experiencing new possibilities, even the old-old; these are people whose deaths would *not* be "tolerable," broadly construed. That he does not consider these "counter-examples" is further evidence that "tolerable death" is merely a philosophical marker, not a (proposed) policy justification. (In retrospect—watching critics pounce on "tolerable death"—we suspect Callahan must wish that he had opted for the inelegant, but serviceable, "non-premature death.")

9. Callahan writes, "The justification I have proposed for the limitation of life-extending resources for the elderly would make little sense, and be unconscionably harsh, apart from the context of an altered vision of the ends of medicine and aging. I would reiterate my objection to a rationing scheme that in the name of cost containment would cut

back on lifesaving care to the elderly without offering a justification based upon some intrinsic benefit for the elderly themselves and some rich understanding of the place of old age in human life" (p. 153; cf. also pp. 197–98).

10. Cf. also Callahan, *Setting Limits*, pp. 116, 209.

11. N. S. Jecker, "Excluding the Elderly: A Reply to Callahan, *QQ: Report from the Institute for Philosophy & Public Policy*, vol. 7, no. 4 (Fall 1987), pp. 12–15; "Disenfranchising the Elderly from Life-Extending Medical Care, *Public Affairs Quarterly*, vol. 2, no. 3 (July 1988), pp. 51–68. Henceforth, references to these articles will appear in the main text. See also the essay by Nancy S. Jecker and Robert A. Pearlman in this volume.

12. See Callahan, pp. 20–24 and the Appendix, "Demographic and Health Care Projections for the Elderly," pp. 225–28.

13. For a discussion of the dangers of this attitude, cf. D. Callahan, *What Kind of Life: The Limits of Medical Progress* (New York: Simon and Schuster, 1990), esp. chap. 2.

14. Jecker offers a second purported counterexample, the case of Sabina; it too fails to constitute a prima facie counterexample. Sabina is not old enough to be excluded. Additionally, it might well be the case that Sabina's pain can be most efficiently relieved by curing her disease—in which case Callahan's SRAPP mandates precisely that.

15. N. K. Bell, "What Setting Limits May Mean: A Feminist Critique of Daniel Callahan's *Setting Limits*," *Hypatia*, vol. 4, no. 2 (Summer 1989), pp. 169–78. Henceforth, references to this article will appear in the main text.

16. Bell's essay concludes with the claim that "setting limits" will have the consequence of making the deaths of certain women "a tragedy and an outrage" (Bell, "What Setting Limits May Mean," p. 176). We take this to be a rejection of Callahan's policy proposal.

17. E. g., see Callahan, *Setting Limits*, pp. 142, 146.

18. Cf. Callahan, *Setting Limits*, p. 170.

19. D. W. Brock, "Justice, Health Care, and the Elderly," *Philosophy & Public Affairs*, vol. 18, no. 3 (1989), pp. 297–312. Henceforth, references to this article will appear in the main text.

20. L. R. Churchill, "Private Virtues, Public Detriment: Allocating Scarce Medical Resources to the Elderly," *Ethics*, vol. 100, no. 1 (Oct. 1989), pp. 169–76. Henceforth, references to this article will appear in the main text. Churchill is sharply critical of those who attribute to Callahan the position that "the old deserve less than the young because they have fewer productive years to be salvaged" (p. 173). We agree with him that

This wrongheaded reading of Callahan is worth noting here because it has occurred several times in national forums. Because he has spoken forthrightly, Callahan seems especially vulnerable to vilification as a nihilist advocating passive euthanasia for the elderly on utilitarian grounds. Those who make such charges against Callahan should not be complimented as having misread him. For anyone who believes that this is his position cannot have read *Setting Limits* at all. (p. 173)

Nonetheless, we take issue with portions of Churchill's claims about Callahan's positions.

21. For this reason, we also reject Churchill's claim that "no reader will benefit from . . . Callahan short of a conviction to face squarely the problem of scarcity in health care" (Churchill "Private Virtues, Public Detriment," p. 171).

22. *Fact Sheet*, (Washington, D.C. Long Term Care Campaign, 1989), p. 2. Henceforth, references to this article will appear in the main text. (The Long Term Care Campaign is located at 1334 G Street, N.W., 3rd Floor, Washington, D.C., 20005.)

6

Justice, Age Rationing, and the Problem of Identifiable Lives

Leonard M. Fleck

Both Daniel Callahan[1] and Norman Daniels[2] argue for an age-based approach to rationing access to health care. In order to avoid being charged with ageism, they both appeal in their own ways to a course-of-life perspective, according to which prudent individuals, early on in life, choosing from behind a veil of ignorance and recognizing that only limited resources were available for purchasing health care as a social good, would allocate more expensive life-prolonging resources to earlier stages in their life in order to maximize the likelihood of their reaching old age, at which time they would then agree to forego these resources. A key moral virtue of this approach is that rationing decisions issue from the autonomous choices of participants, as opposed to being imposed by some in our society on unwilling others.

Baruch Brody does not find this approach to be morally defensible, in part because he does not believe that it can be morally implemented. He writes that "it is one thing to agree in advance that certain care be rationed. It is another thing to accept the rationing when one or one's family is ill and is having care rationed. The difficulty of obtaining patient and family acceptance *at that point* is what drives providers to deceit or at least to minimize awareness."[3] We need to emphasize that Brody is not saying anything here about human nature and weakness of will in the face of death. Rather, his point is that we have no principled basis for making such rationing decisions at the level of the individual patient. As far as he is concerned, a course-of-life conception of health care justice has no moral relevance to *this* patient at *this* point in time. (Brody probably does not have in mind a resource that is scarce in some absolute sense, e.g., a transplantable heart but is thinking of a resource being denied a patient because it is not costworthy from some larger societal perspective. That is, he likely has in mind resources that are relatively scarce rather than absolutely scarce.) Further, the basic reason why Brody rejects such attempts to make such decisions is that they constitute a violation of our society's fundamental commitment to the value of human life, most especially an identifiable human life. The miner trapped in the coal mine or the stranded mountain climber have no claim in justice to the resources needed to save them, but we will still spend millions of dollars to save either, and we seem to believe that it would be very wrong to fail to make that effort, no matter how noncostworthy some flinty eyed economist believes the effort to be. Finally, though Brody does not explicitly make this point, physicians who make rationing decisions at the bedside are really acting as double agents. They can mask that fact only by being deceitful with their patients, hardly a practice worthy of moral commendation.[4]

In short, Brody's basic contention is that the age-rationing proposals by Callahan and Daniels are neither feasible, as a practical matter, nor worthy of being implemented, as a moral matter. Maxwell Mehlman has argued for essentially the same conclusion.[5] His basic claim is that there are formidable transaction costs associated with rationing expensive lifesaving medical treatments at the microallocation level. Those transaction costs are not just economic but legal, administrative, moral, and psychological as well. Like Brody, Mehlman sees the generative source of these costs as being the fact that *identifiable* individuals would be denied these lifesaving therapies. This is in contrast to the "merely statistical" lives that are affected when rationing decisions are made at the level of public policy. Those lives have no names, no faces, and no voice.

My objective is to defend the Callahan-Daniels age-rationing proposals against these criticisms. In the first part of this paper, I briefly consider three unsuccessful strategies for circumventing the criticisms raised by Brody and Mehlman. The criticisms have to be met more directly, which is the task of subsequent portions of this essay. Specifically, it is the "rescue" analogy itself that must be carefully analyzed.

Invisible Rationing Policies

The first way in which we might try to circumvent the criticisms of Brody and Mehlman is by adopting some sort of strategy for achieving our cost-containment objectives that relies upon invisible rationing mechanisms, such as the British have employed with respect to dialysis.[6] As noted by Schwartz and Aaron, the British are able to provide dialysis to only about one-third of the patients in Britain who need dialysis. This has nothing to do with shortages of equipment or personnel. Rather, it has to do with budgetary decisions, specifically, the judgment that health resources are better deployed for meeting other health needs. The result has been that, generally, individuals who are over age fifty-five and have suffered renal failure will be denied dialysis. However, this choice does not represent any government policy. Rather, it is something that has arisen as a "professional understanding" among British physicians, an understanding that has not been a product of any sort of public debate or public moral assessment. In that respect this is a policy for rationing access to dialysis that is "invisible" to the public. The net result of this policy is that individuals who are denied dialysis are also invisible to the public. That is, they are not identifiable victims of some rationing scheme. To themselves, their family, or the public that reads their obituary, they will simply have died of natural causes.

There are other ways in which rationing can be accomplished invisibly. The use of market mechanisms would be one of the more obvious and common of such devices. Calabresi and Bobbitt have probably been among the more outspoken defenders of such invisible rationing mechanisms. Their basic contention is that if rationing of life-prolonging health resources is inescapable, then society is faced with the need to make "tragic choices." These are choices that will necessarily involve the violation of some basic societal value. From their perspective it is morally preferable that such violations are hidden from the public so as not to erode the moral fabric of the community, which is what is accomplished through the use of invisible rationing mechanisms.[7] However, I have argued elsewhere that such mechanisms violate our most central intuitions of justice, according to which *just* policies can be made and defended publicly. This is what John Rawls refers to as the "publicity condition," which is an essential feature of our conception of justice.[8] That feature is certainly one of the most effective devices we have for protecting individuals from arbitrary and capricious treatment. If this is correct, then invisible rationing mechanisms have little to recommend them from a moral point of view, which is to say we cannot use them to circumvent the Brody-Mehlman criticisms referred to above.[9]

A second way of avoiding the problem of having identifiable individuals as the objects of a rationing scheme would be to attempt to devise policies through which all rationing would be accomplished at the macroallocation level, though, I am unfamiliar with any such real-world policies. Moreover, I believe that Haavi Morreim has successfully argued for the claim that bedside rationing, which is microallocation or rationing at the level of identifiable individuals, is ultimately inescapable.[10] In the final analysis all macroallocation policies have to be implemented at the microlevel. They can be made to appear as merely macropolicies only by employing a device at the microlevel that effectively renders the choices there invisible. And if that is true, then this approach to avoiding the Brody-Mehlman criticisms also has nothing to recommend it from a moral point of view.

Third, we could adopt the libertarian strategy of Brody, which would allow patients to make their own choices (assuming they have the financial resources needed to effect their choices). This option, however, can be criticized as being based upon a less than adequate conception of justice. Specifically, it is a libertarian conception of health care justice to which Brody is at least implicitly appealing. I have criticized the adequacy of that conception of justice for health care elsewhere, so I will not repeat those criticisms here.[11] For now it will suffice to say that if access to health care needed for life prolongation is tied to ability to pay, then we have another attempt to employ an invisible rationing mechanism to obscure the fact that an otherwise identifiable individual is being denied needed and wanted health care.

But there is another aspect to Brody's libertarian appeal. In brief, it is the idea that terminally ill patients will gladly give up a lot of these efforts at life-prolongation that have been foisted upon them by physicians who are excessively paternalistic and unwilling to hear their patients' pleas for a more benign death. All physicians have to do is present patients with the option of treatment refusal. Patients will then be making rationing decisions for themselves, but there would be nothing morally problematic about such decisions. And society would thereby achieve its costs containment objectives at no moral cost. The sort of well-known case that I assume Brody has in mind is the case of William Bartling. No doubt there are many such cases in the real world. What is doubtful is that there are enough. There are terminal circumstances that are "really terminal"—nothing is going to turn the situation around. But the more common and more problematic circumstance is one in which the terminal diagnosis is open ended or ambiguous or related to the state of medical technology at that point in time. There is a sense in which all dialysis patients are terminally ill. But it is very hard to imagine a sixty-year-old English gentleman just choosing to forego dialysis if the option is offered to him of that or death. Likewise, if we are successful in developing a totally implantable artificial heart, it is very difficult to imagine that a lot of people will simply forego that option and accept their death, especially if they are not afflicted with other life-threatening ailments, and if the artificial heart itself proves to be no more burdensome in terms of pain and suffering than having bypass surgery. These are precisely the sorts of advances in medical technology that people seem to want and that are the prime source of upward pressure on health care costs, as Callahan has argued quite effectively in his most recent volume.[12] Brody's belief in this situation does not seem to reflect a very realistic understanding of human psychology in terminal circumstances of this sort.

Rescuing Identifiable Individuals

We now need to speak more directly to the objections of Brody and Mehlman. As already indicated, there are a number of distinct criticisms that each raises. However, what seems to be the core of their criticisms, and what seems to be most compelling from a moral point of view as well, is the fact that it is *identifiable* individuals who would be the victims of some rationing scheme. Further, the analogy that both they and a number of other writers on this topic appeal to is the rescue analogy: Some individual has managed to get himself in a perilous situation, perhaps as a result of his own carelessness or ineptitude. It would generally be agreed that that individual has no moral right to be rescued. We (potential societal rescuers) would do nothing unjust if we were simply to ignore his plight. Still, it seems that it would be morally wrong, inhumane, indecent, simply to ignore that individual, even though it would take considerable societal effort and resources to save that individual.

I shall argue that this analogy has no moral relevance in the circumstances that I (along with Daniels and Callahan) envision, when what we are talking about is age-based rationing. I find five disanalogies here. First, rescue efforts of the sort envisioned by Brody and Mehlman are relatively infrequent affairs, whereas the vast majority of us could expect to be rescued by medicine in old age, not just once, but many times, given continued advances in life-prolonging technological research. The sheer quantity of opportunities for rescue in medicine does have moral relevance, especially if there are resource limitations which we are morally obligated to respect.

Apropos is the story that Callahan tells of the proverbial Mr. Smith. Mr. Smith suffers a heart attack at age sixty-five, colon cancer at age seventy-five, a second heart attack at age eighty, a moderately severe stroke at age eighty-two, followed by several other strokes that leave him greatly debilitated in his mid-eighties, until he dies at age eighty-eight in a demented state. The question Callahan asks at the end is when in this continuum Mr. Smith was dying. The questions we wish to ask are, how many times was Mr. Smith rescued from death and how many times are we morally obligated to rescue him from death? The fact is that each time we raise this question we are talking about an identifiable individual. Moreover, if we answer this latter question by saying that we are morally obligated to rescue as long as we have the capacity to rescue, then that would mean that end-of-life, life-prolonging technology would have the potential for hijacking the bulk of our health care budget. It is far from clear that this would be a morally acceptable outcome, much less something that would be morally obligatory. As Callahan points out, medical need is not at all like the need for rescue. "Medical need is not a fixed concept but a function of technological possibility and regnant social expectations. If this is true of medical care in general, it seems all the more true of health care for the aged: it is a new medical frontier, and the possibilities for improvement are open, beckoning, and flexible."[13] We need to emphasize that we are not simply talking about a Mr. Smith here, or a few Mr. Smiths. We are talking about the end-of-life scenario for the majority of us, especially if we live in urban areas where such rescue technology would be readily accessible. That changes by several factors the magnitude of the economic impact of such rescue efforts.

Second, in assessing the moral relevance of the rescue analogy to rationing access to health care, it would be morally ludicrous to encourage those stranded on a mountain to think about accepting death rather than hoping to be rescued, because those individuals are typically in good health except for the fact that they have gotten themselves into life-threatening circumstances. But this is not true for the very debilitated, chronically ill hyperelderly who would be denied certain expensive life-prolonging medical resources by Daniels and Callahan. It is not at all inappropriate to ask that they prepare themselves for death. This is where I believe

Callahan's discussion of something called a "natural life span" is most helpful. There is a fuzziness and indeterminacy about this concept that could be morally problematic in practice at the level of individual decision making, but the alternative seems to be commitment to an indefinitely prolonged life span that is a very definite threat to the just distribution of health resources in our society.

Third, the rescue analogy is very much a black-and-white affair. There are no trade-offs for the person needing rescue. It is rescue or death. But there are important trade-offs that can be offered the very ill elderly, trade-offs that are probably more appropriate to their overall welfare needs, though current reimbursement policies impede the realization of many of these trade-off options and provide instead strong financial incentives for aggressive life-prolonging therapeutic efforts. What I have especially in mind here is the Medicare program, which has been shaped very much by a commitment to high-quality acute health care interventions. As many commentators have observed, that sort of program is not really congruent with the health needs of the elderly, which are predominantly chronic health needs. Some of those needs are for long term care; others are for various forms of supportive care in the community, often care that is more social than medical in nature, but substantially more appropriate to the actual needs of the elderly.[14] These latter programs are costly, though nowhere near as costly as the medical rescue efforts we currently make on behalf of the elderly. Still, we cannot afford to provide all the medical and social care that the elderly want or need. Choices have to be made.

It is worth observing that the rescue analogy may have badly skewed our thinking about these matters in the past, perhaps to the point of thinking that there really was no choice to be made. Perhaps we thought there really was no choice between saving lives and merely improving the quality of lives of the elderly. Then again, perhaps "we" had no right to impose that choice on "elderly others." Perhaps they would see a choice there and like to have the opportunity to make that choice. And if they were to prefer quality-of-life improvements over prolonged life in a demented or debilitated state, then is that not a choice that ought to be respected if we care about the autonomy of the elderly? For the identifiable elderly who would then die "prematurely" would have made that choice for themselves in exchange for other health goods they valued more highly.

It is also morally noteworthy that in the future scenarios envisioned by Daniels and Callahan the now very old would have agreed at an earlier stage in their life to make the trade-offs that will now result in their being denied access to some expensive life-prolonging therapy. Further, they will likely already have derived some benefits for themselves from this trade-off in the form of subsidized community services to the elderly that they otherwise would have been denied. Thus, they not only have no just claim to these life-prolonging resources now, which is equally true of those in most rescue situations, but it would be positively unjust if they were to attempt to press some sort of moral claim now, which would not be true of those in a rescue situation.

Fourth, the need to be rescued is typically a sporadic, episodic, unexpected affair, whereas aging and becoming chronically ill with a disease that will bring about one's death is common, predictable, and ultimately unavoidable. These facts too create a morally significant distinction between what we usually think of as a rescue situation and age-based rationing schemes. We all confidently expect to grow old, whereas few of us expect to be in circumstances that will require a dramatic life-saving rescue. That means we do have the opportunity to plan with respect to our health needs when we are old. More strongly, I would want to argue that we are morally obligated to engage in such planning efforts so as to reduce the likelihood that either we or our surrogates would make unjust demands on the health resources of society.

This last point is one that is in need of being emphasized more explicitly. For the rescue analogy inclines us to think that the value conflict at the core of the health-rescue situation is a conflict between the moral value associated with saving an identifiable human life and the nonmoral value of trying to control escalating health care costs. But in practice the conflict very often is between two basic moral values: saving life and acting justly. A quick example will help to illustrate this point. As things are now, about 28 percent of the Medicaid budget goes to meeting the health needs of the nonelderly poor on AFDC (Aid for Families with Dependent Children); another 31 percent is for programs for the mentally or physically disabled; and another 37 percent is for the long term health needs of the poor elderly. If we allow the rescue analogy to control the flow of health resources to the poor elderly, then the predictable result will be increased pressure to decrease funding for the health needs of the poor nonelderly, especially those health needs that do not involve immediate life and death matters. Some of the health care thereby denied the poor will compromise their prospects significantly for a normal life expectancy; this will mean a premature though apparently natural death. That "natural" death will appear to all as something unfortunate, but in fact it is an injustice that is effectively hidden from moral scrutiny. Those kinds of injustices are not normally part of the ordinary rescue situation, but they are very often a part of health-rescue situations.

There is another feature of the rescue situation that is worthy of careful moral assessment. It has to do with the symbolic value that is attached to the saving of identifiable lives. Economists can readily point out that these dramatic rescue efforts of trapped miners or mountaineers are usually not very cost effective. But efficiency is certainly not something that we regard as our highest moral value. Rather, being able to save a human life, being able to convey the message that each and every individual is worthy of maximal effort by society to save his life, that is what many regard as a powerful symbolic value that is affirmed when large scale rescue efforts are undertaken on behalf of a single individual. Such symbolism, however, sometimes serves to blunt our moral sensibilities or to blind us to serious injustices.

A few years ago we spent several million dollars to free three whales trapped in the Alaskan ice. That can be seen as a powerful symbol of our commitment to animal welfare. Seeing that vividly portrayed on national television, we may fail to consider the innumerable ways in which animals are miserably treated in ways that are judged by our society to be socially legitimate. The same sort of problem can arise in connection with our health care system.

The individuals who are most likely to command our attention for health-rescue efforts are the insured elderly. If their health-rescue budget were wholly independent of the health budgets of all other groups in our society, then we might be able to indulge our passion for such symbols with a clean conscience. But there are no such airtight budgets for the health needs of the elderly. The fact is that if a hospital finds itself underpaid for Medicare DRG patients who can make effective demands for more life-saving medical care, than that hospital is likely to be cut back on the charity care it provides to the poor and the uninsured. That may result in the loss of a substantial number of life-years by the poor and the uninsured, but that is a loss that will likely be invisible, hidden in part by the many ways in which we symbolically and visibly affirm the pricelessness of human life. If that is what our saving of identifiable human lives amount to in practice, then it is hard to understand the justification for attaching high moral praise to such symbols.

There is another point that we need to consider as a reason for preferring identifiable lives or statistical lives. It is what Charles Fried refers to as the "personalist argument." The gist of it is that it is with known lives that we enter into relations of love and friendship. This clearly has a bearing on our health care system, most especially the relationship between doctors and patients. However, the critical point that Fried makes is that "love and friendship do not justify disregarding obligations of justice and fairness, the beneficiaries of which, after all, are real persons too. The generosity of love and friendship is based on giving up what is one's own, not in depriving a third person of his just and fair entitlements."[15] What it seems physicians fail to recognize in our health care system is the extent to which they are distributing *social* resources to which are attached obligations of justice. No doubt our system of health care financing contributes to this problem. It creates the illusion through private insurance policies that these health resources are private entitlements of insured patients, obscuring the very large extent to which our entire health care system is a product of huge *social* investments in building hospitals, training physicians, and supporting medical research.[16]

Finally, with reference to Mehlman's arguments, given our legal and political system, I have to concede that any age-based rationing effort would likely be challenged in the courts. And there would be high transaction costs associated with the defense of such cost-containment approaches, costs that would certainly exceed the resources saved in any individual case. However, this may simply be the price that has to be paid in order to establish the moral and legal legitimacy of such cost-containment strategies. The reader is reminded that the same argument could have been made with regard to the Karen Ann Quinlan case, which no doubt offended the moral sensibilities of many and produced what many regarded as an incorrect interpretation of the law. Still, the fact is that there has now been a long line of cases that has expanded in various ways the decision made in that case. Among other things, this has brought about some important changes in law and public policy, as well as in medical practice and the moral sensibilities of the public. We are currently in the midst of this change, which we should assume will take a generation to accomplish. We should likewise expect that a similar change could be accomplished with respect to the moral issues pertaining to age rationing. Those kinds of changes in public attitude and understanding do not come about quickly, but they do come about, and they should come about when they are morally justified.

We should not, however, leave it to judges to bring about such changes. Rather, there should be a broad-based democratic conversation through which we articulate a comprehensive, coherent, and just set of rationing protocols that we are willing to impose upon our future selves. No doubt those will be identified selves in the future. But, as we have shown in our argument above, the fact that those selves are identified individuals has no moral relevance for determining the fairness of those rationing decisions.

Making Exceptions

In light of all this how should we deal with an alert and vigorous eighty-two-year-old patient suffering from a life-threatening but easily reversed infection? Callahan himself agrees that such a person should get all medically appropriate care, at least through a first round of illness and disease, especially if they have four or five good years to look forward to. Callahan does call this an "exception," and he says the only reason he has for granting it is that he does not think "anyone would find it tolerable to allow the healthy person to be denied lifesaving care."[17] I agree it is morally permissible that the elderly in the circumstances described should receive the lifesaving medical care they need. One might conclude that Callahan abandons his age criterion in favor of considerations of quality of life (see the essay by Sytsma in this volume). But I wish only to argue two points: treating the vigorous elderly is not a requirement of justice, and it is most compelling precisely when it *is* analogous to a nonmedical rescue. In the typical rescue situation (the little girl in the well or the stranded mountain climber) there are no trade-offs or options we can offer these individuals. It is rescue or death. But there are important trade-offs that can often be offered to the very ill elderly, trade-offs that are more appropriate to their overall welfare needs. Such trade-offs are an integral part of the course-of-life conceptions of justice advocated by both Daniels and Callahan. Moreover, these are not just trade-offs that are imposed upon the elderly. Rather, they are trade-offs that they themselves have accepted as prudent rational contractors making resource distributions across the span of their life.

Thus, if we have an eighty-two-year old lady who is somewhat debilitated and who has been living in a nursing home for ten years, and if her family is now insisting she have access to bypass surgery so that she might get an extra three years of life, then it is clear from the Daniels-Callahan perspective that she has no right to that surgery. She has already enjoyed the benefits of a service for which she, in effect, already traded that bypass surgery. On the other hand, there really are no trade-offs that can be offered to the alert and vigorous patient. For her it is the stark choice of rescue or death. That, it seems, is really what compels (morally) the offer of rescue. This suggests a principled explanation for our moral intuitions in these matters; that is, it may be morally permissible to offer life-saving medical therapy to those elderly who have exceeded a natural life span when, for all practical purposes, that is all that can be offered to them.

What exactly is the source of that moral compulsion to rescue this select group of elderly individuals? Is it justice that we see as the compelling moral consideration in what I will call the "typical rescue situation"? I would contend that it is not justice that is ordinarily operative in rescue situations. Instead, it is social beneficence, which I would contend we should think of as a weak social obligation, relative at least to the strong obligations that define justice. As a society it might be an obligation of justice that we have to rescue coal miners trapped in a cave-in. They risk their lives in order to provide for the energy from which we all benefit. But mountain climbers and sailors and balloonists do not seem to have any claims based in justice that would require that they be rescued. Society would do nothing unjust if their plight were ignored, especially if great effort had been made to warn and advise people that no such organized rescue efforts would be forthcoming should they suffer misfortune in their daring exploits.

The elderly, in our relatively affluent society at least, are entitled to have such urgent medical needs considered as a matter of social beneficence. But if they are denied such care, they have not been treated unfairly, especially if the rationing protocols and priorities were adopted by the young and middle-aged for their future elderly selves. If there is any danger in our society as things are now, it is certainly not that the elderly so situated will be denied such care. Rather, the danger is such care will be lavished upon them without considering the just claims to health care of many other groups in our society whose serious health needs are often ignored.

Rationing Openly

I will conclude by outlining briefly what I call an "objectivist social-contract strategy" for implementing the age-rationing proposals of Daniels and Callahan. This strategy would require developing clinical/economic protocols that would eventually be fairly fine-grained and that would govern resource allocation with respect to the very old and very infirm elderly. This is not intended to be cook-book medicine. But it would provide a clinically appropriate basis for managing the flow of expensive life-prolonging resources to the elderly. These protocols would be a product of a consensus process that would have to include both clini-cians and the public at large. There are well-known difficulties associated with this approach, given the uncertainties associated with the practice of medicine, rapid technological change, and the uniqueness of the medical circumstances of each pa-tient—all of which require highly individualized clinical judgment. It will have to be in another paper that I speak to these difficulties. Still, the advantage of this ap-proach is that it reduces opportunities for arbitrariness in distributing health re-sources to the elderly. It is a visible and public approach divorced from any particular payment mechanism, the point here being that linkage to a payment mechanism can too readily corrupt medical judgment. It would, in the final analy-sis, be a principled approach, that being some version of the equal-opportunity conception of health care justice articulated by Daniels and supported by Calla-han. It would likely survive judicial scrutiny, if significant attention were given to the procedures used to implement these protocols in clinical practice. It also as-sumes that there would have been a larger public conversation through which the broad outlines of a framework for health care justice would have been articulated. It is within that framework that these clinical protocols would be developed.[18]

Finally, I note that Daniels and Callahan are their own most astute critics, in that they point out that if their proposed policies were to be implemented to-day, the result would likely be that the elderly would be less well off than they are now. They would be socially abandoned, and, relative to their needs, there would be a less just distribution of health resources. There are a number of practical rec-ommendations I offer to forestall or mitigate the scenarios they fear. First, any ra-tioning or cost-containment policy that targets the elderly must be coupled with equally effective policies that reduce the wasteful use of health resources by the nonelderly. It would certainly be unfair to impose penny-pinching on the elderly while permitting wasteful excesses by the insured nonelderly. Second, any savings realized by denying the elderly marginally beneficial, expensive, life-prolonging health care must be redeployed to better meet the more mundane needs of the el-derly for long-term care or home-based community care. Third, whatever public policy or institutional choices we make relative to age-rationing must be made publicly, visibly, through broad processes of democratic decision making, the general idea being that we choose in the knowledge that we are making these choices for our future selves. That more than anything else protects against the invidious forms of age discrimination that critics of Callahan and Daniels justifiably abhor.

Notes

1. D. Callahan. *Setting Limits: Medical Goals in an Aging Society* (New York: Simon and Schuster, 1987).

2. N. Daniels, *Am I My Parents' Keeper? An Essay on Justice Between the Young and the Old* (Oxford: Oxford University Press, 1988).

3. B. Brody, "The Macro-Allocation of Health Care Resources," in *Health Care Systems: Moral Conflicts in European and American Public Policy,* ed. Hans-Martin Sass and Robert Massey (Dordrecht, Holland: Kluwer Academic Publishers, 1988), pp. 213–36.

4. The classic statement of this position may be found in N. Levinsky, "The Doctor's Master," *New England Journal of Medicine,* vol. 311 (1984), pp. 1573–75, arguing that only the patient can be the doctor's master, not an outside party, no matter what their economic interest. For more recent discussion, see J. LaPuma, "Quality-Adjusted Life-Years: Why Physicians Should Reject Oregon's Plan," in *Rationing America's Medical Care: The Oregon Plan and Beyond,* ed. M. Strosberg et al. (Washington, D.C.: Brooking Institution, 1992), pp. 125–31.

5. M. Mehlman, "Rationing Expensive Life-Saving Medical Treatments," *Wisconsin Law Review,* 1985, pp. 239–303.

6. H. Aaron, and W. Schwartz, *The Painful Prescription: Rationing Hospital Care* (Washington, D.C.: Brookings Institution, 1984), pp. 27–56.

7. G. Calabresi, and P. Bobbitt, *Tragic Choices* (New York: Norton, 1978), pp. 17–28.

8. J. Rawls, "Kantian Constructivism in Moral Theory: The Dewey Lectures 1980," *Journal of Philosophy,* vol. 77 (Sept. 1980), pp. 536–43.

9. L. M. Fleck, "Just Health Care Rationing: A Democratic Decisionmaking Approach," *University of Pennsylvania Law Review,* vol. 140 (May 1992), pp. 1603–17. See also L. M. Fleck, "DRGs: Justice and the Invisible Rationing of Health Care Resources," *Journal of Medicine and Philosophy,* 13 (May 1987), pp. 165–96.

10. E. H. Morreim, "Fiscal Scarcity and the Inevitability of Bedside Budget Balancing," *Archives of Internal Medicine,* vol. 149 (1989), pp. 1012–15.

11. L. M. Fleck, "Just Health Care (I): Is Beneficence Enough?" *Theoretical Medicine,* vol. 10 (June 1989), pp. 167–82.

12. D. Callahan, *What Kind of Life? The Limits of Medical Progress* (New York: Simon and Schuster, 1990), esp. chap. 2.

13. Callahan, *Setting Limits,* p. 134.

14. C. Cassel and B. Neugarten, "The Goals of Medicine in an Aging Society," in *Too Old For Health Care: Controversies in Medicine, Law, Economics, and Ethics,* ed. R. H. Binstock and S. G. Post (Baltimore: John Hopkins University Press, 1991), pp. 75–91.

15. C. Fried, *An Anatomy of Values* (Cambridge: Harvard University Press, 1970), pp. 226.

16. There is much more argument that is needed to justify the claim that I am making here. I offer that in my paper "Pricing Human Life: The Moral Costs of Medical Progress," *Centennial Review,* vol. 34 (Spring 1990), pp. 232–35.

17. Callahan, *Setting Limits,* p. 184.

18. For a more detailed description and justification of this democratic consensus process, see my paper "Just Health Care Rationing," pp. 1617–36.

7

Age Cut-offs for Health Care Entitlements: The Missing Moral Level

Howard Brody

Setting Limits

If one read only the references to Callahan's *Setting Limits*[1] and some of the critical reviews that have appeared, one would think that the entire thrust of this book is to defend the proposition that once individuals reach a certain age, they should no longer have entitlement to life-prolonging medical treatment but should continue to have full access to palliative care and chronic-illness care of the sort that improves quality of life and ameliorates symptoms. It is, therefore, important to remember how little space Callahan actually devotes to this proposal in his book and the secondary position that this discussion occupies in relation to Callahan's main theme. This main theme has to do with the lack of meaning that our society now attaches to the aging process and to the life of the elderly. Callahan argues, I believe quite persuasively, that much of the illogic and impracticality of discussions of aging and the appropriate care of the aged derived from this absence of meaning and the corresponding effort to make old age meaningful by assuming that it is exactly like other stages of the human life span. At its worst, this lack of meaning amounts to a societal denial of the realities of deterioration of function and eventual death.

While Callahan alludes in several places to a narrative or biographical conception of the human life span, his points can be further developed by noting that our society has, in some sense, forgotten how to tell the story of a complete human life. In the ideal life story, each stage of the individual's existence, from birth to death, would play a meaningful and understandable role in coming to know who that individual is, what she has done with her life, and what goods and purposes she pursued. Depending on what popular conception of aging one chooses, the story of a person aged seventy-five in our society today might be told as a continuing effort to keep up function and activity as if one were trying to pretend still to be thirty. Or it might be told as the story of how one is now enjoying the rewards that one thinks one has earned by working hard previously, so that one now is solely on the receiving end and owes nothing back to society at all. Or the story might be that of trying to cheat death by using whatever technology is available to postpone one's final moments. But all of these stories basically indicate that at a deeper level, one has given up hope of trying to make sense of one's life as a whole. These conceptions assume that the only thing that is important in life is the acquisition of pleasurable experiences, one day at a time. Callahan believes that this conception of what life means and how one attaches meaning to one's existence is ultimately empty and self-defeating.

Callahan shows the primacy of the project of restoring meaning to aging in several ways as he discusses his proposals for health care entitlements. First, he mentions that he is opposed to any immediate implementation of his age cut-off recommendation. One practical reason for this that he is strongly opposed to any reduction in medical care for the elderly until there has been a significant increase in the provision of chronic and palliative care. The last thing Callahan wants to justify is the withdrawal of life-prolonging treatment if it is not going to be replaced with more humane and compassionate care aimed at the quality of life for as long as one is going to live. But there is another and deeper reason for the delay; for Callahan realizes there is no practicality in changing the entitlements to life-prolonging health care unless one has already accomplished, at least partially, the reevaluation of the meaning of aging for the society as a whole and of the message that society is giving to the elderly about the meaning and importance of their lives. If society is now telling the aged that their lives don't mean anything, adding to this a message that they are not worth keeping alive is simply one more demoralizing blow. On the other hand, if an adequate message of the meaning of aging could be transmitted, then Callahan's proposal to withhold life-prolonging treatment might be seen as a socially coherent response to the needs and goals of the aged person.

However, the most significant statement Callahan makes regarding the priority of the meaning project is his insistence that his proposal to terminate entitlement to life-prolonging care is not in any way to be construed as a cost-cutting measure. It will perhaps, as a consequence, free up necessary resources to be devoted to the care of younger patients. But Callahan states repeatedly throughout the book that even if resources were full adequate to provide all desired care for all age groups, he would still be in favor of an age cut-off for entitlement. Ultimately, he wants to limit life-prolonging care for the elderly because he believes that such care sends the elderly the wrong message from society about what their lives are about. He is not simply trying to save money at their expense.

Callahan admits that this project would be a slow one, and he envisions that it will take at least a generation to see any substantial progress, assuming that his goal is accepted. Despite his willingness to be patient, or perhaps because of it, a certain air of implausibility comes to surround his entire proposal, both the larger project of reestablishing the meaning of aging and the more limited project of deciding upon entitlements to life-prolonging treatment. This suggests, in turn, that there might be something missing in the conception of society upon which Callahan relies.

Rawls and the Peer Network

I contend that the implausibility in Callahan's project exists because we appear to be lacking in our contemporary picture of how our society functions a critical level of moral inquiry and moral conversation that would be necessary for this project to be carried out satisfactorily. This level of moral conversation is alluded to, but relatively little developed, in John Rawls's *A Theory of Justice.*[2] I have referred to this moral level elsewhere by the unappetizing title of "Life Plan Peer Review Network."[3] For this discussion I will shorten that to "peer network."

The conception of the peer network derives from Rawls's theory of self-respect. Rawls argues that self-respect is the most important primary good, and his principles of justice are stated in the priority order that he gives them precisely because of primacy of individual self-respect. According to Rawls, one has self-respect when one has a rational plan of life that is coherent with one's conception of the good and is realistic when taking into account one's natural talents; when one is making reasonable progress, depending upon where one is in one's life trajectory, toward achieving that life plan; and when both the life plan and one's activities toward it are affirmed by a group of respected close associates.

This group of close associates indicates the socially reciprocal nature of self-respect in Rawls's conception. It is critical to note that these are individuals with whom one voluntarily has chosen to associate, those whose opinion one has voluntarily sought with regard to the rationality and the practicality of one's life plan. This in turn suggests that one would ask individuals (in effect) to be a member of this group only to the extent that one has respect for how they in turn are living their own lives and carrying out their life plans. But having that respect for their life plans entails that they are able to have a maximal degree of self-respect themselves. Thus, these networks of associates engaged in reviewing each other's life plans, based upon reasonable sharing of conceptions of the good life, form a sort of miniature social union. Rawls argues that a just, well-ordered society ought to be seen as a social union of these social unions. At the microlevel, there is a great deal of diversity, since these smaller social unions may have radically divergent views of what counts as a good life. At the macrolevel, there is a great deal of social cohesiveness and cooperation, because all people are convinced that, by adhering to and supporting just social institutions and the general principles of justice that inform the society, they are in turn maximizing their opportunities individually to achieve the goods that they personally desire.

If this description of the activities of the peer network seem somewhat unreal, it may be because most political conceptions that pervade today's marketplace of ideas totally neglect this level of moral discourse. This is true for both traditional liberal and neoconservative conceptions. The traditional liberal can see two levels of moral discourse. One is the individual making his or her own choices in an autonomous fashion, and the other is the government deciding how to carry out useful social activities while still respecting individual rights. At the individual level, it is very hard to say that any action is wrong so long as the rights of others are not violated by it. One may try to persuade someone that what they are doing is a mistake, but if they refuse to accept this, there is nothing more to be said. At the government level, all moral judgment must be based on the least amount of personal knowledge of individuals, and it must be directed toward people as individual social units rather than as full human beings. Any allowance of differential treatment depending on people's conceptions of the good life or on their natural talents and skills would make the national government so intrusive and totalitarian as to be totally unacceptable. Accordingly, the government must deal with individuals as packages of rights rather than as unique human beings.

Neoconservative ideology has seen that something is missing but has been in error about what it is. There has been an effort to insist that the life of the community must be restored by taking away some of the functions now attributed to the national government and redistributing them to institutions at the community level, such as the church, the school, or the city or county government. But the neoconservative conception ignores the fact that, once ideology is put to one side, there is virtually no evidence that the school, the church, or local government is really significantly "closer to the individual" than is the federal government in Washington. Certainly, those community groups do not represent a network with which one has voluntarily chosen to associate except in a very rudimentary fashion. The possibilities for abuse, in having those community groups impose a conception of the good that is very foreign to the individual's own wishes, seem undeniable despite conservative ideology.

In this regard, Rawls's concept of the 'peer network' differs from both traditional liberalism and neoconservatism. The peer network is supposed to affirm an individual's life plan, and this entails that it is not willing to affirm or commend one's each and every desire or whim. In this sense, the level of moral inquiry is at a higher community level compared to the individual. However, this group is much closer to the individual than is any governmental or even community group, because of the close voluntary association and the fact that this network knows the individual uniquely as a person, both in terms of his conception of the 'good' and also in terms of his particular talents and skills and the history of his life up until this point. Their moral judgments about the individual's behavior can thus be fine tuned in a way that no governmental or even community agency is capable of. Moreover, there is an important sense in which they have the power of sanctions over the individual regarding the individual's moral behavior. By withholding their affirmation, they can threaten the individual's self-respect, which is a critical primary good. The individual could, of course, "fire" the peer network and go choose a new one that is more congenial to one's particular desires and plans. If one wants to be a scoundrel, one can go and find a group of scoundrels with which to associate. However, once one has chosen a life plan and has over the years accumulated a group of close associates, a group that functions in the way this network envisions, giving up this group and finding a new one to affirm a modified life plan can be a psychologically wrenching experience, to say the least. Therefore, there is a major sense in which this group has power to at least shape the individual's moral behavior. Psychologically, this seems realistic. I believe that most of us, facing a major moral choice, in one way or another ask ourselves the question, What would those friends whose opinions most matter to me think of me if I were to do this?

The Peer Network, Aging, and Health Care

Callahan's proposal for an entitlement cut-off for life-prolonging health care depends heavily upon his conception of the "natural life span." Callahan believes that there is an age, roughly specifiable for the majority of people, by which one has accomplished most of what one has set out to accomplish in life and has achieved most of what one is going to achieve in terms of interpersonal relationships with family and friends. What the future realistically holds, even though one might go on living for some time, and might indeed enjoy life, is a deterioration in one's ability to carry out any further major projects and the loss of those relationships through death of others or perhaps through deterioration of one's own function. It is, therefore, logical and fitting that once one has reached this time of life, medical care be directed toward maintaining the quality that is possible before death, rather than postponing the time of death itself.

Unfortunately, to implement such a restriction on health care entitlement becomes virtually impossible if one is stuck with the two levels of moral discourse envisioned by the traditional liberal view of society. These choices cannot be left up to the individual, for there is every reason to believe that the individual will, faced with a crisis, cave in to fear or habit and demand life-sustaining treatment. If this is left as an individual decision, one would have to provide this care at public expense so long as the individual makes the choice voluntarily. Alternatively, one can see the federal government enforcing such a rule only by setting a specific age limit, which is likely to be both arbitrary and controversial. No matter which age is chosen, some individuals will have reached the end of their natural life span well before, and others will still have important goals or projects toward which they could contribute in a meaningful way. The injustice of judgments based upon this arbitrary age cut-off will become obvious as soon as individual cases are subjected to public scrutiny, guaranteeing a lack of social support for this proposal.

However, the peer network is precisely the sort of group that could be relied upon to make a meaningful and informed judgment about when one has reached one's natural life span. This group has all along been in the process of monitoring one's life plan and the progress that one has been accumulating toward its realization. When one's major goals have been accomplished, and when one's talents and skills have begun to deteriorate so as to make future accomplishments unlikely, then it is precisely this group that is in a position to gently remind the individual that further prolongation of life will not enhance either self-respect or the cherished goals that have formed this person's life up to this point. In the face of this judgment from the peer network, the *self-respecting* elderly person will then be happy to forgo life-prolonging medical treatment. In the presence of a functioning and recognized peer network upon which one relies for one's ongoing self-respect, the idea of an age cut-off for entitlement to life-prolonging health care makes perfectly good sense. In the absence of such a network, the proposal sounds inherently unworkable.

The Peer Network and Social Reform

I believe that Callahan's proposal to restore meaning to the process of aging and death in our society—and his specific recommendation of an age cutoff for health care—provides only a single example of the importance of the peer network. Were we to find today's society impoverished in terms of its public morality, Rawls would suggest that we have only to look to the absence of any recognition or social promotion of the peer network as a primary reason for this occurrence.

We face in our society today a number of moral issues and problems that share general characteristics with refusal of life-prolonging treatment by the elderly. In all such cases, individuals tend to make choices that do not in any meaningful way promote rational life plans or even that individual's long-term conception of the good. In addition, those choices do a very poor job of developing and taking advantage of the natural talents and skills that the individual happens to possess, particularly in terms of the social contributions that the individual could make. However, in order for government to intervene and to prevent such choices, individual rights would have to be violated, and government would have to become intrusive to an unacceptable degree. I contend that the only way to resolve these problems is to try in every way possible to strengthen an activity that now occurs in an informal and sporadic fashion—the review and affirmation of life plans by these peer networks of close personal associates.

It could easily be argued that the further development and strengthening of these networks is every bit as unrealistic a project as is Callahan's proposal for age entitlement cut-offs. If, however, one feels this way, and one happens to agree with Rawls about the basic structure of society, then one is in effect saying that individuals cannot hope to achieve self-respect in our present social climate. And if one does not adhere to Rawls's conception, one must still agree that we seem therefore stuck between the unpleasant choices of anarchy or fascism when it comes to dealing with many of these moral problems.

I think that Callahan has done us a great service, not only by pointing out the difficulty of attaching meaning to the experience of aging in our contemporary society, but also indirectly by reminding us of a missing level of moral discourse that we, as a society, can no longer afford to ignore.

Notes

1. D. Callahan, *Setting Limits: Medical Goals in an Aging Society* (New York: Simon and Schuster, 1987).

2. J. Rawls, *A Theory of Justice* (Cambridge: Harvard University Press, 1971).

3. H. Brody, *Stories of Sickness* (New Haven: Yale University Press, 1987).

8

Callahan's Medical Rationing Principle: Age or Quality of Life?

Sharon E. Sytsma

There is much in Daniel Callahan's book *Setting Limits* with which I agree.[1] First, I think he is correct that the goal of medicine should never be merely the extension of biological life and that this goal must always be placed in the context of other values. Persons are more than their bodily states; so attention should be directed to the person as a whole, not just as a body. We must resist "vitalism," the view that *all* life, no matter what its quality, is valuable, and the associated enslavement to technology. Thus I too reject "medical need" or "bodily wholeness" as the sole criterion for the administration of health services.

Second, I think Callahan is right that unrestricted spending on health care for the elderly sends the wrong message: that aging and death are great evils to be avoided at all cost. Callahan claims that "the meaning and significance of life for the elderly themselves is best founded on a sense of limits to health care" (p. 116). Constraints on medical spending for the elderly are required, not simply for economic reasons, but for reasons that I believe are *existential*. Life becomes truly meaningful only when we acknowledge that it must end. Unrestrained spending to stave off death masks this existential truth.

Third, I agree that rationing is necessary and that it must be based on moral principles. The need for rationing cannot be eliminated by "cutting the fat" from our medical spending or even by a critical reevaluation of priorities in our societal values. Moreover, our present practice of ad hoc rationing is unjust and should be replaced by a coherent and morally justifiable system.

I do not agree, however, that age-based rationing is the only solution to the problem of the moral distribution of medical resources. In fact, I will argue that rationing by age is morally objectionable and, further, that there is an inconsistency in Callahan's own application of his principle of age-rationing that reveals that he himself resorts to an alternative solution. The inconsistency arises, I believe, in response to his recognition that the consistent adoption of age-rationing as an independent criterion leads to morally unacceptable conclusions. I will show that where the application of age-rationing leads to morally objectionable conclusions, Callahan shifts from the criterion of age to the criterion of quality of life and that all along he really uses the criterion of age as a shorthand reference to quality of life. The suggestion that age should be our principle of rationing is convincing only because there are broad generalizations one can make about a relationship between age and quality of life. Any time an exception arises to the broad generalizations about age-relevant characteristics, age must fall by the wayside.

Callahan's argument for age rationing is based upon the concept of a 'natural life span.' He believes that the notion of a natural life span is commonly, intuitively, and cross-culturally accepted and would not vary according to the ability of technology to prolong life. Rather, it is an idea that evolves, Callahan says, from a "persistent pattern of judgment in our culture and others of what it means to live out a life, one that manifests a wholeness and relative completeness" (p. 65). A natural life span is reached when one has had the opportunity for most of life's major experiences and is a point beyond which death is no longer thought of as being "intolerable."

Callahan states that a person achieves a natural life span somewhere in the late seventies or early eighties. He openly recognizes the dilemma involved in the acceptance of this notion: If we are too precise in our standard, we will not be able to be sensitive to the fact of individual variation among the elderly; but if we are too vague, we will invite accusations of unfairness. He nevertheless maintains that it would be unduly obstructionistic to allow this difficulty to prevent our acceptance of some sort of age standard. His position, then, is that life-saving technology should not be used after a person has reached his or her natural life span. After this point, a person should receive only services that contribute to the relief of pain and suffering.

In order to show how the principle of age rationing (based on the notion of a natural life span) should be applied, Callahan distinguishes seven levels or types of physical and mental status and four levels of care. Levels of care include, from the most rudimentary level, (*a*) nursing care (primarily directed toward relieving suffering and providing care—but not toward the extension of life), (*b*) general medical care (hydration and nutrition, antibiotics, surgery, cancer chemotherapy), (*c*) intensive care and advanced life support, and (*d*) emergency lifesaving interventions. The seven levels that classify patients according to their physical and mental status are: (1) brain death, (2) permanent vegetative state, (3) severe mental dementation, (4) mild to moderate competence, (5) severe illness but mental alertness, (6) physical frailty, mental alertness, and (7) physical vigor.

Age does not function as a criterion for those who are brain dead, for those who are in a permanent vegetative state (PVS), or for those who have suffered from severe mental dementation. Those who are brain dead will not benefit from any level of care. Callahan suggests that we limit the treatment of those in a PVS to nursing or palliative care. Victims of severe mental dementation would receive nursing care but also medical care to the extent that it would contribute to the relief of suffering. So nutrition and hydration would be provided, but antibiotics, surgery, or chemotherapy would not. Age enters as a relevant criterion at the fourth level, with those individuals who have a mild impairment of competence. All such people are, of course, eligible for nursing and medical care, but Callahan claims that for those who have reached their natural life span, advanced life support and lifesaving interventions are not "morally required". Such medical services would however be required for those in this condition who have not reached a natural life span. Similarly, age would be a relevant criterion for those who are severely ill, but mentally alert. Those who have not reached a natural life span would be eligible for all levels of care. Those who have led a full life would not qualify for life-extending and lifesaving treatment, nor would they quality for medical care other than that which would significantly reduce suffering and pain. Those who are physically frail but mentally alert, and who have led a full life, would qualify for nursing and medical care so long as the medical care did not contribute to conditions that seriously detract from the quality of life. They would also occasionally qualify for emergency treatment. Extended attempts to prolong life for such individuals would not be justified.

On the other hand, Callahan makes an exception. He allows that life-extending care should be provided for the elderly who have achieved a natural life span, who are suffering from a life-threatening condition, but who are otherwise "physically vigorous." Callahan makes this exception to his general principle that life-extending care should be withheld from those who have reached the natural life span "because I do not think anyone would find it tolerable to allow the healthy person to be denied lifesaving care" (p. 184).[2] I take Callahan to mean that it would be *morally* intolerable to refuse lifesaving care to an elderly person in good health.

I believe these applications of the principles of medical distribution based on the notion of a natural life span show compassion for the elderly and are consistent with common intuitions about what would be regarded as "appropriate" medical treatment. A closer look, however, will reveal the weakness of Callahan's argument supporting age as a medical rationing criterion.

Callahan argues simultaneously that (1) the achievement of a natural and fitting life span should replace the extension of life as the proper goal of medicine and (2) that we *should* use emergency and life-extending means for the otherwise physically (and mentally) vigorous elderly individual—even though his or her natural life span has been reached. He urges the necessity of adopting age as a criterion for the distribution of medical services, and then, in applying his own principles, he makes an exception for the case of those who have reached a natural life span but are predominantly vigorous in their health. Surely, this is an inconsistency: Callahan's suggested practice contradicts his suggested principle. Further, with regard to the elderly with mild impairment of competence, instead of prohibiting intensive care procedures and lifesaving treatment, he merely claims that we are not "morally required" to provide them. But his primary general principle was that life-extending care should *not* be provided for those who have reached a natural life span, so this application involves not just a "watering down" of his basic principle but a clear contradiction between the principle of age rationing and the application of that principle.

These apparent inconsistencies are revealing. They make it clear, I believe, that Callahan is defending age rationing in such a way that age is to be taken not as an sufficient criterion for the restriction of medical services but only as one *relevant* criterion among others. This clarification of Callahan's position surely points to a need for further clarification of his proposal. If age is not to be a sufficient criterion—if indeed it is obvious that relying exclusively on age would lead to conclusions that violate moral sense—perhaps we should examine *why* it is that age should be relevant at all. Pursuing this question, as I will show, reveals that quality-of-life considerations underlie Callahan's applications. Notice that this criterion provides an alternative for the rationing of medical services that could equally militate against the enslavement to technology and the current of vitalism and, further, could be equally effective as a *rationing* (limiting) principle. If quality of life considerations underlie Callahan's application of age rationing, and if the adoption of quality of life considerations is equally effective at undermining the enslavement to technology and vitalism, and if we are not led to contradictions or to morally objectionable practices in its application (as we are with the criterion of age), then it is the quality of life that should be our moral principle of medical rationing. In pursuing this alternative, let us revisit Callahan's applications.

We have seen that there are only three of the seven levels where Callahan argues for age as a criterion for medical treatment. Why is age not a factor in determining treatment for the *brain dead, permanently vegetative,* or *severely demented?* Because even if such persons were young, intensive or life-saving treatment would not reinstate any quality of life. These people are forever barred from valuable life experiences. With regard to the *mildly incompetent,* we are morally obliged to provide all levels of medical treatment to those who have not reached their natural life span, but not to those who have. Presumably, this is because extending the lives of the mildly incompetent elderly, who have surely fulfilled their capacities and experienced the major opportunities life will afford them, will not contribute significantly to the quality of their lives. Similarly, while we are required to provide emergency or lifesaving treatment to the young, or relatively young, who are *severely ill,* it is much more clear that doing so for the elderly may not only fail to contribute to the quality of lives but may, in fact, detract from it. Finally, for elderly people in a *frail* state of health, it is unlikely that the extension of life is beneficial.

Although the term *frail* remains vague in Callahan's analysis, it is clear that the physically frail are not to be confused with the severely ill. I suppose the distinction is that while the severely ill may recover from one or more ailments, the health of the physically frail is generally impaired. For the physically frail, escape from one problem will just allow another to arise, and this is precisely *why* life-extending procedures are not beneficial. The young who are physically frail, however, benefit more from life-saving or extending treatment because there is so much more for them to learn and experience. Elderly people who are physically frail are already limited with respect to future opportunities and may more readily feel that past experiences have been enough. Age is relevant in these cases because it is logical to assume that because of their age, the physically frail elderly will be less likely to experience quality-of-life benefits from prospective treatment than would younger persons.

Age is a relevant criterion only insofar as it has a bearing in an evaluation of the medical treatment's ability to contribute to the quality of life of the patient. As such, we can see that for Callahan age is really subservient to the broader criterion of the quality of life. This is especially obvious in his warning that we must be sensitive to individual differences among the elderly, so that if a person deviates from the normal processes of aging, and if treatment would have the same likelihood of success as for a significantly younger person, we should go ahead and provide treatment. Callahan's own exception in regard to the physically vigorous elderly allows us to put age within perspective in its use as a criterion for medical treatment. It shows that for Callahan chronological age is relevant only when associated with typical life patterns and should not be used without reference to overall physical and mental health statuses.

It is clear that Callahan's motive for calling for a reexamination of the goals of medicine is to combat that unreflective use of technology that ignores the true needs and desires of human beings. The tendency to use technology "just because it is there" reflects and encourages vitalism—Callahan's prime target. In its place he would like to see an emphasis, not just on the fact of life, but on life's quality. He disapproves of the view that the goal of medicine is the extension of life precisely because that goal is not focused properly on the quality of life. He substitutes "the achievement of a natural life span" as the more appropriate goal of medicine in order to escape the pitfall of vitalism. This ploy, however, is successful only if the notion of a 'natural life span' can function as a practical guideline, and it is necessary only if there is no other way to escape this pitfall.

Doubt is cast on the claim that the "proper" and necessary goal of medicine is the achievement of a natural life span just because, if it is adopted, it appears to be impossible to explain why we are morally required, as Callahan believes we are, to provide higher levels of care (beyond nursing and ordinary medical care) to otherwise healthy people who have already reached that stage. We naturally want to treat such individuals because of the present and likely future quality of their lives. Callahan's proposed statement of the goal of medicine as the achievement of a natural life span backfires: it was designed to ensure a concern for quality of life, but, if adopted consistently as a rationing principle, it ignores the significant quality of life possible for the generally healthy elderly who require life-saving treatment.

Callahan might try to escape this contradiction by suggesting that such persons have not really achieved their natural life spans. He has admitted that the point at which a natural life span is reached varies between individuals, but he says it is reached somewhere in the late seventies or early eighties. Biographies, he says, vary. If he were to admit that it is possible for physically vigorous ninety-year-old patients to have not yet reached their natural life spans, it would suggest that the notion of a natural life span has a greater variability than he specifies. But if the notion is so widely variable, it becomes practically useless, and Callahan's response that to think so is unduly obstructionistic is simply inappropriate.

Callahan's defense of age rationing presumes the legitimacy of the notion of a 'natural life span'. I have argued that the notion is too vague to provide a meaningful and independent guideline. Moreover, it appears that what is at issue, even for Callahan, is really the patient's potential quality of life. Since we have seen that all Callahan's applications can be interpreted in this light, and since it is a meaningful and workable alternative, it follows that age is not a *necessary* criterion, despite Callahan's claims to the contrary (p. 172).

Notes

An earlier version of this argument was developed in an article entitled "Age Rationing of Medical Resources" in the June, 1990, issue of *The World & I.* (Washington, DC, News World Communications, Inc.), some passages of which are reproduced with permission.

1. Daniel Callahan, *Setting Limits: Medical Goals in an Aging Society* (New York: Simon and Schuster, 1987).

2. This sentence is deleted in a revision in the paperback edition of *Setting Limits* (New York: Simon and Schuster, First Touchstone Edition, 1988). His explanation for the exception in the case of the physically vigorous elderly is restated: "public consensus might allow no other course in such cases, and there is no reason why policy could not be formulated to include exceptions—in this or any of the other categories. The open question is whether we could develop exceptions in a coherent, consistent, and reasonable way" (p. 184). The restatement in no way escapes my criticism: the reason public consensus wouldn't allow the physically vigorous elderly to be denied treatment is because they would find that course to be morally objectionable; and such an exception cannot be made in a coherent way, because the exception logically entails another rationing criterion.

9

Designing Ethical Alternatives to Age-Based Rationing

Nancy S. Jecker and Robert A. Pearlman

Increased attention is being paid to the need for rationing health services and to the appropriateness of age-based rationing schemes. If we agree that some form of rationing is unavoidable, given the limited current and future allocation of funds to health care, and we also reject the present informal way in which health care is tacitly and unsystematically denied to various groups, we must explore alternative rationing proposals.

Arguments Supporting Rationing Based on Age

The proposal to ration medical care by age has taken center stage in present debates. This should come as no surprise in light of the phenomenon of an aging society. Since 1900 there has been an eightfold increase in the number of American over the age of sixty-five and almost a tripling of their proportion in the population. Those over the age of eighty-five, the fastest growing age group in the country, are twenty-one times as numerous as in 1900.[1] The elderly are also the heaviest users of health services. Persons sixty-five and over, 12 percent of the population, account for one-third of the country's total personal health-care expenditures (exclusive of research costs).[2] Of course, the fact that the ranks of older Americans are swelling and the cost of their care is disproportionately high does not suffice to make limiting health care to the elderly rational or just; it merely focuses attention on this group and makes them an obvious target.

Many arguments can be marshalled both for and against rationing based on age. Arguments favoring an age criterion can be usefully grouped into three categories: productivity arguments, person-centered arguments, and equality arguments:[3]

Productivity Arguments. Productivity arguments advise us to maximize achievement of some end or goal. One such approach puts a premium on efficient output and measures the worth of individuals in terms of their productive work or contribution to the social order.[4] Older individuals generally contribute in fewer areas and function less efficiently where they do contribute. For example, older people generally cease professional work and take leave of active participation in other social roles, such as parenting. According to this argument, then, in order to maximize public welfare, scarce medical resources should be aimed at prolonging life for the young, who are relatively more productive and efficient in their contribution to society.

Another kind of productivity argument takes reducing health expenditures as its goal and justifies denial of care to the elderly as the most effective means to achieve this. This argument highlights the fact that the financial savings that could be achieved if the elderly were excluded, not only from life-extending care but from various other forms of care as well, is disproportionately high, owing to the fact that the elderly as a group are much more frequent utilizers of health services than are other age groups. For example, as Kilner notes, if only those over fifty-five years of age were excluded from treatment for renal disease in the United States, 45 percent of the costs of the renal-disease program would be saved. In other areas, such as intensive care, a tremendous financial gain could be realized by excluding the elderly.

A final version of the productivity approach invokes as a goal maximizing return on life-years saved. One way of spelling this out is that the young have, on average, many more years ahead to live than older people do. Therefore, life-extending technology applied to the young will yield, on average, a greater return on investment, where return on investment is measured in terms of life-years saved. Even supposing an old and a young person have the same number of years remaining, still the quality-adjusted value of future life-years is generally higher for the younger person. For example, younger years typically include a lower incidence of disease and disability, which have a negative impact on quality of life.[5]

It is a credit to each of these utilitarian-style arguments that they proffer an objective scale by which to gauge the relative value of distributing goods to different age groups. The issue before us, however, is not to furnish an empirical argument but to furnish an ethically defensible one. Measured in these terms, the foregoing arguments encounter formidable obstacles. First, both the functionally-based argument and the argument based on maximizing life-years or quality-adjusted life-years oversimplify the ways in which we actually value persons. We value persons, not merely as means to productive or efficient output, but as ends in themselves. We view older and younger persons as possessing equal worth and dignity, despite discrepancies in their efficiency and productive contribution. For instance, in our society murderers are not punished less for killing sixty-five-year-olds than for killing twenty-five-year-olds.[6] We believe that people of all ages possess an underlying equality of value.

Second, the argument based on maximizing quality-adjusted life-years is difficult to sustain because methods for rating life quality are notoriously controversial.[7] For example, large discrepancies have been found between the life-quality ratings that the general population assigns to various diseases and disabilities and the ratings assigned by persons who actually experience these conditions. Dialysis patients, for example, rank quality of life with dialysis much higher than non-dialysis patients do.[8] This suggests that the population at large may be prone to underestimate the quality of life associated with diseases and disabilities. If so, we can expect to find the quality-adjusted value of life in old age to be underestimated as well.

Third, even if the social worth of persons is simply a function of their productive contribution, many older people could be far more productive than they are now if social barriers were removed. As Spitter points out, many older persons who seek and are capable of carrying out vocational or artistic tasks are treated with patronizing amusement, indifference, or neglect. The commonly held stereotype that older people have no role to play in the social system becomes self-justifying; it is a basis for denying older persons opportunities to continue to make productive contributions.

Finally, the productivity argument that appeals to the principle that excluding older persons produces disproportionate savings is satisfying only if one assumes that greater return on monetary investment is the most appropriate measure of whether medical treatment is ethically warranted. An alternative approach asserts that the aim of medicine should be not to maximize returns on investments but, rather, to compensate for the deficiencies of opportunity and happiness wrought by disease and disability. If these deficiencies fail disproportionately to a certain group then it is ethically legitimate for medicine to serve that group disproportionately, rather than to underserve it as rationing by old age implies.

Productivity arguments generally can be faulted on various other grounds: (1) in the process of identifying and promoting maximization of some end, they unacceptably demean people;[9] and (2) since the elderly are not a monolithic group, but an extremely heterogeneous one, it is unfair to discriminate against some older people on the grounds that their group as a whole is not a productive investment.[10]

Person-Centered Arguments. If these objections to productivity arguments are convincing, we should then explore alternative justifications for rationing by age. Use of an age criterion has been championed recently on person-oriented grounds by philosophers such as Daniel Callahan,[11] Harry Moody,[12] and Norman Daniels.[13] Holders of person-oriented views claim to respect individuals for their own sake, regardless of the goods they produce. For example, Daniel Callahan maintains that denial of health care to elderly persons is consistent with respect for the elderly. This is because, in old age, death is often not an evil to the one whose death it is. According to Callahan, death is tolerable once a "natural lifespan" has been reached, provided that an individual has discharged filial duties and that his or her dying process does not involve tormenting or degrading pain. In situations where death is tolerable, it is tolerable as well to allow death to happen, for example, by withholding government-financed life-extending care.

Harry Moody advances a similar person-oriented argument. He reasons that if we were forced to choose between living in (1) medical institutions that provide excellent palliative and other sorts of care aimed at improving life quality, but provide no life-extending care, and (2) medical institutions that afford mediocre palliative care and mediocre life-extending care, the former would have distinct appeal for older persons. In other words, from the perspective of older people themselves, the opportunity to optimize life quality is often esteemed more than the opportunity to lengthen life. If so, then barring the elderly from life-extending care in order to make possible a better quality of life does not display a lack of respect. Even if the cost of optimizing quality of life in old age is a shorter life, this cost is one older people themselves would be willing to bear. To illustrate this point, Moody asks us to imagine a large and well-endowed volunteer nursing home, spectacularly equipped with all the medical equipment and staff support that could be imagined, but the nursing home lacks basic equipment of an intensive care unit. In this situation, failure to provide intensive care reflects a rational decision to spend finite resources enhancing the quality of life for the residents (most in their eighties), rather than providing life-saving technologies to extend life during a medical crisis.

Finally, Norman Daniels also focuses on respect for individual old people who may be denied beneficial care. He holds that if individuals view their lives as a whole (from a "life-time" perspective), rather than from a particular moment in time (a "time-slice" perspective), they would sometimes prefer distributing life-extending medical resources to earlier, rather than later, years. This would be so, for example, whenever increasing one's odds of living beyond normal life expectancy results in diminishing one's chance of ever reaching normal life expectancy.

Person-oriented arguments offer the clear advantage of exhibiting respect for individuals. But this approach still fails to provide a sound basis for rationing by age. In the first place, as Churchill points out, these arguments routinely presuppose a larger health care system that is cohesive, just, and meets broader social needs of the elderly. For example, as Daniels himself notes, the justification for age-based rationing works only on the contrary-to-fact assumption that individuals live the duration of their lives under a closed health care system (and a system to which a fair share of public funds has been allocated). Only then will it make sense to say that taking life-extending resources away from older age groups results in individuals having access to more life-sustaining services in younger life. If individuals move from one health system to another, say, from a state or federal insurance plan to a health maintenance organization, then the disadvantages they experience at one point will not be offset by advantages at some other point. Similarly, Callahan's and Moody's arguments support an age-based criterion for life-extending care only on the assumption that older people who forego life-extending care will gain more appropriate services, such as better rehabilitative and chronic care. But policies explicitly linking these trade-offs are not presently forthcoming; thus the elderly would be foolish to agree to such sacrifices at the present time.

Additional objections to person-centered arguments include the following. First, Callahan's argument fails to distinguish between rights, on the one hand, and best interests, on the other hand. Even supposing we accept Callahan's view that death in old age is sometimes tolerable, this does not suffice to establish that allowing death to happen is consistent with respecting an older person's rights. It merely shows that letting death occur may be consistent with promoting a person's best interest.[14] Second, Callahan's argument also can be faulted on the grounds that attainment of a natural lifespan is not itself a sufficient condition for the disenfranchisement of older persons from life-extending care; other considerations emerge as ethically important.[15] For example, if an older person chooses to continue living or personally experiences life as worth continuing, disenfranchising that person from the means to extend life would be objectionable.[16] Third, Daniels's argument can be faulted on the ground that it presupposes controversial definitions of health and disease, and these definitions skew the resulting account.[17]

Equality Arguments. A final set of arguments supporting rationing of medical services based on age appeals to the principle of equality. The thrust of this approach is that ageism is not objectionable in the way it is usually thought to be. Unlike sexism or racism, differential treatment by age is compatible with treating individuals equally. For example, as Daniels notes, "If we treat the young one way and the old another, then over time, each person is treated both ways. The advantages (or disadvantages) of consistent differential treatment by age equalize over time." But although differential treatment by age does not imply unequal treatment between persons over a lifetime, equality arguments are no more convincing than productivity or person-oriented arguments. Even if the opportunities that different ages have to gain health care services are consistently age based, this will not always serve to equalize the actual benefits individuals enjoy. First, a young person with a serious disease may have already received a great deal of medical care, while a relatively healthy older person may have received very little. It would not be accurate to say, in this particular case, that the younger party has not been given as great a chance to live as the older person.[18] Second, men and women do not enjoy equality of opportunity under age-based rationing, because women reach older stages of life with greater frequency, anticipate more years of life ahead when they reach old age, and rely to a greater extent on public insurance to cover their health care costs.[19]

Arguments against Rationing Based on Age

Despite the fact that unstinting support for age-based rationing is forthcoming in many quarters, the various arguments on behalf of such a policy are encumbered by serious objections. Countering these arguments, however, represents only the barest beginnings of a sustained argument against such a basis for rationing. Three positive arguments are put forth to show that rationing by age is not an ethical option. These arguments appeal to disproportionate need, invoke special duties, and make the charge of invidious discrimination.

Needs-Based Arguments. First, needs-based arguments underscore the fact that geriatric patients experience a greater incidence of disease and disability than do those in other age groups. Needs give rise to duties, in this case, because the vast majority of old people do not possess the financial wherewithal to meet the increasingly high costs of basic medical services. A growing number of elderly people rely heavily on government programs, such as Medicare. The crux of a needs-based approach is to establish that society is obligated to meet the essential needs of citizens if these needs would otherwise go unmet.

One way of establishing this is to invoke the ethical perspective outlined by Rawls.[20] According to this perspective, just principles are those that would be chosen by individuals in an "original position." In this position, rational agents make choices without knowledge of such things as their gender, class position, social status, natural assets or liabilities, intelligence, rational plan of life, or the particular circumstances of their society. Presumably, in an original position persons are additionally ignorant of their present age, and so they are unsure how the advantages and disadvantages of principles affect their age group. From this perspective, it could be argued, individuals would be concerned to guarantee, as far as possible, that the essential needs of persons of all ages are met. For to the extent that essential needs are left unmet, persons are prevented from carrying out the particular plan they have set for each stage of life. Thus, persons in the original position would prefer to ration whatever constitutes more extravagant, higher cost care with respect to a given society in order to underwrite a decent minimum of care and meet the essential needs of citizens.

Arguments Appealing to Special Duties. A second argument opposing rationing based on age invokes the idea of special duties. In one account, described by Kilner,[21] special duties to provide medical care to older persons derive from the relationship of the older individual to the community:

> Whereas the utilitarian view . . . conceives of the social good atomistically in terms of individual (mainly job-related) contributions summed over the breadth of society . . . this view presupposes a social network of interpersonal relations within which one becomes more and more an essential part the older one becomes. The more personally interwoven a person becomes with others through time, the greater the damage done to the social fabric when that person is torn away by death.

So, for example, if one cannot avoid choosing between saving the lives of two individuals, an older person should be saved before a neonate because the former has more social responsibility and is more deeply integrated and finely fastened within a network of social relationships.

One difficulty with this view is that it appears to depend on the idea that interpersonal relationships are sustained throughout old age. It could be contended, however, that as one moves further into old age the relationships one forged earlier are increasingly severed: spouses and friends die, work associates retire and go their separate ways, and offspring mature and refocus energy toward new family members they wed and parent. But, in response to this, it could be held that even if relational ties are cut or recede in significance in extreme old age, still the depth and character of past participation should be respected. Such respecting calls for refusing to neglect or disown those who at one time occupied a significant place in the social web.

Another way of mounting an argument for special duties to older persons appeals to the fact that the elderly as a group have made past contributions to the social good that entitle them to present acknowledgment. Jonsen elucidates such an argument in the following way.[22] He begins with the premise that the process of having lived through a history, regardless of how calamitous or satisfying it was, is itself an achievement. The second premise asserts that should the society in which that personal history has been lived refuse to acknowledge it in an effective way, resentment—experienced as injustice or the feeling that one is not given adequate recognition—will be generated in those who have lived those histories. The touchstone of the argument is stated in the next premise: this experience of injustice is not a mere epiphenomenon; it reflects a genuine right to acknowledgment. The argument supporting this last premise states that the elderly themselves, as members of society even though not necessarily as individuals, have participated in the creation of social goods. The present state of science, technology, medicine, and culture are the results of their having lived communally through their histories. The conclusion of the argument maintains that effective recognition of the elderly's contribution makes imperative the application of science, technology, medicine, and culture to benefit the elderly.

As it stands, the ability of Jonsen's argument to establish the relative priority of health needs for older persons is unclear. It would seem that the entitlement for the elderly that this argument generates is a prima facie entitlement only: older persons, no matter how old, are prima facie entitled to health care along with everyone else. This would seem to follow from the fact that Jonsen's argument offers a counterpart to the utilitarian position discussed earlier, that is, the view that the young have priority because of potential future contributions. The counterpart to this argument makes evident that older persons as a group are on roughly equal footing in respect to social contribution, because their past contributions offset their lack of future ones. Also, not rewarding the elderly for their past contributions may discourage younger members from making their own contributions.

Arguments Charging Invidious Discrimination. A final sort of defense of the principle that we ought to include, rather than exclude, older groups makes much of the idea that rationing by age represents invidious discrimination. The guiding theme of this view is that discrimination based on age is invidious either because it is buttressed by negative attitudes toward older persons or because it will inevitably engender such attitudes. According to the former account,[23] rationing based on age is supported by nefarious cultural prejudices against older persons. For example, it is unusual to watch an hour of television, without noting offers for products designed to rid our bodies of the signs of aging. The message such sentiments convey is clear: old age is synonymous with ugliness. This attitude allows us to develop the belief that older people, as a group, are different; next, we consider them not equal; finally, we think of them merely as objects to be passed over. Clearly, if these emerge as the underlying reasons why age-based rationing is heralded, rationing based on age should be vigorously opposed, and ageism replaced with an attitude of proper respect.

The second version of an anti-ageist view holds that even if rationing of health care based on age is justified on other, more cogent, grounds, instituting it as a widespread policy would impart a dangerous message. It would be interpreted by many as signaling that older persons are less worthy human beings and so can be legitimately disenfranchised from other essential goods, such as housing and food. In other words, age-based rationing of medical care would constitute a first step down a slippery slope of age-based exclusion in many areas of life. It would also strengthen negative attitudes already present toward personal aging: aging panics people, is experienced as calamitous, and so on. By contrast, enfranchising older persons in the area of health care would impress on people the importance of according respect to all persons, regardless of their age. It would thus foster positive virtues, instill a sense of responsibility for aging parents, and encourage personal celebration of the ripening of human life, as well as its birth and beginning.

In summary, there are many reasons for continuing to include older persons, including the extreme old, within the rubric of publicly financed health care, whether life-extending or palliative. To the extent that scarcity forces rationing, older persons should not be excluded because they are old.

Alternatives to Age-Based Rationing

If the above arguments are persuasive, then age does not constitute an ethically sound basis for limiting care. Yet rejecting an age criterion leads us to ask, What alternative rationing criteria are ethically defensible? In this section, we introduce an ethical framework for thinking about different rationing standards, and we evaluate several alternatives to age-based rationing.

The Ethical Framework

We propose grouping different ethical criteria under two broad categories. The first we call "resource-centered" rationing. Resource-centered criteria ignore differences among persons and instead rest rationing decisions on features of health services themselves. Relevant features may include the price resources command, the newness or technological sophistication resources display, or the rehabilitative, curative, palliative, or preventive function resources serve. In general, appeals to resource-centered criteria occur between different health care categories. For instance, it might be argued that Medicaid dollars should be invested in basic or preventive health care, rather than costly acute care services. The individuals authorized to make resource-centered rationing decisions typically include policy makers, legislators, hospital administrators, and state and federal governments. One appeal of resource-centered rationing is that it offers a way of avoiding controversial comparisons between persons. Of course, this aspect of resource-centered rationing cuts both ways: to the extent that morally relevant differences exist among individuals, resource-based rationing can be faulted for ignoring these.

A second ethical basis for rationing is "patient-centered." Patient-centered rationing claims to identify morally relevant qualities of individuals and make these the determining ground of individuals' entitlement to health care. A person's age, ability to pay, place of residence, life expectancy, needs, past or future contributions, and lifestyle choices are examples of patient-centered standards. In general, appeals to patient-centered criteria occur within health care categories. For example, a particular person may be denied a liver-transplant because that person has a history of alcohol abuse. Persons directly involved with patient care and management are most likely to assume responsibility for patient-centered rationing decisions. The challenge of certain patient-centered rationing is to guard against a tendency to denigrate the worth of certain individuals or groups and to avoid resting rationing on differences among persons that are arbitrary from a moral point of view.

Resource-Centered Criteria

Rationing High-Technology Services. One form of resource-centered rationing holds the success of recent medical technology chiefly responsible for problems of distributive justice in health care. For example: diagnostic technologies, such as magnetic resonance imaging; curative procedures, such as organ transplantation; and therapies, such as total parental nutrition, raise rationing problems that did not exist previously. This approach regards rationing publicly financed high technology as a natural antidote to our present health care crisis. "High technology" usually refers in this context to apparatus and procedures based on modern sciences, as opposed to the simpler healing arts. High technology also connotes: new, as opposed to long accepted; scientifically complex, as distinct from common sense; costly, rather than inexpensive; and limited, rather than widespread, expertise in using a particular technique. Advocates of rationing publicly financed high-technology medicine defend their view by pointing, first, to a growing consensus among intellectual leaders in the health care field that much technologically advanced curative medicine costs a great deal in comparison to alternative health purposes.[24] Subjective factors, such as practice style or the prestige associated with new technologies, have been suggested as influencing clinical treatment much more than does scientific evidence. As Abel-Smith writes, "If a physician wants to order diagnostic tests or use surgery . . . he expects the sky to be the limit. But if he were to decide to prescribe . . . just a concrete ramp to enable a wheel chair patient to get in and out of his home the physician's expectations and the public's suddenly become circumscribed."[25] In the academic setting especially, centers of excellence depend upon enterprising groups of individuals becoming experts and specialists in the latest technologies. Critics charge that high technologies are sought primarily to advance professional careers, rather than to provide medical benefits to patients. Strategies for controlling runaway technology include adjusting the way physicians are reimbursed to reduce the incentive to use expensive technologies,[26] improving technology assessment and eliminating nonbeneficial or only marginally beneficial technologies, preventing physicians from profiting from referrals to high-technology service centers,[27] educating clinicians to be more prudent in judging the costs and benefits of new technologies,[28] and curbing citizens' demands for high technologies.[29] In general, these authors maintain that the burden of proof in high-technology medicine should be shifted to those who urge proceeding with it full speed ahead.

Further support for rationing medical technology is based on the belief that no one has a right to receive the latest medical technologies in the first place. Such a stance is consistent with beliefs we hold in other areas. For example, in the area of education, we do not think that students' rights are infringed because public schools do not provide them with ergonomic chairs or the latest computer software. Likewise, in the area of health care, denying public support for the development of leading edge technologies does not imply that our health care system treats patients unjustly.

Despite its appeal, the proposal to ration publicly supported high technology can be faulted on several grounds. First, although certain forms of health care are above and beyond what society is morally obligated to provide, the practical difficulty is to identify forms of care that fall under this heading. Technological sophistication alone is not an adequate gauge. Especially where technology is defined broadly, to include technical complexity, newness, costliness, and related features, such as scarcity and professional expertise, it is not a sensitive tool.

Second, much of the criticism directed against public support for high-technology medicine speaks to the unwarranted use of medical technologies in clinical practice.[30] These objections do not establish that technology per se should be rationed. The soundness of limiting the use of technologies will depend upon the extent of medical benefits those technologies afford in specific, clinical applications and whether they qualify as basic or nonbasic forms of medical care. (We discuss these criteria in more detail below.)

Finally, a major drawback of rationing publicly financed high technology is that today's high technologies are tomorrow's low technologies. Developing new technologies is important as a pathway to improving the overall level of health care in society. For example, if Congress had failed to extend Medicare to cover the cost of hemodialysis, then many patients who can now live happy and productive lives would have died prematurely.

Rationing Nonbasic Services. A second form of resource-centered rationing advocates rationing nonbasic services that exceed a basic floor.[31] On this model, those whose primary concern is guaranteeing a basic floor depend on the imposition of a ceiling for the resources they need. The floor is elaborated in a variety of ways. Some elaborate the floor in terms of the government's minimum obligation defined as the least health services the public feels compelled to provide individuals, merely because they need help.[32] Others identify the floor as including those services most people use most of the time. Still others judge that the basic floor should encompass primary care generally and include such items as immunizations, basic health education, inexpensive curative therapies, relief for chronic conditions, emergency care, and palliative care.[33] Finally, some associate basic care with less technologically sophisticated services.

We submit that basic health care refers to health services that prevent, cure, or compensate for deficiencies in the normal opportunities persons enjoy at each stage of life.[34] We define the normal range both *biologically,* in terms of typical species functioning, and *socially,* in terms of the level of health care resources available in the society at large. For example, in old age, disabilities in activities of daily living can restrict normal opportunities; home health care is a form of basic care that can compensate for these restrictions. Yet basic care does not include the most advanced form of computer-assisted rehabilitative care. Although the most advanced form of computer-assisted rehabilitative care may compensate for opportunities that are normal for a typical member of the species, such care does not restore opportunities that are normal within the context of our society, that is, given our present level of technological development and the amount of money we devote to health care.

In contrast to basic care, nonbasic care either aims to improve conditions unrelated to normal opportunities or aims to correct or compensate for deficiencies in normal opportunities but is ineffective in doing so. Efforts to improve conditions unrelated to normal opportunity include face lifts, breast augmentation, or genetic engineering designed to enhance athletic skill or physical beauty beyond some average baseline. By contrast, using penicillin to treat a viral infection is an example of an ineffective effort to improve a condition (viral infection) that has the potential to impair normal opportunities. Another example of an ineffective effort is maintaining on a respirator a patient who is in a permanently vegetative state. So long as normal opportunities remain forever beyond the patient's reach, treatment merely continues the patient's unconscious existence.

Proposals to ration nonbasic health care are justified, first, by establishing that government is responsible to provide basic health care; and, second, by arguing that society must ration publicly financed nonbasic care in order to prevent the cost of basic health care for all citizens from becoming prohibitive. In support of the first claim, it has been argued that society should provide a decent standard of health care because failing to do so works against the interest of all of us. For example, persons who lack adequate health care are less able to make productive contributions to the economy and community.

A principle of enforced benevolence lends further support to the claim that the public should shoulder a responsibility to ensure that citizens' basic health care needs are met.[35] On this view, there exists a moral obligation of charity or beneficence to help those in need, including providing the needy with certain forms of health care. However, private acts of charity are rarely adequate to provide many important forms of health care, such as technologies that require coordination of diverse groups or large-scale interdisciplinary programs. The conclusion of this argument is that government mechanisms to ensure that sufficient contributions and coordination take place are justified.

Third, it has been claimed that basic health care is a societal obligation for the reason that individuals have a right to basic health care. A right to basic care may be held to follow from the fact that considerable public dollars are spent on health care. Although some have argued that physicians own the medical services they sell,[36] it can be argued, to the contrary, that public dollars underwrite a significant share of the cost of medical education and medical research and the demand for medical services. Public institutions also afford the environment in which and the structure through which much medical activity occurs. A right to basic health care also might be thought to follow from a more general property right to natural resources.[37] This argument begins with the claim that all members of society own natural resources, such as viruses, molds, minerals, and plants. It proceeds with the observation that many basic health care resources are produced from these resources. According to one estimate, one in four prescription drugs in the United States comes from natural resources.[38] This implies that the public partly owns many health care resources, although those who invest the labor needed to create usable products out of national resources also own a share of these resources. The conclusion of this argument states that people possess rights to basic health care and that a government that fails to ensure access to basic health care violates these rights.

A fourth and final argument supporting the idea that the responsibility for basic health care should be shouldered by the public is that the alternative of letting basic care be bought and sold on a free market is unacceptable. In the first place, distributing health care on a free market runs afoul of long-standing ethical traditions in medicine. In its very first Code of Medical Ethics, the American Medical Association called upon physicians to offer care to individuals in indigent circumstances in a free and cheerful manner.[39] More recently, a 1987 American Medical Association House of Delegates affirmed this tradition by approving a policy that urged all physicians to share in the care of indigent patients.[40] Furthermore, if all citizens partly own health care goods, then the sale of health services on a free market violates the rights of all citizens who do not share in the profits of free exchange.

If we accept the claim that there is a social obligation to provide basic health care, the corresponding claim that rationing nonbasic care is essential to make basic health care affordable gains support on several grounds. First, if health care is to occupy a responsible place in our common life, we must not allocate so much of our national wealth to health that we impoverish support of other social goods, such as education and the environment. This argument continues that a government that chooses to pay the cost of nonbasic, as well as basic, care will be forced to shirk its responsibilities in other areas. The remedy is for government to limit its sights to basic health care and broaden its perspective to include the full range of social goods.

Another way of mounting an argument for rationing nonbasic health care appeals to the idea that persons have no right to receive extravagant health services in the first place; hence, rationing publicly funded nonbasic care to make more basic care affordable is consistent with justice. For example, no one has a right to receive luxurious treatments, such as liposuction or a face lift, at the public's expense. Therefore, denying public support for such care violates no one's rights. Presumably, persons also have no right that society pay for other kinds of medical services that do not fall under the heading of basic care. For example, a patient with irreversible respiratory disease who is in the intensive-care severely obtunded state, who cannot be weaned from the ventilator despite repeated efforts, and who will never recover to survive outside an intensive-care setting, has no right to receive continued care at the public's expense. Under the circumstances, continued treatment does not represent a form of basic health care that the patient can claim as a matter of right.

Patient-Centered Criteria

Rationing Services to Patients Who Receive the Least Medical Benefit. Once public policies governing resource-centered rationing are enacted, persons who interface more directly with patients may employ patient-centered standards to distribute health care within specific categories. Patient-centered criteria highlight specific characteristics of individuals and regard these as the ultimate support for rationing policies. Under this heading fall rationing policies that seek to provide scarce services to individuals likely to receive the greatest medical benefit while denying them to patients likely to gain the least.

A medical-benefit standard should be distinguished from a standard, such as Oregon's, that rations medical care for different illness categories based on whether that care, on average, offers greater improvements in health and quality of life per dollar spent. Oregon's plan treats as homogeneous conditions falling under the same disease category, even though these conditions may have diverse etiologies, and treatments may offer dissimilar medical benefits. For example, Aaron and Schwartz[41] make the point that under Oregon's proposal, all stages of esophageal stricture are placed in one category in order to determine whether the state should pay for them. Yet degree of stricture of the esophagus can vary widely and require widely different interventions that have diverse benefits and costs. Similarly, Oregon lumps together all patients with renal failure, while ignoring a wide range of factors that affect outcome and benefits. Although some generalizing will of course be needed to put a medical benefit standard into practice, under a true medical-benefit standard it will be medical benefit, not disease category, that is the basis for generalizing.

Oregon's proposal also departs from a medical-benefit standard because it would allow excluding from coverage many treatments that are clearly beneficial. This is because no set of benefits is guaranteed under the plan.[42] Instead, whether beneficial treatments are provided would depend upon the budget available in each biennium.

A foreseeable consequence of rationing by medical benefit is that certain visible groups may be denied specific treatments because these treatments can be more beneficial, on average, to other patient groups. For example, rationing intensive-care-unit (ICU) services according to medical benefit may result in denial of these services to elderly persons in chronically poor health and with poor short-term survival rates.[43] However, a medical-benefit approach is not the same as utilitarian approaches that incorporate social worth criteria. Whereas utilitarian approaches ask which use of resources produces the greatest benefit to *society at large,* a medical-benefit approach is patient centered and asks which use of resources produces the greatest benefit to *particular patients or patient groups.*

Several arguments can be put forward in favor of rationing according to medical benefit. First, confining selection criteria to medical benefit avoids making comparisons among persons in terms of social worth. Second, not excluding outright any group from medical consideration also avoids invidious discrimination against particular groups. Finally, rationing on the basis of medical benefit builds on the idea that physicians' obligation to offer care strengthens as the quality and likelihood of benefits increase, yet no physician is obligated to offer futile treatment. "Futile treatment" does not refer only to situations where the physician literally cannot do anything that will have any effect at all. It also includes cases in which medical benefits are highly improbable and situations where, although the likelihood of some benefit may be good, the quality of benefit is extremely poor. For example, we agree with those who argue that medical treatment is futile where there is a negligible chance that a patient will wake up from a coma, or where the best that can be hoped for is survival that requires the patient's entire preoccupation with intensive medical treatment.[44]

One objection to rationing based on medical benefit invokes the substantial difficulty of designing accurate and feasible tools for assessing benefit. Efforts to do so are often exceedingly cumbersome and difficult to implement. For example, Engelhardt and Rie[45] developed an apparently simple equation for measuring societal obligation to pay for a patient's treatment in an ICU: societal obligation = PQL/C. In this equation, P refers to probability of successful outcome, Q to quality of success, L to length of life, and C to the cost required to achieve therapeutic success. However, the difficulty in measuring likelihood of success, quality of success, and length of survival is formidable. Rather than viewing this problem as decisive, however, we believe it points to a need to target research to developing accurate methods for assessing medical benefit.

A second objection to rationing by medical benefit insists that persons who knowingly choose to engage in unhealthy behaviors, such as excessive drinking or smoking, are less deserving of the medical benefits health services provide.[46] Yet this objection is uncompelling. Much illness occurs at random, may be much is genetic.[47] Also, an individual's ability to consider the effects of decisions is itself an acquired skill that lower socioeconomic and educational groups may be at a disadvantage to acquire. Thus, focusing on individual responsibility for health is likely to mask deeper social ills, such as poverty and lack of education, that influence the choice of risky lifestyles.[48] In addition, we are far from being able to tell accurately whether particular patients' health problems are caused by prior behaviors or would have occurred in the absence of these behaviors. More importantly, refusing health services to persons who live unhealthy lifestyles is at odds with our considered judgements about ethical medical practice. We would not accept the practice of physicians routinely refusing therapy to consumers of cholesterol, persons with venereal disease, those who choose to live in polluted urban areas, or the sedentary portion of the population.[49] Our society's emphasis on liberty of the individual also places limits on any far-reaching effort to compel or pressure people to lead healthy lives.

A final objection to rationing by medical benefit is that this approach does not incorporate the perspective of patients. According to this objection, medical benefit can be distinguished from patient benefit. "Medical benefit" refers to success in achieving significant goals of medicine, such as weaning a patient from a respiratory or improving the patient's overall physiological condition. Determining whether or not a particular intervention will yield medical benefits requires the exercise of medical judgment and expertise as well as familiarity with medical facts and research findings. By contrast, "patient benefit" refers to success in achieving the goals of a particular patient.

The difficulty with this objection lies in the sharp distinction it tries to draw between patient and medical benefit. Properly understood, a medical-benefit standard takes into account the values and goals a patient holds as well as the physiological effects treatment will have for a particular patient. Thus, medical benefit does not mean the same thing as medical effect, nor is it merely equivalent to what the patient wishes. This broader interpretation of medical benefit does take the patient's perspective sufficiently into account.

Rationing Services That Are Not Equally Available. Unlike the patient-centered proposals glimpsed thus far, a principle of equality focuses on similarities, rather than differences, among persons. The guiding idea of this approach is that all individuals possess an equal worth and dignity. Thus, differences in persons' income, social productivity, or wisdom do not imply that individuals are more or less worthy. In the area of health care, such a perspective lends support to the view that persons are equally entitled to receive health services. According to one interpretation, equal entitlement implies a principle of equal access. This principle states that whenever a health service is available to any individual, it should be effectively available to any other person who has similar medical needs.[50] A second interpretation of equal entitlement allows some inequalities in health care but seeks to eliminate differences in nonbasic care. This approach either categorically restricts high levels of health care consumption or requires that consumption at high levels benefit those who are least advantaged. For example, according to the latter approach, if artificial hearts were likely to become available to the least advantaged in the future, then funding their selective use now can be ethically justified.

Both forms of an equality argument have merit. The first form resembles a medical-benefit criterion in several key respects. Just as medical benefit implies that persons who will benefit equally from a particular treatment have an equal claim to receive it, a principle of equal access specifies that persons with equal needs for health care are equally entitled to that care. Both standards allow rationing health care to persons who would benefit less. Thus, much of the assessment given in connection with medical benefit applies to equal access as well. The alternative interpretation of equality, which favors imposing a ceiling on health care consumption, is made convincing by considering that our hesitancy to restrict access to high levels of health care may simply reflect the fact that we envision the possibility of ourselves being in a position to need and receive such care. Allowing or even applauding high levels of consumption keeps alive for us the idea of some day having access to such care ourselves. If correct, this explanation bolsters the equality argument that calls for placing a ceiling on health care consumption. It reveals that our tolerance of inequalities is based more on the prospect of personal advantage than on ethical considerations of justice and fairness.

Summary and Proposal

We have framed a variety of proposals concerning the just management of scarce health care resources in terms of resource- and patient-centered rationing. We now are prepared to evaluate this framework and weigh the strength and weakness of different rationing proposals. It is our hope that the framework we have identified affords clearer direction to present rationing debates and that the proposals we support furnish an ethically viable alternative to the old age-based rationing proposals that are currently championed.

Our framework aims to achieve two central goals. First, it intends to clarify the context in which different rationing criteria apply. Proposals to ration high-technology or nonbasic care generally apply to legislators, hospital administrators, and governmental bodies who make choices about the distribution of scarce dollars between different health care categories. Proposals to ration based on medical benefit or the equality of persons generally apply to settings in which persons more directly involved with patient care and management distribute scarce health care resources between patients. A second goal of this framework is to highlight the ethical bases for different rationing choices. Arguments for rationing may point to ethically relevant features of resources themselves or to ethically important differences between persons.

We now turn to the specific rationing criteria explored throughout the paper. These include rationing high-technology services, rationing nonbasic services, rationing services to patients who receive the least medical benefit, and rationing services that are not equally available. In light of the arguments discussed above, we submit the following four-point proposal.

First, we reject resource-centered rationing that calls for limiting the development of publicly financed high-technology medicine. As noted above, the critical flaws with this method are that it is insensitive to medical benefit and slows or even stops medical progress. Such progress holds out the hope of raising the level of health care for all. Rationing the use of high technology may be ethically defensible, but it should not be done in a categorical fashion or any manner that ignores relevant patient-centered factors. Neither the development nor the use of medical services should be rationed on the grounds that they are high-technology services.

Second, we endorse resource-centered policies that place limits on publicly financed nonbasic health services. The practical problem will be determining which services fall under basic and nonbasic health care categories. Making this determination requires qualitative assessment in which specific health services are classified as basic or nonbasic. The classification is not static but relative both to the amount of money available to spend on health care and the level of medical technology available in the society at large. Nonetheless, it is possible to put forward a general standard: basic health care prevents, cures, or compensates for deficiencies in the normal range of opportunities people enjoy at each stage of life.

Third, we hold that a medical-benefit standard should be used to distribute health care resources among persons. Successfully implementing a medical-benefit standard requires improving technology assessment in order to better predict the likelihood, magnitude, and duration of medical benefits to particular patients and patient groups. Here the goal should be to reduce, rather than eliminate, uncertainty.

Finally, we propose equality as the goal in the provision of basic health care. This means that departures from equal basic care will require a special justification. For example, a nonbasic health service that is on the leading edge of medical knowledge may be a candidate for public support if it promises eventually to improve basic health care for all. Generally speaking, the justification for support of nonbasic services must be linked to improvements in basic care.

It is our view that inability to pay should not be a basis for excluding patients from basic health care. Instead, basic health care should be guaranteed. However, ability to pay can be used as a means to distribute nonbasic health services. As noted above, funding of nonbasic care is more accurately thought of as an act of supererogation, rather than a requirement of justice. Although people may ideally like government to pay for all the health care they desire, rationing nonbasic care to persons who cannot afford it does not violate those persons' rights. It also seems unlikely that individuals would be willing to give up completely their present freedom to use their own resources to purchase medical services. Individual freedom is an important value, and a viable approach to rationing must balance ethical factors against pragmatic considerations.

In summary, the cornerstone of our proposal is a commitment to basic care and patient-centered standards. Although age-based proposals represent a patient-centered approach, our proposal improves on the shortcomings of age-based rationing in several key respects. First, by emphasizing medical benefit, rather than age, our proposal is sensitive to differences between patients at each stage of life. For example, *within* age groups patients may have wildly different life prospects and health status. And *between* age groups, healthier older persons may stand to gain much more than younger, sicker patients. Second, our proposal underscores the idea of equality and the related idea that persons at all ages possess an incalculable worth and dignity. By contrast, discriminating on the basis of age may denigrate the value and worth of persons or it may signal that older persons can be legitimately disenfranchised from goods other than health care. Finally, our proposal supports funding basic health services for all age groups. Although tentative in nature, we believe our proposal constitutes a first step toward fashioning an ethical approach to rationing health care.

Notes

This essay is a synthesis of two previously published articles by these two authors. "Ethical Constraints on Rationing Medical Care by Age" appeared in the *Journal of the American Geriatrics Society*, vol. 37, no. 11 (1989), pp. 1067–1075, copyright American Geriatrics Society, and is used by permission. "An Equal Framework for Rationing Health Care" appeared in the *Journal of Medicine and Philosophy*, vol. 17, no. 1 (1992), pp. 79–96, and is used with permission.

1. C. Mills, "The Graying of America," *QQ: Report from the Institute for Philosophy & Public Policy*, vol. 8 (1987), pp. 12–15.

2. U.S. Senate Special Committee on Aging, *Aging, America: Trends and Projections* (Washington, D.C.: Public Health Service, Department of Health and Human Services, 1985–86).

3. J. Kilner, "Age as a Basis for Allocating Lifesaving Medical Resources: An Ethical Analysis," *Journal of Health Politics, Policy and Law*, vol. 13 (1988), pp. 405–23.

4. M. Spitter, "Growing Older in America: Can We Restore the Dignity of Age?" in *Bioethics and Human Rights*, ed. E. Bandman and B. Bandman (Boston: Little, Brown and Co., 1978), pp. 191–96.

5. J. Avron, "Benefit and Cost Analysis in Geriatric Care: Turning Age Discrimination into Health Policy," *New England Journal of Medicine*, vol. 310 (1984), pp. 1294–1301.

6. N. Bell, "Ethical Considerations in the Allocation of Scarce Medical Resources," (Ph.D. diss., University of North Carolina at Chapel Hill, 1978).

7. Spitter, "Growing Older in America," pp. 191–96.

8. D. L. Sackett and G. W. Torrance, "The Utility of Different Health States as Perceived by the General Public." *Journal of Chronic Diseases and Therapeutics Research* vol. 31 (1978), pp. 697–704.

9. J. Kilner, "Age as a Basis for Allocating Resources," pp. 405–23.

10. Kilner, "Age as a Basis for Allocating Resources," pp. 405–23.

11. D. Callahan, *Setting Limits: Medical Goals in an Aging Society* (New York: Simon and Schuster, 1987).

12. H. Moody, "Is It Right to Allocate Health Care Resources on Grounds of Age?" in *Bioethics and Human Rights*, ed. E. Bandman and B. Bandman (Boston: Little, Brown and Co., 1978), pp. 197–201.

13. N. Daniels, *Am I My Parents' Keeper? An Essay on Justice Between the Young and the Old* (New York: Oxford University Press, 1988).

14. N. S. Jecker, "Should We Ration Health Care?" *Journal of Medical Humanities,* vol. 10 (1989), pp. 77–90.

15. N. S. Jecker, Disenfranchising the Elderly from Life-Extending Care. *Public Affairs Quarterly,* vol. 2, no. 3 (July 1988), p. 51.

16. N. S. Jecker, "Excluding the Elderly: A Reply to Callahan, *QQ: Report from the Institute for Philosophy & Public Policy,* vol. 8, (1987), pp. 12–15.

17. N. S. Jecker, "Towards a Theory of Age Group Justice," *Journal of Medicine and Philosophy,* vol. 14 (1989), pp. 655–76.

18. Kilner, "Age as a Basis for Allocating Resources," pp. 405–23.

19. N. S. Jecker, "Age-based Rationing and Women," *Journal of the American Medical Association,* vol. 266 (1991), pp. 3012–15.

20. J. Rawls, *A Theory of Justice* (Cambridge: Harvard University Press, 1971).

21. Kilner, "Age as a Basis for Allocating Resources," pp. 405–23.

22. A. Jonsen, "Resentment and the Rights of the Elderly," in *Aging and Ethics: Philosophical Problems in Gerontology,* ed. N. S. Jecker (Totowa, N.J., Humana Press, 1991), pp. 341–52.

23. P. Brickner, "Older People, Issues and Problems from a Medical Viewpoint," in *Bioethics and Human Rights,* E. Bandman and B. Bandman (Boston: Little, Brown and Co., 1978), pp. 191–96.

24. D. Price, "Planning and Administrative Perspectives on Adequate Minimum Personal Health Services," *Milbank Memorial Fund Quarterly,* vol. 56 (1978), pp. 22–50; J. E. Wennberg, "Dealing with Medical Practice Variations: A Proposal for Action," *Health Affairs,* vol. 3, no. 2 (Summer 1984), pp. 6–32; B. Abel-Smith, "Minimum Adequate Levels of Personal Health Care: History and Justification," *Milbank Memorial Fund Quarterly,* vol. 57 (1978), pp. 212–13.

25. Abel-Smith, "Minimum Adequate Levels of Care," pp. 212–13.

26. W. Hsiao et al., "Results and Policy Implications of the Resource-based Relative Value Scale," *New England Journal of Medicine,* vol. 319 (1988), pp. 881–88; W. Hsiao et al., "Estimating Physicians' Work for a Resource-based Relative-value Scale," *New England Journal of Medicine,* vol. 319 (1988), pp. 835–41.

27. D. A. Hyman and J. V. Williamson, "Fraud and Abuse: Setting Limits on Physicians' Entrepreneurship," *New England Journal of Medicine,* vol. 320 (1989), pp. 1275–78; E. H. Morreim, "Conflicts of Interest: Profits and Problems in Physician Referrals," *Journal of the American Medical Association* 262 (1989), pp. 390–94; J. S. Todd and J. K. Horan, "Physician Referral: The AMA View," *Journal of the American Medical Association,* vol. 262 (1989), pp. 395–96; F. H. Stark, "Physicians' Conflicts in Patient Referrals," *Journal of the American Medical Association,* vol. 262 (1989), p. 397; A. Relman, "Practicing

Medicine in the New Business Climate," *New England Journal of Medicine,* vol. 316 (1987), pp. 1150–51.

28. S. B. Soumerai and J. Avron, "Principles of Educational Outreach ("Academic Detailing") to Improve Clinical Decision Making," *Journal of the American Medical Association,* vol. 263 (1990), pp. 549–56.

29. A. Brett and L. B. McCullough, "When Patients Request Specific Interventions: Defining the Limits of the Physician's Obligation," *New England Journal of Medicine,* vol. 315 (1986), pp. 1347–51; D. Callahan, *What Kind of Life: The Limits of Medical Progress* (New York: Simon and Schuster, 1990).

30. B. Jennett, *High Technology Medicine: Benefits and Burdens* (New York: Oxford University Press, 1986).

31. T. C. Schelling, "Standards for Adequate Minimum Personal Health Services," *Milbank Memorial Fund Quarterly,* vol. 57 (1978), pp. 212–13.

32. G. Rosenthal and D. M. Fox, "A Right to What? Toward Adequate Minimum Standards for Personal Health Services," *Milbank Memorial Fund Quarterly,* vol. 56 (1978), pp. 1–6.

33. L. R. Churchill, *Rationing Health Care in America: Perceptions and Principles of Justice* (Notre Dame: University of Notre Dame Press, 1987).

34. N. Daniels, *Just Health Care* (New York: Cambridge University Press, 1985).

35. A. Buchanan, "The Right to a Decent Minimum of Health Care, in *Securing Access to Health Care,* ed. President's Commission for the Study of Ethical Problems in Medicine and Biomedical and Behavioral Research, vol. 2 (Government Printing Office, Washington, D.C.: 1983), pp. 207–38.

36. R. Sade, "Medical Care as a Right: A Refutation," *New England Journal of Medicine,* vol. 285 (1971), pp. 1288–92.

37. B. A. Brody, "Health Care for the Haves and Have Nots: Toward a Just Basis of Distribution," in *Justice in Health Care,* ed. E. E. Shelp (Dordecht, The Netherlands: Reidel Publishing Company, 1981), pp. 151–60.

38. L. L. Altman, "Tracking a New Drug from the Soil in Japan to Organ Transplants," *New York Times,* Oct. 31, 1989.

39. American Medical Association, "Code of Medical Ethics," in *Ethics in Medicine: Historical Perspectives and Contemporary Concerns,* ed. S. J. Reiser, A. Dych, and W. J. Curran (Cambridge: MIT Press, 1985), pp. 26–34.

40. G. D. Lundberg and L. Bodine, "Fifty Houses for the Poor," *Journal of the American Medical Association,* vol. 260 (1988), p. 3178.

41. W. B. Schwartz and H. J. Aaron, "The Achilles Heel of Health Care Rationing," *New York Times,* July 9, 1990.

42. Office of Technology Assessment, *Draft Report on Oregon's Health Care Plan.* Reported in R. Pear, "Study Questions Oregon's Plan to Ration Health-care Services," *New York Times,* Feb. 25, 1992.

43. W. A. Knaus, E. A. Draper, and D. P. Wagner, "The Use of Intensive Care: New Research Initiatives and Their Implications for National Health Policy," *Milbank Memorial Fund Quarterly,* vol. 61 (1983), pp. 561–83.

44. L. J. Schneiderman, N. S. Jecker, and A. R. Jonsen, "Medical Futility: Its Meaning and Ethical Implications," *Annals of Internal Medicine,* vol. 112 (1990), pp. 949–54.

45. H. T. Engelhardt and M. A. Rie, "Intensive Care Units, Scarce Resources, and Conflicting Principles of Justice," *Journal of the American Medical Association,* vol. 255 (1986), pp. 1159–64.

46. E. Loewy, Letter to the Editor, *New England Journal of Medicine,* vol. 302 (1980), p. 697; J. H. Knowles, "The Responsibility of the Individual," in *The Sociology of Health and Illness,* ed. P. Conrad and R. Kern, 3d ed. (New York: St. Martin's Press, 1990); R. Blank, *Rationing Medicine* (New York: Columbia University Press, 1988).

47. D. Price, "Planning and Administrative Perspectives on Adequate Minimum Personal Health Services," *Milbank Memorial Fund Quarterly,* vol. 56 (1978), pp. 22–50.

48. R. Crawford, "Individual Responsibility and Health Politics," in *The Sociology of Health and Illness,* ed. P. Conrad and R. Kern, 3d ed., (New York: St. Martin's Press, 1990).

49. C. E. Atterbury, "The Alcoholic in the Lifeboat: Should Drinkers be Candidates for Liver Transplant?" *Journal of Gastroenterology,* vol. 8 (1986), pp. 1–4.

50. A. Gutmann, "For and Against Equal Access to Health Care," in *Securing Access to Health Care,* ed. President's Commission for the Study of Ethical Problems in Medicine and Biomedical and Behavioral Research, vol. 2 (Washington, D.C.: Government Printing Office, 1983), pp. 51–66.

III

Planning for the Future

10

A Values Framework for Health System Reform

Reinhard Priester

The American health care system is under great stress. The long litany of concerns can be summarized into the broad problems of inadequate access to needed services, the high cost of health care services, and the unknown quality of services provided. These problems have raised widespread criticism of the present system, with which virtually everyone is dissatisfied. Over the past three years, an astounding number and range of health care reform proposals have been put forward. Many suggest quick-fix economic or financing solutions within the present system without addressing its inherent shortcomings. Others argue that incrementalism is no longer appropriate and call for dismantling either the entire system or portions of it. Clearly, the consensus that something needs to be done does not extend to what should be done.

Superficially, the frustrations with health care stem from runaway costs and an increasingly complex yet unresponsive system. At a deeper level, they arise from disagreement and confusion about the values that should shape America's health care system. Most proposals for change ignore or uncritically adopt the current framework of values underlying our health care system. If we do not make explicit the values we should adopt, discussion of change will be hollow, and consensus for reform nearly impossible. We as a society will more likely agree on strategies to resolve the fundamental problems of our health care system once we agree on the values on which it should be based.

Why Focus on Values? In our contemporary culture, the term *value* is frequently used in a confusing way. In the simplest and most popular usage, *values* refer to what is desirable or what ought to be—not what is, was, or will be. From this perspective. "health care value" is a concrete phrase referring to what is thought to be good or desirable in our health care system. The framework of values proposed here refers to the configuration or arrangement of values that should guide U.S. health care policy.

Robert Veatch argues that values are unavoidable, since policy making "logically requires a system of values."[1] Reforming or restructuring the U.S. health care system must therefore begin with values. The only interesting question is whether the values should be explicit or implicit.

An explicit values framework will advance health care reform more rapidly and more effectively. Without such a guiding framework, our health care policy has been incremental, piecemeal, and reactive and thus has failed to resolve the fundamental problems of inadequate access, high cost, and unknown quality. Systems based on explicit, highly publicized values, such as those in Canada, Norway, and several other Western countries, more effectively provide affordable, high-quality health care to all. Furthermore, explicit values can help us reach agreement on what we should reasonably get out of the system, make clear the trade-offs we face, and force us to have more realistic expectations.

Placing an explicit values framework at the forefront of reform will enable the public to hold policy makers accountable, so that policies promote and do not detract from underlying values. Without an explicit framework, the expressed goals of health care policy can be changed indiscriminately. Such a framework can also function as a "yardstick" to evaluate proposals for reform, providing a perspective for analysis and criteria for comparison.

A focus on values illuminates why the United States is the only Western country that does not assure universal (or near-universal) access. The United States shares with Canada and Western European countries many cultural, theological, philosophical, and democratic traditions. These countries are demographically similar in age, wealth, and income distribution as well as in types of health care personnel (nurses, technicians, and other health professionals), structure of medical education, and types of technology. Information on advances in research and treatment is quickly shared among these countries. Given these similarities, differences in values alone probably explain why the United States stands separately with a patchwork system that leaves one of every eight people uninsured. Direction for health care reform in the United States can come from better understanding the values underlying systems in other Western countries. All Western health care systems—except for ours— share a commitment to universal access. Furthermore, all of these systems are undergirded by the belief that nations are obliged to provide a strong network of social benefits to all their citizens. The social welfare systems in Western European countries promote the dignity and well-being of all persons and promote the welfare of society as a whole. In contrast, the United States embraces individualism, sees provider autonomy as the preeminent value, and neglects community-oriented values.

Current Values Framework

A set of six influential values has shaped the U.S. health care system since World War II:[2]

1. Professional autonomy includes both clinical autonomy of practitioners (that is, independence in making treatment decisions) and regulatory autonomy of the profession.
2. Patient autonomy refers to patients' right to information that is material to making an informed decision about medical care—including the right to refuse care.
3. Consumer sovereignty includes individuals' freedom to choose both their health insurance plan and their own physician.
4. Patient advocacy connotes a mix of values, including caring, service, benevolence, beneficence, fidelity, and effacement of self-interests. It requires health care professionals to single-mindedly pursue the best interests of individual patients, regardless of costs or other societal considerations. The advocacy role has traditionally been limited to benefiting patients (some suggest, patients who pay) and has not included the ill who are not someone's patients.
5. High-quality care, historically has been assessed with reference to its process and structure (i.e., how and in what setting medicine is practiced). In the past few years, this focus has broadened to include outcome (i.e., the effect of care on patients' functional status and quality of life).
6. Access to care, relative to the other five values, has been vaguely defined. Confusion over its meaning is compounded by the mingling of two separate but related aspects of access. One refers to providing care to more people (universality); the other, to offering more services (comprehensiveness). Most policy discussions on access have focused on the progress toward universal access. Determining those services to which people should have access has come to the fore only since resources have been declared finite.

These six health care values have been shaped by the values of our broader society, among them a strong faith in individualism, a distrust of government and a preference for private solutions to social problems, a belief in American exceptionalism, a standard of abundance as the normal state of affairs, the power of technology, and the uniquely American frontier orientation. Although these values are not universally or consistently adhered to throughout the United States, they do form part of the ethos of many elements of our society—including the health care system.

The six values continue to function as ideals that the system never fully realized; indeed, given the inherent tension among these values, it is impossible to implement all of them simultaneously. Maximizing professional or individual autonomy, for example, interferes with maximizing access to care. Nonetheless, the values were thought to be reasonable, achievable goals. A common perception is that the explosive growth of managed care, aggressive cost containment, shifts toward prospective payment, and other changes no longer permit us to exercise these values. In reality, the system never fully implemented them, except for physician autonomy. Recent changes in health care delivery and financing have broadened the gap between the expressed values and their realization.

Recent changes also have altered our conception of some of the values and threatened the importance of others. For example, because of finite resources, many argue that the patient's well-being should be only the primary, not the sole, allegiance of health care professionals.[3] The gatekeeper role in a managed care plan, which requires the gatekeeper to balance a patient's needs against the managed-care tenets of cost consciousness, similarly challenges the traditional advocacy role.

Reduced Commitment to Current Values. Three problems with the current values framework justify the need for a new one to guide health care policy. First among these is a reduced commitment to the current values framework. Ideally, values should guide the development and implementation of health care policy. But the values that have formed the foundation of our health care system have not served that function. There has been a marked lack of commitment to pursuing and implementing them; indeed, discussion of underlying values has been confused and incomplete. U.S. policy over the past two decades has been guided more by economics than by the six values. Most notable has been an erosion of the already modest commitment to access. Efforts to expand access were superseded by aggressive initiatives to contain—and sometimes merely to shift—costs. Health policy aimed at controlling costs through Medicare's prospective payment system (PPS) and managed care. During the 1980s, profits, market share, competitiveness, and other more commercial and less service-oriented goals eclipsed the value of access. In fact, the meaning of access has never been agreed on. Some argue for a right to health care, others suggest a societal obligation to assure access, while still others view health care as a private consumption good distributed through free markets. We continue to espouse the same six values, while retreating from them in reality. For example, in today's more market-driven environment, practitioners want to have professional autonomy and pursue patient advocacy, yet they are also directly responsible to, and called to account by, cost-conscious government and corporate payers. Cost-containment initiatives restrict hospitals' ability to provide care to uninsured patients, for whom consumer sovereignty is moot. Even insured patients wonder about patient advocacy and quality when their providers have economic interests in the clinical laboratories or imaging centers whose services and products they prescribe. The overriding concern to contain costs is the root of the reduced commitment to our traditional health care values. As James Morone has suggested, we have let our economics come before our ethics.[4]

Misplaced Order of Values. A second problem with the current framework is that it does not hold the value of access paramount. Access should be the driving value because of health care's special importance in promoting personal well-being, avoiding irreversible harm, and preventing premature death.[5] Everyone should have access to health care to cure or prevent illnesses, mitigate symptoms, and ease pain and suffering.

Norman Daniels has cogently argued that health care derives its moral importance from its effect on the normal range of opportunities available in society. Health care meets basic human needs, as do food, clothing, housing, and education. In his words, an individual's range of opportunities "is reduced when disease or disability impairs normal functioning. Since we have social obligations to protect equal opportunity, we also have obligations to provide access, without financial or discriminatory barriers, to services that adequately protect and restore normal functioning."[6] However, since World War II, U.S. health policy has consistently subordinated access to other values, most notably to professional autonomy, patient autonomy, and consumer sovereignty. Professional autonomy has been the dominant value in physicians' decision of what specialty to enter, where to practice, which patients to serve, and what fees to charge. The ethical obligations of informed consent, truth telling, and respect for privacy and confidentiality became (in the past two decades) the ideals governing doctor/patient relationships. Similarly, consumer sovereignty has been upheld in consumers' ability to select a health care plan and provider. Finally, in distributing health care resources, the United States, unlike every other Western industrialized country, relies heavily on choice in the marketplace.

The idea of access for everyone conflicts with several more deep-seated values, such as a strong resistance to government involvement in the health care sector and physicians' autonomy to choose their patients. Although the value that care should be provided to poor and disadvantaged people is long standing, its ethical obligation is limited to providing charity for the so-called worthy poor. Unlike the value of access, the charity ethic complements other values of American medicine. Individual and institutional providers are free to select which of the patients unable to pay are worthy of receiving free care. The concept of the worthy poor derives from the peculiarly American notion that for many poor people, poverty is somehow deserved.[7] From this perspective, access to necessities such as health care, and clearly to all life's luxuries, depends on personal effort, achievement, or merit.

After World War II, many government programs (e.g., the Hill-Burton Program and the Health Professions Education Assistance Act of 1963) had the limited goals of expanding health care resources and services. Other government initiatives (e.g., Medicare, Medicaid, favorable tax treatment of employer contributions to employee health benefits) provided individuals with the financial means to obtain services from the private sector. However, reluctance to interfere with professional autonomy and consumer sovereignty limited the government's ability to resolve perceived inequities in access.

Entitlement programs such as Medicaid, for instance, gave great weight to preserving the freedom of patients to choose their providers and of providers to choose to participate. The unwillingness of some providers to treat those programs' patients leaves them with restricted access. The widespread state practice to underreimburse providers further strapped Medicaid's services to nonelderly enrollees. Although these cost-conscious policies probably saved some money, they also reduced provider participation, with the side effect of restricting access. Fewer than 40 percent of the people below the federal poverty line are enrolled in Medicaid today. Some states now seek to increase the number of Medicaid enrollees but restrict their access to certain services. Such changes in the breadth and depth of coverage are a clear retreat from Medicaid's original intent to provide poor persons with equal access to the same services as are offered to persons with higher incomes.

Our lukewarm commitment to access has also eroded in the private sector. As employers and government sought to control health spending, providers could no longer shift to paying patients the cost of caring for uninsured patients. This environment has also challenged the traditional social commitment of hospitals to provide emergency services to uninsured people. Many private hospitals responded by "dumping" such patients to a public hospital or by having no emergency facilities.

Omission of Community-Oriented Values. Individualism and personal autonomy have superceded community values in American society. These concepts reflect the views that each individual is his or her own best judge of what is of value or interest and that government is a necessary evil, not a natural vehicle for achieving common aspirations. The needs of the individual have been given priority over those of the community.

The patient-centered Hippocratic tradition is the core of our current values framework. This "ethical individualism" has singularly focused on encounters between an individual practitioner and an individual patient. The provider's responsibility—as the patient's advocate—narrowly and exclusively centers on the individual patient. Respect for patient autonomy has become (in theory if not always in practice) the guiding principle for provider/patient encounters. The impact of the individual's treatment choice on the distribution of health care resources or its effect on the interests of others has been considered irrelevant.

Unlike most other Western countries, a community perspective has not been strong in the United States. Criticisms of our excessive individualism and calls to incorporate community values abound, both inside and outside the health care system. For instance, the Catholic Health Association describes human rights, including the "right to a basic level of healthcare," in terms of the interdependence of personal and social life. Health care from a community-oriented perspective is viewed as necessary for society to sustain essential social harmonies and ensure its viability.[8] Marion Danis and Larry Churchill argue that in the context of scarcity, "ethical concerns about the fair distribution of health care resources cannot remain detached from the ethics of individual patient care."[9] When health care resources are limited (i.e., scarce relative to needs), individual treatment choices affect the resources available for others. Using resources for one patient necessarily means that fewer resources will be available to treat others.

In the United States, broad, community-oriented conceptions of human good have generally seemed unobtainable rationally and totalitarian if imposed politically. Nonetheless, Daniel Callahan argues, "we will not be able to work out the problems of our health care system unless we shift our priorities and bias from an individual-centered to a community-centered view of health and human welfare."[10] The objective is not to get rid of individual autonomy but to temper the significance of free choice and individualism according to the good of the whole— to keep autonomy from being such a "moral obsession" that it "pushes other values aside."[11]

Proposed New U.S. Values Framework

The proposed new U.S. values framework retains all six old values, but it reorders and redefines some of them, reemphasizes several that have been neglected, adds some new ones, and offers more guidance on which values take priority and how to resolve conflicts among competing values. The added values come from many sources, including selected Western countries, several states' initiatives, national reform proposals, and the professional and popular literature. Some of these have been around for a long time, albeit largely neglected. Others, although absent in our health care system, have been prominent in foreign systems. Three nations, in particular, offer credible models for determining the values underlying a health care system. The Canadian model has long been championed by critics of the U.S. system as an attractive and viable alternative. Norway, like Canada, is among the few Western countries to delineate explicitly the values that should guide its health care system. Of all Western systems, (formerly West) Germany's perhaps most closely approximates the U.S. system: it is professionally dominated and relies on private insurance carriers ("sickness funds"). These carriers offer employer-financed services through private physicians and hospitals, while the federal government establishes the system's ground rules and provides a safety net for those who do not receive the employer-financed coverage. Some of the values of these three countries are somewhat alien to the U.S. system (e.g., social solidarity and personal security), but these values should be added to our own framework, after they are first negotiated and interpreted through American society and culture.

Comprehensive and well-known national health care reform proposals (such as those from the National Leadership Commission on Health Care, the Pepper Commission, and the American Medical Association) are additional sources of values. So are state reform proposals. Oregon, Massachusetts, New York, Minnesota, and Hawaii are among the states at the cutting edge of health care reform.[12] All of the national reform proposals and state initiatives are based

TABLE 1

Proposed Values Framework for the U.S. Health Care System

Essential Values	Instrumental Values
Fair access	Personal responsibility
Quality	Social solidarity
Efficiency	Social advocacy
Respect for patients	Provider autonomy
Patient advocacy	Consumer sovereignty
	Personal security

Note: Ordering rules for these values are as follows: (1) each essential value should be maximized, to the degree possible without threatening any other essential value, but fair access should be preeminent; (2) essential values should be achieved before instrumental values, except insofar as instrumental values are means to achieve essential values.

primarily on the current values framework, although the relative rankings of specific values vary; some reforms incorporate values (such as efficiency and personal responsibility) that go beyond the current framework.

These health care systems, proposals, and plans yields a master list of potential values that can then be pared down to a set of eleven values to guide the restructuring and reform of our health care system (table 1). The first five are essential values, fundamental for any health care system: without them a system would be deficient. The next six are instrumental values, primarily a means to help achieve the essential values.

Essential Values

Fair Access. Each person should have access to an adequate level of health care. This requires minimizing financial, geographic, and cultural barriers to care; distributing health care resources in a manner acceptable from an impartial point of view; and treating similar health care needs similarly, without regard to the patient's membership in a group or class. Assuring access to health care, regardless of cause of source of need, is society's collective responsibility.

While everyone ought to have access to health care, this does not require universal access to all potentially beneficial care. No society can afford to provide every service of potential benefit to everyone in need. And although total resources devoted to health care could be increased, clearly there is a limit (which some argue we have already passed) beyond which our ability to spend money on other important and desirable societal goals, such as education, transportation, and housing, would be constricted. This limit—plus the continued development of new, efficacious, and often expensive technologies; our aging population; acquired immunodeficiency syndrome (AIDS); and other factors fueling the demand for health care—would mean that we still could not provide all services to all who could benefit.

In the context of scarcity, everyone should have access to a level of health care "that would permit [them] to achieve sufficient welfare, opportunity, information, and evidence of interpersonal concern to facilitate a reasonably full and satisfying life."[13] Defining fairness as access to an adequate level of health care is the only way to avoid either an impossible commitment of resources or the abandonment of at least some help to everyone. Each person, regardless of his or her ability to pay, would have access to an adequate level of health care.[14] The specified level would function only as a floor below which no one should fall, not a ceiling.[15]

Inherent in the very idea of an adequate level is that it is acceptable for different people to receive different levels of care, depending on where the levels are set. It is unacceptable to have some people receive a very high level of care while others receive virtually no care at all. But it is acceptable to have some people receive a very high level of care while others receive less care, David Eddy has argued, if the lower level of care covers everything that is considered adequate.[16] This is also acceptable if public policy only defines the adequate level while permitting—but not defining—the higher levels. Services not considered basic would be available for purchase in the health care market. Public education offers an analogy: while every American child is assured access to publicly funded education, individuals are free to purchase additional opportunities, such as private music lessons or college classes.

Despite widespread support for the concept of an adequate level of care, there is no consensus regarding what, precisely, it should include. There clearly is a level of services below which a system would be ethically unacceptable, even if the universal access requirement were met. Defining the level to which everyone ought to have access is absolutely crucial for specifying a morally acceptable system. This is where the health care reform debate ought to move to, following these substantive guidelines for specifying an adequate level of care. First, the available budget should not drive the definition of what is adequate; instead, only after the level is defined should attention turn to how to pay for it. If resources can assure universal access to only a portion of the defined adequate level of care, then this should then be explicitly acknowledged. Second, the process for deciding what is adequate should assure accountability. Those who define the adequate level should be bound by the definition, even though they may use their own funds to purchase additional coverage. Otherwise, the procedure would be biased: as Daniels states, "the 'haves' deciding what is 'important' to give to the 'have-nots.' "[17] Also, a representative cross section of those who will actually receive services deemed adequate should be involved in the process. Third, since it should apply to all, the adequate level should not be defined with reference to a particular group. Finally, regardless of how adequate care is defined, its content should be constantly revised to incorporate changing information on technology and consumer preferences. The revisions should apply to all.

Universal access requires, first and foremost, that everyone have the financial means to obtain needed care. Since only the relatively affluent are able to pay for their health care services out of pocket, this will require some form of universal health insurance coverage. Universal coverage (through public or private health insurance or some combination) would make it easier for minorities, legal immigrants, illegal aliens, and other underserved people to obtain care, but it would not necessarily result in universal access. Language handicaps, cultural barriers, and unfamiliarity and distrust of the system would continue to inhibit access. These nonfinancial barriers along with the financial barriers, must be overcome.

For access to be nondiscriminatory, health care needs should be treated similarly, without regard to the patients age, gender, race, religion, national origin, education, place of residency, sexual orientation, ability to pay, or presumed social worth. Oregon's reform proposal, for instance, would violate this requirement. It expands Medicaid coverage to all Oregonians below the poverty level by providing them with a less comprehensive level than is currently prescribed under Medicaid. However, it explicitly exempts from the reduced benefits blind, disabled, and elderly Medicaid enrollees—who will continue to receive the current (higher) level of benefits. Doling out benefits in this way is discriminatory.

Individuals and the private sector should be involved in enhancing access, but the ultimate responsibility rests with the federal government. Unless it assumes this responsibility, the health care needs of many will remain unmet. Although widespread activity on health care issues is under way in most states, there is mounting evidence that such state efforts, although pioneering and sometimes initially successful, may fail.

Quality of Care. Health care should maximize the likelihood of desired health outcomes for individuals and populations, be consistent with current and emerging professional knowledge, and be humanely and respectfully provided. This definition of quality, adapted from the Institute of Medicine's report *Medicare: A Strategy for Quality Assurance,* has several important characteristics.[18] First, high-quality care is an ideal. Second, emphasis on current and emerging knowledge underscores the constraints placed on health care by technical, medical, and scientific developments. Health care professionals must keep abreast of new information and use the best knowledge base available. Third, the definition highlights the growing importance of outcomes. Previously, quality assessment and assurance focused on the process and structure of care. High-quality care was that provided by a competent practitioner (with certain qualifications, training, and experience), in the appropriate setting, using commonly accepted procedures, in accordance with accepted medical practice. Outcomes are now an integral component of quality assessment and assurance, and they must be linked to the process of care. Desired outcomes obtained by serendipity do not indicate high-quality care. Fourth, the preferences and values of individual patients should help to determine which interventions and associated outcomes are desired.

Efficiency. The health care system should be efficient—that is, should achieve desired outcomes with the least expenditure, thereby providing good value for money spent. Efficiency has two important dimensions, as defined by Mark Pauly and his colleagues: minimizing the cost of whatever services are provided and choosing the services leading to the maximum excess of benefits over cost.[19] An efficient health care system is not necessarily the least expensive, but it obtains the greatest benefit (defined in terms of desired outcomes) for the lowest cost.

Efficient use of resources has not been part of the culture of the medical profession or of the health care system. Few resources are devoted to evaluating medical technologies, and there is much uncertainty about their effectiveness. Consider a prime example of inefficiency: uninsured people obtain much of their primary care in emergency rooms, instead of physicians' offices and other less costly settings, because their access to care is restricted. They also often delay obtaining care, thereby turning less costly problems into expensive ones. Unnecessary care, the duplication and oversupply of health care facilities, escalating administrative costs, and the malpractice "system" further contribute to inefficiency.

Among the reasons efficiency has not been an important value is that most Americans have long believed that abundance, rather than scarcity, is natural. Concerns about efficiency are incompatible with the perception of virtually unlimited growth in knowledge and unlimited availability of useful health care resources. Only in the past decade has it been widely acknowledged that resources are limited and that all needs may not be met. When all health care needs cannot be met, it is inappropriate merely to try to hold down costs—which was the focus of cost-containment initiatives in the 1970s and 1980s. We need to look beyond "minimizing the cost of whatever services are provided" (the first dimension of efficiency noted above). We must also pay attention to what works in health care and then add incentives to achieve desired outcomes with the least expenditure.

Respect for Patients. The elements of this value are fourfold: First, patients have the right to information to make informed decisions about their care, including information about their provider's potential conflicts of interest. Second, patients have the right and responsibility to make informed, voluntary decisions about their care (including the right to refuse care); no care can be initiated without the patient's (or surrogate's) informed consent. Third, patients have the right of access to their medical records and the right to protect and control personal information about their health and health care. Finally, patients have the right to be treated with respect and dignity.

Respect for a patient's autonomy has had a brief, very recent, but powerful history in our current values framework. Historically, medical paternalism prevailed in provider/patient relationships. Now, the relatively modern doctrine of informed consent is generally promoted. Informed consent has two basic parts: first, certain information must be disclosed to the patient before consent is obtained; second, no procedure may be performed on a patient without consent. Informed consent is also a legal doctrine, first articulated by a California court in 1957 and since adopted by statue or court opinion in all states. But despite widespread support, informed consent rarely has been fully implemented, so its impact on fostering greater respect for patient autonomy is uncertain. Although respect for patient autonomy has appropriately become an important value, it should not trump other values. In health care policy, the demands of justice, which require fair access, can (in narrow circumstances) outweigh respect for patient autonomy.

The individual's right to protect and control personal information requires confidentiality, which, in its simplest terms, means respect for people's secrets. Confidentiality has never been absolute. Many statutes specify the circumstances in which confidential information can be released in order to protect others (e.g., health care providers must report certain communicable diseases and evidence of child abuse). Professional codes of ethics incorporate such restrictions. The American Medical Association's (AMA's) Principles of Medical Ethics, for example, provides that a physician "shall safeguard patient confidences within the constraints of the law." Rules of confidentiality have also been developed from the standpoint of patient (for example, the American Hospital Association's Patient's Bill of Rights).

But patient confidentiality is now under considerable threat—beyond the narrow legal exceptions. Major challenges include centralization of medical records, utilization review and other forms of oversight by parties other than the physician and patient, and the intrusive effects of litigation. Hundreds of people—medical records personnel, health care providers, claims processors, health plan administrators, even the patient's employer—may have access to patient records. One study found that more than one hundred hospital staff could have legitimate access to a patient's hospital record and concluded that such sharing of information has diluted confidentiality beyond meaningful existence.[20]

Despite such challenges, confidentiality is crucial, because the effectiveness of provider/patient encounters depends on the patient's willingness to reveal information essential to proper diagnosis and treatment. Assurance of confidentiality encourages full disclosure and is essential for effective treatment. Confidentiality should also be protected simply out of respect for patients' "right to privacy."

Patient Advocacy. Health care providers should zealously promote their individual patients' best interests within established, recognized constraints. Physicians, it has often been said, cannot serve two masters; circumstances that present potential conflicts of interest should always be resolved in favor of the patient. This expansive view of advocacy enshrined the provider's ideal role as single-mindedly serving the patient's interests. However, this view is not appropriate today, even as an ideal. Since health care resources are clearly finite, treatment choices for an individual patient will affect the resources available for others. Some patients, therefore, may appropriately receive less than the maximum if this is necessary to conserve resources to assure universal access to an adequate level of care.

The provider's advocacy role should be altered in two aspects. First, in addition to serving their own patients, providers must promote the fair and judicious use of resources and advocate for the needs of individuals and groups that have traditionally been left out of the health care system. Second, providers should not do everything that may benefit an individual patient, since doing so may interfere with the ability of other patients to obtain basic services; rather, providers should treat each patient with as full a range of resources as is compatible with treating patients yet to come. But providers should not be required to balance at the bedside the patient's interests against those of others or of society. They should only be required to adhere to previously established constraints, including a managed care plan's practice guidelines for appropriate care and coverage limitations of third-party payers. Providers should also be involved in establishing such allocation rules and regulations. However, they should do so as health care administrators, managers, and members of professional organizations—not in their capacity as bedside clinicians. In short, providers should help develop allocation rules and then play by the rules. Within those rules, they should continue to advocate zealously for their individual patient's interests. If providers believe the rules are detrimental to their patients, they should work to change them.

Many argue that asking providers to abide by rules that reflect an organization's or program's obligations to meet the needs of groups (e.g., enrollees in a managed care plan) raises unacceptable conflicts of interest. This criticism is misplaced. Providers have always faced conflicts of interest. For example, in the traditional fee-for-service system, a provider's income depends on the number and cost of procedures performed. There is little reason to believe that the new conflict between patient and group interests is potentially more harmful than the former conflict between patient and provider interests.

Instrumental Values

Personal Responsibility. This value has two aspects: individual and institutional. First, each person should, within his or her means, share in the costs of health care. Individual financial responsibility requires all people to help bear, to the extent possible, the cost of adequate health insurance and services and the cost of the system as a whole. The financial burden should be progressive: any premiums, copayments, deductibles, or taxes should be based on the ability to pay. Premium subsidies for lower-income people, for instance, could be on a sliding scale based on gross family income to assure that health coverage will be available to all people while still requiring (almost) everyone to pay at least some of the premium.

Individual financial responsibility can also encourage more appropriate and parsimonious use of services by consumers. A system providing "free care" (that is, no out-of-pocket cost to the individual at the point of service) often leads to overuse. Cost-sharing provisions, such as copayments and deductibles, can encourage rational economic behavior among consumers without denying them necessary care.[21] However, to assure decreased use of inappropriate services, more information for consumers regarding the outcome of services should accompany such cost-sharing provisions. Moreover, even modest levels of coinsurance adversely affect the health of people who are both sick and poor. Cost-sharing requirements need to be carefully crafted to encourage more appropriate use of the system but discouraged underuse, overuse, or other inappropriate use. Cost sharing should not apply to cost-effective prevention measures.

The second aspect of personal responsibility involves providers, the health care system, and society, and their capacity to enable each person to take greater control over his or her own health. Americans are largely free to engage in any number of dangerous activities that place them in need of health care services. But the traditional emphasis on individual freedom needs to be balanced with a corresponding emphasis on personal responsibility. Providers, employers (as purchasers of group health insurance), and insurers are exploring policies to attach financial consequences to people's lifestyle or behavior when it affects their health. Options include direct taxes on tobacco products, alcohol, and other dangerous substances and higher insurance premiums for those who smoke or take other risks with their health.

However, policies that hold individuals responsible for their injuries and illnesses are open to criticism. First, they presuppose in-depth understanding of causal relationships, but we cannot always be certain that attributions of responsibility are accurate. Second, they conflict with the traditional ethos of physicians and nurses to treat all patients with the same understanding, compassion, and clinical expertise—without regard to the patients' role in the origin of their ailments. Third, they can deteriorate into "victim blaming," that is, locating the causes of social problems within the individual, rather than in social and environmental forces. Claims of individual responsibility may fail to recognize that a lack of education, lack of funds, deep-seated cultural traditions, or other barriers may make it difficult for individuals to take responsibility for their health.

The thrust of the value of personal responsibility, therefore, should be to enable people to take appropriate steps to maintain and improve their health—without attaching blame if they fail to do so. First and foremost, providers, the health care system, and society in general should provide information on risks associated with certain behaviors, offer health-promotion programs, and implement similar strategies that contribute to good health. Only then may it be appropriate to take additional steps to discourage unhealthy behaviors through economic penalties. The penalties, however, should not be so onerous as to prevent or discourage anyone from obtaining needed medical care.

Social Solidarity. The health care system should engender a sense of community. Social solidarity represents a commitment to bridging the gaps among different segments of society by including them in a community. Our public education system, for example, has long reflected this value and promoted community concerns. People without children, or whose children have grown, still vote on school bond issues, and most of them share a sense of responsibility for the educational system. But social solidarity is rarely mentioned in discussions of U.S. health policy.

This value is much more familiar to many Europeans, who argue that economic and class differences should not be exacerbated by or reflected in the health care system. In Norway, for example, various commissions have insisted that the health care system must remain a force for societal unity. Norwegians are keenly aware that theirs is a relatively young and geographically isolated nation and that the health care system is one of the most powerful forces unifying the citizenry. The United Kingdom's health care system serves much the same unifying role. Those who use the National Health Service rarely complain about long waits for elective procedures or the dilapidated conditions of some hospitals (increasingly, however, signs of discontent are emerging). They feel it would be wrong to complain about a system that has treated them fairly, even if it cannot provide everything they might want or need.

Fairness is clearly the central driving factor behind the value of social solidarity. Leaving any group, class, or segment of society outside the health care system is seen as unfair. But social solidarity also provides a nation with a common rallying point. It affirms that all citizens count, and society sees itself as having a stake in each citizen. In Norway, social solidarity means that everyone has access to roughly the same level and quality of care. In the United Kingdom, it means that everyone has access to at least the same minimal package of services. In both countries, the government has an obligation to ensure that health care is available to all in need, regardless of their station or lot in life.

The United States should transfer its sense of social consciousness to support a fairer health care system. Social solidarity provides a common bond among those who use a nationally sponsored health care system and a means to make each person a "stakeholder" in the system. But social solidarity does not simply result from creating a nationalized health care system or insurance program. To flourish, this value requires all citizens to be involved and feel a sense of ownership of their system. It also requires a political mechanism to allow the public to have a real say in how well or how poorly the system serves their needs.

Social Advocacy. Health care providers should advance the health of the public and recognize and provide for the health care needs of poor, underserved, and other vulnerable individuals and groups. The preamble to the AMA's 1980 Principles of Medical Ethics acknowledges that the medical profession has "long subscribed to a body of ethical statements developed primarily for the benefit of the patient" but then states that "a physician must recognize responsibility not only to patients, but also to society."[22] However, recent changes in the AMA's principles regarding the latter responsibility reinforce a narrower, patient-centered focus. Section 1 of the 1957 medical ethics principles states that "the primary objective of the medical profession is to *render service to humanity* with full respect for the dignity of man" (emphasis added). Section 1 of the 1980 principles, in contrast, eliminates any mention of obligations to humanity and thus appears to focus physicians' responsibility more narrowly on their individual patients; it states merely that "a physician shall . . . provide . . . service with compassion and respect for human dignity."

The value of social advocacy calls on providers to renew their commitment to advocate for the health care needs of underserved people and of society in general. (This is in addition to their long-standing obligation to advocate for their patients at the bedside.) Providers should advance the health of the public, broadly construed. They should also recognize and help to meet the specific health needs of vulnerable underserved individuals and groups. Providers may fulfill these responsibilities in many ways, for example, by participating in health-policy making, educating the public on health issues, or being active in organizations that address the health care needs of vulnerable populations.

Provider Autonomy. Providers should have freedom to practice medicine to the best of their ability without undue interference from others. Providers should have the freedom to refuse patients (except in emergencies or if refusal is discriminatory) and the opportunity for just compensation for services rendered. Each health care profession should have the freedom to control its education, set criteria for entry into the profession, and control professional certification processes and standards.

The autonomy of providers—especially of physicians—has traditionally been the dominant value of our health care system. It includes both the clinical autonomy of individual practitioners and the regulatory autonomy of the professions. Many believe professional autonomy was conferred on American medicine around the time of the Flexner report (1910). One reviewer noted that "in essence, organized medicine was granted broad, monopolistic powers over the health care industry (such as it was at the time), in exchange for its promise to provide quality medical care and eliminate the sad state of affairs described by Flexner."[23] Others argue that conferring autonomy was based on the public imputation of medicine's "extraordinary trustworthiness" to promote the public's interest rather than practitioners' self-interest.[24] Although recent bureaucratic and institutional changes chip away at provider autonomy, it still remains the dominant value of our health care system.

Inherent in conferring autonomy, Frederic Wolinsky states, is the "potential revocation of that autonomy at any point at which the public imputes that the profession has not lived up to its side of the bargain."[25] That is the situation today.

The public was promised too much; our system, driven primarily by the value of provider autonomy, has failed to meet individuals' and society's needs. Provider autonomy, though important, should be a means to promote more crucial values, not an end in itself.

Consumer Sovereignty. Consumers have the right to information to make informed choices among health care providers (including information on the quality and efficiency of providers) and, where appropriate, the right to select a provider. Consumer sovereignty includes individuals' freedom of choice in both the market for services (and providers) and the market for insurance (and plans). The clear trend has been toward greater restriction of choice in both markets. Commercial insurance plans initially preserved consumers' freedom to choose among providers; only for enrollees in prepaid group practices was this freedom significantly restricted. Today, however, restricted choice of providers is a central element of managed care plans and of many commercial insurance plans. It is often "enforced" through significant financial penalties imposed if individuals choose outside an identified group of providers. Choice of insurance has been similarly restricted. The vast majority of privately insured Americans now have group (usually employer-provided) health insurance; their choice of plans is thereby limited to those offered by their employer. These plans directly reflect the purchasing decisions made by employers and other group purchasers (ostensibly acting as the consumer's agent) and only indirectly the decisions of individual consumers.

Consumer sovereignty should remain a value because it functions as a check on the system. Freedom of choice helps make the system responsive to consumers' references regarding the times, places, and quality of care. In contrast, a system unresponsive to consumers' preferences would be guided much more by providers' preferences and thus would lack accountability to patients. Nevertheless, some restrictions on consumer sovereignty are acceptable. It may no longer be feasible in our complex system for individual consumers to make informed, responsible choices among providers, for which consumers would need provider-specific information on the quality and efficiency of care. Individuals rarely have such information or the expertise to evaluate it. Furthermore, acting in isolation, individual consumers do not have the market power to compel changes in the supply side. To preserve an appropriate level of consumer sovereignty, large group purchasers could evaluate all providers and exclude those with poor performance. They should then offer meaningful (albeit limited) choices within the overall plan(s) they offer, so that consumers could make well-informed choices of efficient, high-quality providers.

Personal Security. The health care system should protect individuals' peace of mind and financial security by meeting their health care needs without impoverishment. The two interrelated elements of this value—peace of mind (knowing that health care needs will be met) and financial security (not being impoverished after paying the bill)—are endorsed in all countries that have some sort of national health system. From the German government's perspective, for example, feeling safe and secure is "inconceivable" without a health care system that provides needed medical treatment. Although Germany's workers must contribute to the cost of their health insurance, the mandated comprehensive benefits and liberal public safety net for unemployed people assure that no one has to worry about the financial side of being ill.

Certain health care programs and policies have addressed concerns for personal security of specific groups in the United States. Testimony from older people about their great fear of being unable to obtain needed care was a driving force to get Medicare enacted. Because elders face chronic and terminal illness more immediately than the rest of the population, a sense of personal security is of particular concern for them. But despite Medicare and other programs assuring access for specified groups, the peace-of-mind element of personal security has not been a value for overall U.S. health care policy. Nor has financial security been upheld; indeed, through the spend-down provisions in Medicaid, for example, eligibility is conditioned on impoverishment.

Interrelations among Values

The relations among the proposed new framework's values are complex. While the essential values often are mutually reinforcing, they may conflict in some circumstances. Since it may not be possible to provide beneficial care of the highest quality to all persons in need, quality may conflict with fair access. Respecting patients' choices, such as the wishes of many patients to receive extremely costly, labor-intensive care of only marginal benefit, may undermine fair access and quality. Respect for patients may also conflict with efficiency; if patients are free to choose between two equally effective treatments, but one costs much more, they may not always select the most cost-effective, or efficient, treatment. Two ordering rules should help resolve possible conflicts.

Coexistence of Essential Values. First, each essential value should be maximized, to the degree possible without threatening any other essential value. But fair access should be preeminent. The preferred strategy to resolve conflicts among the essential values is to modify a simple balancing approach. The essential values should be equal in their priority—each should be maximally satisfied, consistent with respect for the other essential values—but fair access should be first among equals.

The main conflict is between fair access and autonomy (reflecting the classic confrontation between justice and freedom). In our society the weight of the tension has usually been resolved historically in favor of autonomy. But under the proposed new framework, it would usually be resolved in favor of fair access instead. Individual freedom may thus be restricted if it interferes with assuring access to an adequate level of care for everyone. One patient should not be entitled to every potentially beneficial treatment if it consumes resources to which another patient has a greater claim. The need for health care services that are part of the adequate level of care presents such a greater claim.

When a patient selects a treatment from among the alternatives offered by the provider that is beyond the adequate level of care, and, as a result, another patient is denied access to services included in the adequate level of care, the first patient's choice should be restricted. In practice, this means that until everyone has access to an adequate level of care, no one may receive services that are not part of the adequate level. Once universal access to an adequate level of care is achieved, however, individuals may obtain (with their own resources) additional services—but only if this does not deny more basic services to another patient.

As a general rule, if achieving universal access to an adequate level of care requires restricting the freedom of choice of an individual provider, patient, or consumer, restricting this aspect of individual autonomy is permissible. But fair access should not override the value of autonomy altogether. Specifically, the pursuit of fair access should not override a person's right to bodily integrity, which our society has held nearly inviolate. The field of transplantation illustrates the high value placed on this aspect of individual autonomy. Despite the chronic shortage of transplantable tissues and organs, one's freedom to refuse to be a live donor has taken precedence over the need to increase access to transplants.

Priority of Essential Values. Second, essential values should be achieved before instrumental values, except insofar as instrumental values act as means to achieve essential values. The five essential values are fundamental to a health care system; without them, a system would be deficient. Without quality, for instance, patients may be harmed, resources may be used inappropriately, and needs may go unmet. The instrumental values function primarily as ways to help achieve the essential values; some may also, themselves, be values that a health care system should pursue and implement where possible, but not at the expense of any of the essential values. Many people suggest that provider autonomy, for instance, is a value in and of itself. But if fair access cannot be assured without imposing restrictions on a provider's freedom to choose her or his patients, then provider autonomy may be restricted, for example, by requiring providers to see a minimum number of Medicaid enrollees or other underserved people.

In the proposed framework provider autonomy is valued insofar as it supports the provider's role as the patient's zealous advocate and to promote quality of care. Daniels sees that granting providers "considerable autonomy in clinical decision making is necessary if they are to be effective as [advocates] pursuing their patient's interests."[26] Further, providers' freedom in determining (jointly with the

patient) the medically acceptable and appropriate treatment—with minimum interference by government, courts, third-party payers, and administrators—fosters
high-quality care.

The other instrumental values similarly promote one or more of the essential values. Consumer sovereignty fosters greater efficiency and promotes quality.
When free to choose among health care plans and providers, and armed with appropriate cost and outcome data, consumers could select plans based on their efficiency, quality, and services. Or group purchasers (as consumers' agents) could
selectively contract for specific services with particular health care institutions in
order to obtain efficient, high-quality care. The three community-oriented values—social advocacy, personal responsibility, and social solidarity—help to temper our excessive individualism. Adding these values, in Philip Clark's view, will
help the current system to break out of the "narcissistic individualism" that
presently undermines "any meaningful public dialogue on what the goals of [our
health care system] should be and the appropriate means for achieving them."[27]

The value of social solidarity is more complex and fundamental than the
proposed framework's other instrumental values. It fosters among all citizens a
recognition of their social, political, and economic interdependence, as well as a
perception of shared ownership, and thereby helps to promote a health care system holding the value of fair access preeminent. Social solidarity will help to shift
U.S. health policy away from its excessive individualism; in fact, its presence in our
social value system may be necessary for such a shift to occur. The health care systems in Canada and Western European countries are committed to universal access in part because social solidarity undergirds their social value systems. The
value's possible role for the United States is similar. Given the long history of individualism in the United States, a robust social solidarity principle may help us
to establish a fairer health care system. Once established, a strong sense of community will continue to support a health care system that provides universal access
to an adequate level of care.

Conclusion

Recent health care policy—based on an excessively individualistic values
framework and driven by an overriding emphasis on cost containment—has failed
to remedy the interrelated problems of inadequate access to needed services, the
high cost of health care, and the unknown quality of services provided. To develop
and implement comprehensive and consistent health policies to address these problems, we need a new framework of values and a commitment to take it seriously.
Our society must adopt a values framework with "a new blend of ethical priorities,"
in Richard Botelho's words, and then place it at the forefront of health care reform.[28]

The proposed new U.S. values framework squarely establishes fair access as
the preeminent value, reemphasizes several neglected values, adds several community-

oriented values, and offers rules to resolve conflicts among competing values. This framework should serve as the moral foundation of American's health care system and explicitly guide health care policy. It can be a rallying point to build consensus for reform, offer a perspective for analysis, provide criteria for comparing reform proposals, and help to hold policy makers accountable.

Notes

Published in *Health Affairs,* vol. 11, no. 1 (1992), pp. 84–107, and reprinted with permission.

The author, as project director, thanks the members of the Center for Biomedical Ethics' "New Ethic" research project, whose participation made this paper possible. Members include: Sheila Leatherman (cochair), Arthur L. Caplan (cochair), Mila Aroskar, Dianne Bartels, Paul Bearmon, Paul Bowlin, Mary Brainerd, Amos Deinard, Bryan E. Dowd, Ann Dudero, Rodney Dueck, Barbara Elliott, John R. Finnegan, Ellen Z. Green, Representative Lee Greenfield, Rosalie A. Kane, James F. Kohrt, Peg LaBore, Lisa Latts, Carl P. Malmquist, Daniel J. McInerney, Jr., Steven H. Miles, Steve Mosow, Charles Oberg, Dorothy E. Vawter, Cindy Yess. The research project was supported in part by the Deinard Memorial Law and Medicine Fund.

1. R. Veatch, "Value Systems: Their Roles in Shaping Policy Decisions," in *Health Policy, Ethics and Human Values,* ed. Z. Bankowski and J. H. Bryant (Geneva: CIOMS, 1985), pp. 84–86.

2. Center for Biomedical Ethics, *Rethinking Medical Morality: The Ethical Implications of Changes in Health Care Organization, Delivery, and Financing* (Minneapolis: University of Minnesota, 1989).

3. L. R. Churchill, *Rationing Health Care in America* (Notre Dame: University of Notre Dame Press, 1987).

4. J. A. Morone, "American Political Culture and the Search for Lessons from Abroad," *Journal of Health Politics, Policy and Law,* vol. 15, (1990), pp. 129–43.

5. President's Commission for the Study of Ethical Problems in Medicine and Biomedical and Behavioral Research, *Securing Access to Health Care: The Ethical Implications of Differences in the Availability of Health Services,* vol. 1, *Report* (Washington, D.C.: Government Printing Office, 1983).

6. N. Daniels, "Why Saying No to Patients in the United States is so Hard," *New England Journal of Medicine,* vol. 315, (1986), pp. 1380–83.

7. R. Sidel, *Women and Children Last: The Plight of Poor Women in Affluent America* (New York: Penguin Books, 1987).

8. Catholic Health Association of the United States, *With Justice For All: The Ethics of Healthcare Rationing* (St. Louis: CHA, 1991).

9. M. Danis and L. R. Churchill, "Autonomy and the Common Weal," *Hastings Center Report,* vol. 21, no. 1 (1991), pp. 25–31.

10. D. Callahan, *What Kind of Life? The Limits of Medical Progress* (New York: Simon and Schuster, 1990).

11. D. Callahan, "Autonomy: A Moral Good, Not a Moral Obsession," *Hastings Center Report,* vol. 14 (Oct. 1984), pp. 40–42.

12. Oregon's bold reform proposal has captured the nation's attention as the first government initiative to explicitly distribute limited health care resources. Oregon Health Services Commission, *Prioritization of Health Services: A Report to the Governor and Legislature* (Salem: Oregon Health Services Commission, 1991). The goal of Massachusetts's Health Security Act (H.5210; chap. 23 of the Acts of 1988, enacted Apr. 13, 1988) is to provide universal access without major restructuring of the health care system. (Primarily due to the state's severe economic downturn since the act's passage, implementation of most of it was postponed in 1991 for three years.) New York's UNY*Care proposal would radically reform the system by establishing a single-payer network, while retaining existing payors and employer-based insurance coverage (D. E. Beauchamp and R. L. Rouse, "Universal NY Health Care: A Single-Payor Strategy Linking Cost Control and Universal Access," *New England Journal of Medicine,* vol. 323 (1990) pp. 640–44. The 1991 health care access bill in Minnesota (passed by the legislature but vetoed by the governor) would have established a state plan to provide health care coverage for the uninsured and required all state residents to obtain coverage for at least the level of benefits provided by the state plan (chap. 335 [House File 2, 1991]). Hawaii enacted a health insurance program in 1990, for people who are not working, to complement its existing legislation on mandated employer-based health insurance. Thus, Hawaii is now the only state capable of assuring universal access.

13. President's Commission, *Securing Access to Health Care.*

14. Whether this should include all inhabitants (including illegal aliens), all residents, or only all U.S. citizens is a thorny but unresolved issue.

15. President's Commission, *Securing Access to Health Care.*

16. D. M. Eddy, "What Care is 'Essential'? What Services are 'Basic'?" *Journal of the American Medical Association,* vol. 265 (1991), pp. 782–88.

17. N. Daniels, "Is the Oregon Rationing Plan Fair?" *Journal of the American Medical Association,* vol. 265 (1991), pp. 2232–35.

18. Committee to Design a Strategy for Quality Review and Assurance in Medicare, *Medicare: A Strategy for Quality Assurance* (Washington, D.C.: National Academy Press, 1990).

19. M. V. Pauly et al., "A Plan for 'Responsible National Health Insurance,'" *Health Affairs,* Spring 1991, pp. 5–25.

20. M. Siegler, "Confidentiality in Medicine: A Decrepit Concept," *New England Journal of Medicine,* vol. 307 (1982), pp. 1518–21.

21.W. Manning et al., *Health Insurance and the Demand for Medical Care: Evidence From a Randomized Experiment,* RAND Research Report, R. 3476–HHS, Feb. 1988.

22. American Medical Association, *Principles of Medical Ethics* (Chicago: American Medical Association, 1980).

23. F. D. Wolinsky, "The Professional Dominance Perspective, Revisited," *Milbank Memorial Fund Quarterly,* vol. 66 (1988 suppl. 2), pp. 33–47.

24. E. Freidson, *Professional Dominance: The Social Structure of Medical Care* (New York: Atherton Press, 1970).

25. Wolinsky, "Professional Dominance Perspective."

26. Daniels, "Saying No to Patients."

27. P. Clark, "Ethical Dimensions of Quality of Life in Aging: Individual Autonomy vs. Collectivism in the United States and Canada," *Gerontologist,* vol. 31 (1991), pp. 631–39.

28. R. J. Botelho, "Overcoming the Prejudice Against Establishing a National Health Care System," *Archives of Internal Medicine,* vol. 151 (1991), pp. 863–69.

11

Limits and Equal Access to Basic Health Care: Suggestions for Comprehensive Reform

Robert J. Barnet

In a *New York Times* essay, A. M. Rosenthal lamented the state of emergency room care in New York City. He related that he "spent many boyhood months in a huge stinking charity ward."In asking what has gone wrong, he said that nobody told him he "could not have a bed—nobody said that."Today they do.

It is clear that in the United States there is a crisis in the delivery of health care. Millions have no health insurance; millions of others are underinsured. Others are excluded or limited because they do not have the financial means. Many who do obtain care end up with major financial burden. We spend the highest percentage of gross national product on health care of any industrialized country and continue to have an unacceptable level of infant mortality and a life expectancy less than that of countries who spend half to two-thirds of what we do.

If our citizens have a right of access to basic health care, as I believe they do, a solution to our dilemma must be found. We cannot consider the problem of health care for the aged separately from health care for the rest of society. If our health care system is fundamentally flawed, as I believe it is, we cannot continue to defer reform, but we do.

Unfortunately, both major political parties have been unwilling to challenge the conventional wisdom. George Mitchell, Senate majority leader, when asked about the Physicians for a National Health Program proposal, replied that:

1. we as a nation cannot afford more for health care
2. the free enterprise system insures better health care
3. the current system delivers through high-tech medicine a superior level of health care

None of these statements is patently true. Too many millions are unserved, underserved, and poorly served. Too many other countries spend far less and have comparable or better health care. It is not simply that our total financing is inadequate. Our free market approach has failed; a revolutionary rethinking is required. Patchwork approaches are no longer acceptable. Our current health care system is seriously stressed, if not in chaos. More important, it is not a just system. It is fragmented, too technical, too specialized, too expensive, depersonalized, and often lacking in compassion as well as in clear benefit. Regardless of the political rhetoric, solutions must be found. Justice and compassion require that.

The Right to Basic Health Care

In the United States today, there is a right of access to basic health care. It is a derivative moral right, not a constitutional or natural right. In explaining the basis of this right, I will rely on my understanding of the current state of American society and my experience as a physician, and I do this from a perspective rooted in the concept that we are all members of a community with a particular history and identity. It is my claim that part of that narrative is the recognition of the worth and dignity of every single person and of the concept of 'equality'. One of the roles of community is to meet the needs of its members—all of its members. I accept the position articulated by Rawls and others, including most religious groups, that basic human needs have the first claim against the goods of society. This finds expression in such phrases as a "preferential option for the poor" and "special concern for the least advantaged".

Society has gradually broadened what it has included in its concept of 'rights'. There are limits to our resources, hence it is inappropriate to argue that there is an unlimited right to all types of health care. There is, however, a right of access to basic health care, for which, in my judgement, we do have sufficient resources. There are far too many who are unable to exercise even that basic right, while at the same time others receive excessive, often unproven, harmful, and expensive services. Available financial resources are being depleted increasingly by for-profit segments of society, including the medical profession. Often, even those who submit to the health care system and exercise their right do so inappropriately because they are, or feel, impotent to manage many of their own difficulties. The medical profession and other elements of the medical-industry complex have redefined (and expanded) what we know as health care. Society has too easily accepted this, compounding the problem.

The notion of a right to health care is a relatively recent concept. The necessity of confirming that concept has come about because of changing human experience and societal development over the last hundred years. Ideas on social justice in this and other areas have at the same time evolved, reflecting a new and different reality. Since the 1970s, developments in medical technology, as well as changes in health care delivery patterns, have left much of American society with a tenuous grasp on what it perceives as necessary to assure a healthful life. This insecurity is most prevalent among those who, especially when ill, are the most vulnerable—the poor, minorities, the young, the elderly, and the marginally employed. Today more than thirty-seven million people have no health insurance. Even for many who do have insurance, health care costs remain a major burden.

During the past forty years, because of scientific development and the greater effectiveness of medicine, our ability to provide significant improvement in health has expanded. With this has come the reality, arising out of the institutionalization of health care and the medicalization of many aspects of our lives, that access to health care is something that is necessary for our general well-being. Modern media and marketing have gone further and have fostered not only this perception but often false needs and false expectations. Without this entitlement we often feel impotent, deprived, and not truly happy. We perceive that we cannot find in our community by ourselves, or by mutual association, adequate health care. As a nation, unfortunately, we have become dependent on professionals for those goods and services that make up health care. Access to basic health care has become a real need.

We have moved from a time (the nineteenth and early twentieth century) when a right to health care was not even considered, to a time (the 1950s and 1960s) when it was assumed to be a right. But now, for many, especially the young and the elderly, the dreams that they would be secure about their needs for health care have faded. The promises have not been kept. Today, more than thirty-four million people in the United States live in poverty, as measured by any plausible standard. Another twenty to thirty million are needy, if not destitute. The increasing burden of even the basic premiums for Medicare combined with the deductible amount and cost of medications, took in 1989 almost 25 percent of the median annual social security payment of $6,150. Hence, the typical social security recipient has approximately $380 a month for all other expenses, including food, shelter, and clothing.

Changing the Health Care System

Society and especially those involved in health care have a mandate to do everything possible to bring about a reordering of priorities to insure that the basic needs of all members of society are met. Physicians must recognize that it is primarily their decisions that result in health care resources being encumbered. Neither their financial nor decision-making autonomy can continue unfettered.

Michael Walzer has pointed out in *Spheres of Justice:* "So long as communal funds are spent, as they currently are, to finance research, build hospitals and pay the fees of doctors in private practice, the services that these expenditures underwrite must be equally available to all citizens."[1]

David Smith in his book *Health Care in the Anglican Tradition* continues with the same theme:

within their own frame of reference our medieval forefathers did a better job of communal provision than we do, for they acknowledged in principle a social duty to meet the most fundamental need of everyone.

Then, as now, these needs cannot be met without cost, and one cost, central to the American tradition, will be liberty—notably, in this case, the market liberty of physicians. Just as the medieval church could not begin to deliver on its social responsibilities if clergy were completely free to function as unchecked entrepreneurs, so some kinds of constraints will be necessary to assure that less-attractive specialties, populations and geographical areas receive adequate medical care. For the sake of need, some trade-offs against liberty are justified.[2]

Those trade-offs may well involve less income and less power for physicians. Critical to the changes will be a reappraisal of professional roles, motives, and values. Physicians must return to a tradition that acknowledges their limits; there is a time at which they are no longer "healers"but "hand-holders."

Changes in the roles, responsibilities, and reimbursement of physicians are crucial to meeting the basic health care needs of all our citizens, but a more comprehensive restructuring of the system is necessary. This restructuring should be guided by the following imperatives:

1. Recognize limits for all, not disproportionately for any particular group
2. Remove financial considerations as the basis of decision making
3. Acknowledge that the right of universal access to basic health care is an entitlement, not charity or the granting of a welfare benefit
4. Recognize the importance of community-based identification of needs
5. Strive to deinstitutionalize and demedicalize the health care so that individuals and communities gain greater control
6. Resist the lure of high-tech medicine and concentrate on the humanization of aging and dying

Let me suggest eight more concrete initiatives that might help to bring about a more just health care system.

1. We should encourage the development of a consensus expressed in clear, simple, and forceful statements of principles about what the informed community itself, not the health care profession nor the medical-industrial complex, sees as the important priorities in health care. A dialogue on the importance and meaning of the concepts of demedicalization and deinstutionalization should be part of this effort. With this, the education and empowerment of the general public should be fostered.

2. Public policy should give its highest priority to the encouragement and support of providing access to decentralized, community-based, and community-integrated health services designed to deal with immediate and basic health needs. This should include the use of direct federal funding, transfer of Medicaid funds, or block grants when necessary. It may be useful to convert some closed or marginal facilities to federally funded primary care clinics, staffed with salaried or National Health Service physicians and other personnel, especially during a transition period. Enlightened and innovative use of community facilities such as schools, churches, and other centers chosen and accepted by the members of the community could be especially important. Services should be available to all. Restructuring of health care services should involve the rejection of free-market principles and profit incentives as the basis for decision making. Basic health needs, rather than economics, must determine the priorities.

3. We should encourage and fund programs involving nurse practitioners, pharmacists, midwives, and other auxiliary personnel as primary deliverers of health services, not simply as physician extenders. More responsibility for basic procedures and care should be assumed by such individuals. This reorientation should include clarification and redefinition of the role of specialists so that, rather than taking charge of the patient's care, they would function as consultants to those involved in primary care.

4. There should be a reemphasis on a community-based approach to health services. We should concentrate on primary care medicine and associated programs directed toward enhancing home and community-based care, rather than focusing on high-tech, acute care in the hospital. I characterize primary care as that level of health care currently delivered by family practitioners, internists, pediatricians, nurse practitioners, physician assistants, and the like. Such a program should involve, as a first step, the expansion of nonprofit community health clinics, staffed when possible by community, neighborhood, or family volunteers, nurse practitioners, and other health auxiliaries who would provide first-level care.

5. We should undertake intensive review, sponsored and funded by the federal government, of current therapies and procedures to determine their clinical efficacy. When interventions or medications are available that have comparable efficacy and safety, the use of the least expensive should be encouraged. There should be renewed systematic efforts at prospective, not retrospective, evaluations.

6. Resources should be redirected from esoteric high-technology medicine to first-level primary care, public health, preventative medicine, and child and maternal health. Priority should be given to providing basic services to those who are the least advantaged. A careful review of current research policies and funding should be part of the reappraisal. Government funding of high-

technology medicine not clearly benefiting society or yielding significant improvement in health should be discontinued. The decision-making process on the use and introduction of procedures and technology should include the meaningful involvement of the community.

7.   There should be a comprehensive appraisal of the effect of statutory regulations and malpractice litigation on health care delivery. Legislative action should be sought to encourage rather than hinder the delivery of low-cost health care. Legal constraints that tend to restrict individual access to basic drugs and health services should be removed.

8.   We should recognize that we do have excellent federal programs involved in the delivery of health care. Rather than privatizing or eliminating those existing federal services, such as the Indian Service, veteran and military hospitals, and clinics, efforts should be made to strengthen them so that they can continue to play an important and perhaps expanded role. Reappraisal and reform of their bureaucracy may be needed if they are to play an important role in the new system.

Conclusion

There is a right of access to basic health care in the context of our current historical setting. Under current patterns of care, however, there is inadequate access to basic health services for too many members of American society. These individuals are typically the least advantaged and often, because of their standing in society, the most needy. Reallocation from the elderly is not an appropriate solution to the problem.

I have included "reform"in the title. Perhaps I chose the wrong term. Reform typically refers to removal of faults and abuses, and this is not sufficient. What is required is a reorientation with fundamental, comprehensive, and probably radical changes. That defines revolution. But it should be a revolution that recognizes and preserves, as far as possible, the virtues of the present system.

The changes necessary will require some modification of the expectations of those who seek entitlement, as well as a restructuring of benefits so that more accrue to the least advantaged and less to the entrepreneur. One such system that may meet that condition is a targeted national health service concentrating on primary care. National health *insurance* alone is unacceptable, since it would only serve to perpetuate what is a basically flawed system.

Health care resources are finite; what can be accomplished with them has limits. Science and technology cannot be presumed to be capable of totally resolving all human problems. A just distribution of health care resources is possible only if the reality of limits is recognized by all three groups: those who seek health care, those who provide it, and those involved in social planning. Justifiable limits, however, will not exclude anyone from access to basic health care.

Notes

1. Michael Walzer, *Spheres of Justice: A Defense of Pluralism and Equality* (New York: Basic Books, 1983).

2. David Smith, *Health Care in the Anglican Tradition* (New York, Crossroad Publishing Company, 1986).

12

Just Caring: Lessons from Oregon and Canada

Leonard M. Fleck

This is an essay in health care justice. It is not aimed at providing a philosophically elegant account of the subject. Rather, an objective is to identify the articulate judgments of health care justice that will allow us to assess specific proposals for health reform at either the state or national level. I deliberately refrain from speaking of anything as noble as *principles* of health care justice, for that term has the unfortunate tendency of eliciting an ideological response. What is needed in making health policy are moral judgments that are pragmatic, tentative, fine grained, and contextualized. To be sure, we can talk about something called the "framework" or "sphere" of health care justice, but most of the work we will be doing in this essay will be in the moral interstices of that framework.[1] If philosophers are to have anything morally relevant to say with respect to the more important policy debates in our society, then they will have to become considerably more skillful in fashioning the nonideal, contextualized, micromoral judgments needed to guide and advance policy debates from a moral point of view. My hope is that this essay will serve as an example of what such moral analysis should be.

Health Reform and Rationing

There are two major goals of health reform that must be achieved simultaneously. First, we must expand access to our health care system because there are thirty-seven million Americans without health insurance, another twenty million who are inadequately insured, and a considerable number of unmet or inadequately met health needs among the poor, the elderly, and the chronically ill.[2] Second, we need to contain escalating health care costs, which jumped from $26 billion (5.2 percent of GNP in 1960) to $838 billion in 1992 (14 percent of GNP), and are projected to hit $1.7 trillion by the year 2000 (17 percent of GNP). These two goals are in obvious tension with one another and are reasonably thought to constitute *the* central dilemma of health reform. To the extent that we wish to provide more health care of high quality to more people, we must expect higher aggregate health costs. This is the "equitable access" aspect of health reform. To the extent that our primary objective is to control costs, fewer health services of lower quality will have to be made available to a smaller number of patients. This is the "cost containment/rationing" aspect of health reform.

There is an intense debate among health policy analysts about whether cost containment necessarily implies the need for health care rationing. For some, health care rationing has been a ubiquitous and unremarkable part of our health care system for at least three decades. Rationing is nothing more than the making of allocation decisions at the level of the individual. On the private side we have rationed by price—those unable to pay for needed health services would often simply be denied them. On the public side, for example, in the Medicaid program, we have rationed access to care through setting eligibility levels, or by varying the scope of benefits, or by restricting payment to providers for certain services (thereby reducing their incentive for providing these services), and in many other ways—all of which have failed to elicit very much in the way of moral or political outrage, though we have every reason to believe that such practices have caused considerable premature death and unnecessary suffering.[3]

Though some see health care rationing as a ubiquitous and unremarkable phenomenon, others see health care rationing as a morally and politically abominable innovation that is nothing more than an easy and expedient way out of a cost crisis at the expense of individuals who are sick and vulnerable and poor. Lawrence Brown is one such critic, and the state of Oregon, which all would agree has been the focus of the rationing debate in health care, is the object of his criticism. The conception of rationing he sees as embodied in Oregon is what he describes as "cost-effective retrenchment," or "the deliberate, systematic withholding of beneficial goods or services from some elements of the population on the grounds that society cannot afford to extend them."[4] Medicaid recipients in Oregon are the elements of the population that would be most directly affected by the package of policies that has been approved by the state legislature. Brown contends that there are numerous other ways in which health care costs can be contained that are not morally objectionable, because they spread the burden of controlling costs over the entire population instead of imposing the bulk of that burden on the sick poor. Second, he argues that states like Oregon have been forced to come up with these inequitable ways of controlling health care costs because we have failed to muster the political will to effect fundamental health reform at the national level.[5] His conclusion is that "American policymakers have not earned the right to ration health care," that this is a spurious issue that should certainly not be at the center of the health policy debate.[6]

The Oregon Plan

Despite Brown's misgivings, the fact is that Oregon is very much at the focus of health policy debates. For some, Oregon is a model for reform efforts at the national level.[7] There are two basic reasons for this accolade. First, Oregon recognized that there was something fundamentally unjust about the fact that only 58 percent of those below the poverty level were covered by the Oregon Medicaid program (which was better than most states). Further, there were several hundred-thousand Oregonians who were employed and without health insurance because they were in low-wage jobs without health benefits, which is to say they did not have the financial ability to purchase health insurance on their own. To remedy this situation the Oregon legislature passed a package of bills that would (1) cover everyone below the poverty level with Medicaid, (2) require all small businesses to either buy health insurance for their employees equal to the Medicaid benefit package or pay a payroll tax that the state would use to purchase insurance for those individuals, and (3) create an affordable insurance pool for all those individuals who were denied health insurance because of preexisting medical conditions. The intended result of this legislative package was something very close to universal health insurance coverage. Needless to say, this package had implications for tax-payers. This brings us to our second reason why some would see Oregon as a model for national health reform.

In order to control health care costs, Oregon committed itself to an explicit process of health care rationing, although limited to recipients of Medicaid under the age of sixty-five. More precisely, this was a priority-setting process that aimed at rank-ordering 709 condition-treatment pairs that covered the bulk of possible medical interventions. The ranking was done in accord with cost-effectiveness considerations, community values, and quality-of-life-after-treatment considerations.[8] The legislature was not allowed to adjust the ranking of items; their sole re-sponsibility was to set a budget for Medicaid, which would then determine how far down the list services could be offered. Because Medicaid is a state-federal pro-gram, a waiver was required from Congress for this experiment. To assuage con-gressional anxieties, the governor of Oregon promised Congress that Oregon would fund down to item number 587 on that list for at least five years.

What earned Oregon national attention for this effort was the fact that they were engaged in an *explicit, politically accountable* process of rationing instead of the implicit, invisible, unaccountable process of rationing that is otherwise pervasive in our health care system. Further, the contention of the architects of this plan, such as Dr. Kitzhaber, the physician-president of the Oregon Senate, was that they were making the process of rationing fair and rational. Instead of relying on arbitrary, piecemeal rationing, which is what happens when an individual is denied eligibil-ity for *all* Medicaid benefits, even those that are needed and costworthy, this process of rationing would deny to all Medicaid beneficiaries those medical services that were judged to be least cost-effective, least likely to yield enough medical benefit relative to other health needs of the Medicaid population and treatment options.[9]

At this point the reader should recall Brown's definition of rationing as "the deliberate, systematic withholding of beneficial goods or services." The "deliber-ate and systematic" part of that definition has earned Oregon substantial praise, while the "beneficial" nature of the services denied has earned Oregon moral and political condemnation. This later point, of course, is what makes rationing so controversial. If the services denied under a rationing practice were medically futile, there would be little basis for moral or political objection. But the fact is that for the most part rationed medical services offer "some" chance of benefit, though the benefit (or likelihood of benefit) may be very small and the cost very high. Still, a chance of benefit is a chance of *benefit*, and often enough that benefit will be life itself, as when the judgment is made by Oregon that six-hundred-gram premature infants will not be offered intensive care because there is less than a 10 percent chance of producing an intact survivor, and the cost of producing any survivor (intact or seriously handicapped) will be in excess of $400,000. With this example in mind, it is easier to understand why rationing would be morally and politically problematic.

In order to appreciate the painfulness of the dilemma of health care reform and health care rationing we need to keep in mind that very few health care services are merely wanted. Rather, most often patients see themselves as *needing* health care services. Consequently, when we speak about the desirability of reducing the provision of health services in order to control costs, what we are really saying is that there are some health needs that will go unmet. Expressed in suitably monotonal rational abstract academic prose this consequence may not seem terribly disturbing. Hence, what the reader must imagine is that it is your own intense headache of two weeks duration that the emergency room physician is refusing to diagnose via magnetic resonance imaging (MRI) because you are unable to pay the $1200 cost of the procedure. Further, you find hollow the reassurances of the emergency room physician that it is very unlikely that you have a brain tumor, even if a close friend of yours died with a brain tumor two months ago. From an outsider's perspective a legitimate argument can be made that you do not really *need* that MRI, though you will probably not be persuaded by the rationale for that judgment, especially if what is conveyed to you is that "someone" (a distant bureaucrat, or worse, a formula we use) has concluded that your health needs are less important than someone else's health needs. That is, the $1200 worth of uncompensated care that you are seeking from this hospital represents $1200 worth of care that this hospital will not be able to provide to someone else whose health needs are substantially more likely to be met since there is less than a 1 percent chance that you really do have a brain tumor.

The point of this example is that cost containment means care containment. Cost containment means that the health care needs of some patients are not going to be met. How can a society that claims to be just and caring allow something like that to be called health reform? How can a society allow a seven-year-old boy named Coby Howard to die of leukemia when there is a 20 percent chance that he could be cured with access to a bone marrow transplant that would have cost Medicaid $150,000? This is in stark form the problem of health care rationing.

It was the state of Oregon that made the decision not to fund the bone marrow transplant for Coby Howard through their Medicaid program. The argument that was made to justify this decision was that there were greater health needs for more Medicaid patients that could be met with these same resources.[10] Was Coby Howard treated unjustly? On the face of it, there is something morally unseemly about allowing a seven-year-old boy to die under these circumstances. But we need to be very careful about locating what is morally problematic with this case. Certainly it would be too quick and crude a moral judgment to say that Coby Howard had a moral right to all the health care that he needed. In a world of limited resources no one has a moral right to all the health care that they might need. Still, this is a seven-year-old boy, and all he needed was $150,000, not unlimited health care. Surely the state of Oregon must have that available somewhere. This brings us a little closer to the source of our moral discomfort.

If bone marrow transplants were scarce in some absolute sense, as is the case with transplantable solid organs, and if only one in ten individuals could receive a life-saving bone marrow transplant because of that absolute scarcity, then the deaths of those other nine individuals would be unfortunate and regrettable, but they would not be morally problematic (assuming that all had a fair chance to receive the bone marrow transplant). But this is contrary to fact. The only thing that limits the number of bone marrow transplants is the availability of funds to pay for them. Still, if we knew precisely what other health services were purchased with the $150,000 that was denied Coby Howard—if we knew, for example, that more lives were going to be saved with that $150,000 and that there was more than a 90 percent probability that those lives would be saved—then that would alleviate our moral discomfort. But this too is contrary to fact, or at least not entirely congruent with the facts as they were then.

The state of Oregon had decided that soft tissue transplants would not be funded under the Medicaid program, that this would generate a savings of $1.1 million, which would be used to fund prenatal care.[11] One of the primary objectives of prenatal care is to prevent the birth of very premature infants, for those born at less than one-thousand grams or less than twenty-seven weeks gestation are at very high risk either of death or of serious mental and physical impairments resulting from bleeding in the brain. There are many causes of prematurity, but among the more significant are smoking and substance abuse. These are extremely difficult behaviors to alter under ideal circumstances; this raises the question of how confident Oregon is that it achieved results through this program that morally justified the sacrifice of the life of Coby Howard (as well as some number of other anonymous individuals). Given what is at stake, this should be a source of moral discomfort.

Finally, what must also be a source of moral discomfort is the fact that there are other children in Oregon, just like Coby Howard, whose parents have private health insurance that will purchase for them that chance of survival that Oregon is denying Coby. Our basic sense of fairness is that similar individuals similarly situated should be treated alike, most especially when life itself is at stake. It would be unfortunate and regrettable if the societal judgment were made that the probability of success of bone marrow transplants in these circumstances was too low and the cost too high and that there were other medical interventions more deserving of these resources, the result being that some number of individuals would be effectively condemned to a premature death. But it would not be obvious that something unjust had been done, because there were no arbitrary or invidious distinctions that had been made among individuals in this class. In the case of Coby Howard, however, we are talking about a child who, through no fault of his own, is associated with parents who must rely upon Medicaid for their health care. Further, the state, which is supposed to be the ultimate protector of the equal rights of all, is in this case the originator of the policy that will deny Coby the resources he needs for a chance at continued life.

Rationing Must be Systematic, Open, and Just

What is the moral lesson that we ought to draw from the case of Coby Howard? It is that rationing decisions made in a piecemeal, uncoordinated fashion are very likely to be arbitrary and unjust. At the time that Oregon made these decisions there was a decided lack of moral justification necessary for such a grave decision. But Oregon did remedy this deficiency subsequently through the development and adoption of a comprehensive, systematic, and deliberate approach to health care rationing.

There is a second moral lesson to be drawn from the case of Coby Howard, namely, that rationing decisions made publicly are open to critical assessment and correction. It should be obvious to everyone that Oregon was not the first state to permit the denial of life-sustaining medical care to a Medicaid patient. This is surely a routine occurrence in Medicaid programs throughout the United States and for patients who are without health insurance.[12] But the denials are effected subtly and in ways that are essentially hidden from public scrutiny, as well as scrutiny by the patient himself or herself, which is to say there is ample opportunity for invidious discrimination.[13]

Thus far we have drawn two generalizable lessons from Oregon regarding just health care rationing, namely, that rationing must be deliberate and systematic and that it must be done openly, publicly. A third lesson is that health reform in general, and rationing specifically, must be guided by explicit *moral* considerations, most especially considerations of health care justice. There were eight such principles that were at the heart of the Oregon reform effort.[14] If health care were merely another consumer good, there would be no reason why health care should be an object of special moral concern. We could simply allow markets to distribute health care in accord with individual ability to pay. But I have argued, as have a number of other philosophers, that health care is a moral good; and, consequently, it does matter how health care is distributed.[15] Markets may do a splendid job of distributing goods efficiently, but they offer no assurances at all that equity will be preserved or enhanced through these transactions.

The larger claim implicit in the Oregon reform effort and worthy of national recognition is that the problem of health reform is fundamentally a *moral* problem, as opposed to being primarily an economic or organizational or managerial problem. The point of this claim is threefold. First, tinkering with economic incentives or organizational structures to achieve health reform will result in symptomatic relief at best, unless those economic and organizational adjustments are governed by a shared understanding of what will count as just alterations of our health care system.

Second, there are thousands of children and adults in the United States, just like Coby Howard, whose lives are threatened by a deadly illness and whose lives could be prolonged if they had access to some expensive life-prolonging medical technology, such as a bone marrow transplant. Whether they have a just claim to that technology or not will not be settled by an appeal to an economic equation or organizational theory or more clinical data. We need to address that issue directly as a moral problem. Further, allocational problems caused by advancing medical technology are not just an oddity in our health care system today. Rather, they are at the heart of twentieth-century technological medicine. As Callahan has astutely observed, each innovation in medical technology creates whole categories of new health needs, often costly needs.[16] Infants with necrotic small bowel syndrome, for example, will usually die around the age of two because the hyperalimentation that will initially save their lives (at a cost of $500,000 per year) will ultimately destroy their livers. But we can give those infants another couple of years of life if we do a liver transplant at a cost of $250,000. Is this a medical intervention that our society ought to underwrite? Some of these infants are born into very poor families that have their medical needs met through Medicaid. Given the very limited budgets of many state Medicaid programs, and given the proclivity of many states to balance their Medicaid budgets by raising eligibility requirements in order to exclude more of the poor from the program, should infants like this be denied Medicaid support because they are doomed to a premature death no matter how much we spend to sustain their lives? Would such infants be treated unfairly under such a proposal? Would their right to life have been violated? Again, these sorts of questions are central to any proposal for health reform in a society where health care has no intrinsic moral or political right to command unlimited resources, which is what Oregon says explicitly in one of its eight principles.[17]

Third, to describe the challenge of health reform as a moral problem is to say that all of us as citizens of what should be a just and caring society need to take responsibility for health reform, as opposed to simply handing the problem off to some assortment of experts, especially in the matter of health care rationing. Needless to say, all sorts of expert knowledge may be essential for intelligent rationing decisions, but expert knowledge is not a suitable replacement for public moral judgment and public moral responsibility for the making of fair rationing judgments.[18] This is really the fourth moral lesson for national health reform that ought to be drawn from Oregon, which we may refer to as the principle of community for health care rationing.

Rationing and Community

The general idea behind this principle of community is that rationing decisions are more likely to be fair if they are decisions that are self-imposed rather than ones that are imposed by some (healthy individuals) on others (sick and vulnerable individuals). What needs to be noted is that embedded in this principle of community must be a principle of autonomy with respect to health care rationing. What this principle says is that just rationing decisions must be freely self-imposed. These two principles must be inextricably linked with one another as a practical matter and as a moral matter.

We might imagine that everyone should just make their own rationing decisions for themselves in accord with their personal budgets. But this would be no more than rationing by ability to pay, which is the denial that there is a problem of justice so far as the distribution of access to health care is concerned. Alternatively, the state can establish a health care budget for each individual that would correct for income inequalities, the assumption being that this would be that individual's fair share of resources for meeting his health care needs. Individuals could then make rationing decisions for themselves. The moral and practical difficulty, however, is that individual health needs vary enormously in any given year and over the course of a life. Thus, an average allocation to each individual for health needs will be more than adequate for some and grossly inadequate for others who will have disproportionate health needs, like Coby Howard.

If health budgets are completely individualized by the state to actual or prospective health needs, then all capacity for effectively controlling costs is lost, at least as long as individuals judge for themselves what will count as a health need. On the other hand, if the state determines what will count as a legitimate health need, it appears as if we have sacrificed respect for individual autonomy.

What the Oregon approach recognizes is that a budget for meeting health needs must be communally accepted. As noted earlier, there is no perfectly objective way of identifying and counting up health needs at any point in time, because there are value considerations necessarily bound up with that determination and because emerging medical technologies are constantly adding "new" health needs. This means there is no perfectly objective way of determining that communal health budget. That will require a balancing judgment that takes into account other important social needs that have a claim on social resources. In a democratic society all should have the opportunity to participate in the making of that balancing judgment, since all will be affected by the results of that judgment.

Justice and costworthiness are two of the fundamental value considerations pertinent to framing a health budget, and for the most part these considerations must be highly relativized and contextualized. There is no external ideal of either health care justice or health care costworthiness that we can appeal to as a normative gold standard. Instead, what we must ultimately rely upon are processes of informed democratic decision making to come to some fair agreement regarding our health care priorities. A considerable degree of impartiality is achievable in real world democratic conversations about health care priorities, since the vast majority of us are ignorant of our future health needs. In order for the process to be fair, all who have a voice in shaping health priorities and rationing protocols must be ongoing members of the community, ones who are more or less equally subject to their own rationing schemes.

In this vein it is significant that Oregon did not allow legislators to alter the rankings of those 709 condition-treatment pairs. This too is a critical element in preserving the overall fairness of the system. This is a way of avoiding special pleading by more powerful health interest groups who might be advocates for patients with certain forms of cancer or heart disease or whatever. No collective judgment of what our health priorities ought to be is going to be perfectly correct. There will be some degree of arbitrariness in whatever ranking we can agree to. But that degree of arbitrariness will be "fair enough" just by virtue of the fact that we agreed to it. Further, all those rankings are relativized to one another. Thus, there is a kind of moral integrity to the rankings as a whole. It is this integrity that is threatened when, for example, an advocacy group seeks to get special public funding that would be used to try to sustain the lives of extremely premature infants (less than 600 grams) in the neonatal intensive care unit.

If, for example, care for such infants were ranked at item number 647, and if the legislature had provided a budget that would fund down to item number 587, then to provide public funds for those infants would mean that there were fifty-nine other condition-treatment pairs that were judged as having a greater claim on our health care budget from a shared value perspective of the community and that those claims were simply being ignored through this special pleading. This would be a violation of the fairness and integrity of the priority-setting process. Thus, if the Oregon legislature were convinced that those premature infants were deserving of funding, then they would be morally (and legally) obligated to fund all the intervening condition-treatment pairs.

Rationing in Oregon: A Critical Assessment

As already noted in passing, the Oregon approach to health reform and health care rationing has been subjected to intense moral and political criticism. I wish to discuss briefly some of the more important criticisms that have been made, especially those that I would judge to be fair criticisms. The net result of this discussion will be that Oregon ought not to be taken as a model for health reform at the national level *in toto*. That conclusion, however, does not take away from the many positive contributions of Oregon to the health reform debate.

Clearly the most frequently voiced criticism of Oregon is that the poor were exploited in order to achieve health reform. That is, Oregon committed itself to achieving nearly universal access to health care and hoped to pay for it by imposing a rationing system on the poor, that is, those who were least well off. The objective was clearly laudable, but the means to the objective were unjust.[19] I have defended Oregon on this point at some length.[20] Briefly, I have pointed out that this policy choice must be assessed from the perspective of non-ideal justice, not some idealized conception of justice. More precisely, Oregon can justifiably argue that the poor as a class are better off under the reform proposal than they are under the current Medicaid program, which covers only 58 percent of the poor. The critical piece of empirical information is that there is significant churning among the poor in terms of whether they are above or below that 58 percent mark. A poor person who obtains a low-wage temporary job rises above that 58 percent mark and then has no health coverage at all. Under the Oregon reform proposal, such a person would always be assured access to a basic package of health services but would have given up assured access to services that, although formerly available, now fall below item number 587 on the priority list. It is also morally relevant that rational poor persons, suitably informed, would autonomously choose this reform package over the current Medicaid program.

Henry Aaron raises another objection to the Oregon plan that requires comment. Specifically, he contends that the 709 condition-treatment pairs are not nearly adequate to account for the complexity of clinical medicine.[21] To approach adequacy, there would have to be 30,000 such condition-treatment pairs, which would be an administrative nightmare. As things are now in Oregon's proposed system, there might be patients in a high-priority category who are very likely to derive substantial benefit from that treatment, and, hence, the goals of fairness and efficiency would be well served; and there will also be in that category patients who, because of complex medical circumstances, are very unlikely to achieve more than minimal benefits from that treatment. Yet they would seem to have a "just claim" to that treatment, though neither justice nor efficiency would be well served by providing the treatment to them, since there are clearly other patients who could benefit much more if those resources were saved for them.

This is a fair criticism of Oregon. Still, we need to be careful in drawing a lesson for national health reform. Remember that the basic purpose of setting priorities is to identify *in general* those services that ought to be included in a benefit package that is guaranteed to everyone. The decision to include a service and rank it in a certain position is, in effect, the judgment that this is in general a costworthy use of health resources and that patients in general have a just claim to it. These judgments, however, are not nearly precise enough for clinical applicability, if our concern is to preserve fairness and efficiency at that level. Hence, they need to be supplemented by specific, public, democratically approved clinical protocols and broad clinical guidelines that will identify "outliers" for a specific condition-treatment pair, that is, individuals who need a high-priority service but are very unlikely to benefit very much from having access to that service. Consequently, neither justice nor efficiency would warrant their being provided that service. We need to keep in mind that no manageable set of such protocols can obviate the need for careful clinical judgment *of individual patients and their overall medical circumstances.* This means that there is opportunity for individual physicians to game the system on behalf of "their patients." Further, if challenged, they can offer as a moral rationalization for their gaming that they are being uncompromised advocates of the best interests of their patients. However, if there are hard global budgets in place, then physicians will have countervailing moral motivation for respecting just cost-containing clinical protocols and guidelines. This is because hard budgets in a closed system mean that resources saved by denying this patient here and now marginally beneficial services will result in those resources being used to meet other health needs that can be met more efficiently and that have a stronger moral claim.

Hard global budgets and clinical-practice guidelines must be taken together to achieve fair and efficient results. Hard global budgets alone will not yield that result, because they fail to inform physician judgment *in a systematic way that reflects community values and patient-approved trade-offs.* As we shall see later, this particular deficiency is to be found in Canada as well as Oregon.[22] Canada may be able to tolerate these inefficiencies because they are currently spending only about nine percent of GNP on health care, but these inefficiencies may mask inadvertent distributional injustices that ought not to be tolerated.

The next criticism we need to consider is that of discrimination against the disabled by Oregon. The basic problem is this: If different health outcomes are going to be differentially valued, if part of that differential valuation is an assessment of the quality of life after treatment, and if it is the able-bodied public at large that is primarily responsible for making these quality of life assessments, then will not the result be a systematic disvaluing of the lives of the disabled? That is, will they not be disproportionately the victims of rationing protocols?[23]

Perhaps the more basic question to be raised is this: Should quality of life considerations have any relevance at all in making rationing decisions? An initial response would be to ask: What is the alternative? Should we allocate health care dollars so as to maximize the number of life-years saved, no matter what their quality? Would such a rule more adequately guarantee fair treatment for the disabled so far as their health needs were concerned? It is not obvious that this would be the result. Such a rule would require us to spend one million dollars to sustain the life of Nancy Cruzan in a persistent vegetative state for ten years rather than to use those same funds to purchase a million dollars worth of devices that could be used by variously disabled individuals to achieve a mechanical functional equivalent for whatever their disability might be. Such devices would improve substantially the quality of well-being of these individuals, though they would do nothing at all to add to length of life. In a world of limited resources for meeting health needs, it would seem that prudent disabled individuals would choose funding for these devices for their future selves over sustaining their possible future selves in a persistent vegetative state. This would seem to be a fair choice (because it enhances and protects fair equality of opportunity) and a rational choice that disabled individuals would freely make for themselves, based in part at least on quality-of-life assessments. If this is so, then quality-of-life considerations cannot be ruled inherently discriminatory and unjust in formulating rationing protocols.

The claim can be made that Oregon's cost-effectiveness approach to priority setting systematically devalues the lives of the disabled, because any medical treatment applied to them will yield quality-adjusted life years that will have only a fraction of the value of the life-years generated by that same treatment applied to an individual who is not disabled. This, however, is a complete misrepresentation of Oregon's efforts. As Hadorn observes, "It is the *change* in quality of life, or net benefit, realized from *treatment* that matters, not the *point-in-time* quality of life of a *patient*."[24] From this latter perspective disabled individuals are not treated unfairly. It must be emphasized that any set of rationing protocols will catch up disabled individuals who, for example, will be denied a bone marrow transplant for breast cancer, just as their able-bodied counterparts with the same medical condition will be. This is exactly what fairness requires. If the disabled were given special consideration in these circumstances, perhaps out of a misplaced sense of compassion, then this would be unfair to everyone else in a health care system with fixed budgets.

Should Oregon serve as a model for national health reform? We are asking our question from a moral point of view. Hence, a clearer framing of our question would be: Is the Oregon approach to expanding access to health care and controlling costs by rationing just—not perfectly just, but more just than any feasible alternative? I believe it is not just enough for simple translation to the national level, though we have seen clear moral lessons from Oregon that ought to be adopted nationally. One of the unique features of the Oregon priority-setting process was that it was intended to be a broad-based democratic effort. This too has been an object of repeated criticism. But I believe that the flaws were in the execution, not in the concept, which I see as essential for health reform at the national level.

The Canadian System

Though there may have been as many as fifty proposals for national health reform introduced in Congress during 1992, in mid-1993 there are only two that can be taken seriously as political possibilities: a single-payer system, like Canada's, and the managed-competition approach that will be recommended by the Clinton Administration. Proponents of a single-payer system argue that it is morally (and economically) superior to its policy competitors because it offers universal comprehensive coverage at less than the cost of our current system (Canada spends less than 10 percent of GNP on its health care system) with less intrusiveness in the doctor-patient relationship and without the need for health care rationing as the principal mechanism for controlling costs.[25] If Oregon should not be taken as a model for national health reform from the perspective of health care justice, then should Canada?

The basic features of the Canadian health care system are easy enough to outline. Though we are accustomed to saying that Canada covers all its citizens with a single very comprehensive health care package, the fact is that it is the responsibility of the provinces to provide this package of benefits, and there are slight variations among the provinces in the benefits packages. But the federal government coordinates all this. Hence, as a practical matter it is a national health insurance system that prevails in Canada. There is a single standard of care for all, and virtually no opportunity to buy health insurance over and above the comprehensive package guaranteed to all, which is a way of conveying the equal moral worth of each Canadian citizen so far as health care is concerned.

There is a single payer for all health claims in Canada, as opposed to the fifteen hundred health insurance plans we have in the United States, which means that large administrative efficiencies are achieved. From the perspective of health care justice, not simply efficiency, it is problematic that we in the United States spent $83 billion on excess administrative costs in 1992—billions that failed to provide a dollar's worth of health benefits to anyone—at the same time that we tolerated the failure to meet adequately the health needs of the poor, the elderly, and the uninsured in our society.

Since Canada's health plan is universal, there is no risk rating of individuals. That is, no one is excluded from health care coverage, in whole or in part, because of any preexisting medical condition or any future predictable health needs. Universal coverage assures that those with the greatest health needs will receive the health services they require. It also means that Canada, unlike the United States, offers no opportunities for cost-shifting, which generates both inequities and inefficiencies. It is noteworthy that there are virtually no copayments or deductibles in the Canadian health care system; thus individuals are encouraged to seek needed primary care, rather than putting themselves at risk through inappropriate self-diagnosis.

Physicians are paid on the basis of negotiated fee schedules that are worked out with the government by the different specialty groups. These fees constitute payment in full, which means physicians are not allowed to "extra bill" patients. This is one way in which costs are effectively controlled in the system. The other major form of cost containment is the use of global budgets for hospitals and other institutional providers. This creates a closed health care system, which means, as noted above, that the moral integrity of physicians is better protected. This is be-cause physicians know that the savings achieved by denying a patient before them now some marginally beneficial health service will be redeployed in the health care system to meet the weightier claims of some other patient—and the patient before them now is not treated unfairly because that patient was likely in the position of receiving such redeployed benefits at an earlier point in time. It is of moral signif-icance that there is much less governmental and managerial interference in the clinical autonomy of physicians in Canada, quite unlike the United States, which means physicians are not faced with incentives for compromising the quality of care they provide their patients.

The dissemination of medical technology is clearly more effectively con-trolled in Canada. Again, global budgets would provide incentives for institutions to cooperate with one another in sharing expensive technologies rather than com-peting with one another.

The financing of the health care system is done primarily through taxation at the federal and provincial level in Canada, which means there is a fair share of the cost of the system in accord with ability to pay. Consider, by way of contrast, that there are clear injustices in the way we choose to finance health care in the United States, the most obvious being the very large "tax subsidy" that benefits the middle class at the level of $58 billion in 1992. This represents the tax rev-enues the federal government would have collected from the middle class if the value of the health benefits package provided by their employer were taxed as part of their income. The injustice is that the working poor in low wage jobs are not provided with health insurance as a benefit by their employer, which means that if they wish to purchase health insurance, they will have to do that with unsubsi-dized after-tax dollars.

Our final point concerns health care rationing in Canada. Clearly ra-tioning occurs, mostly through the use of queues for certain expensive services and diagnostic procedures, such as bypass surgery and MRI scans. It seems that this occurs as a matter of "medical judgment" regarding who will likely derive the most benefit from access to specific services. I believe it is fair to describe this as invisible rationing, which is a major moral deficiency in the Canadian health care system. Unlike Oregon, Canada has had no public debate over what sort of rationing protocols or cost containment mechanisms or health priorities within a global budget or trade-offs among competing health goods Canadian patients would choose for themselves. Debates like this are potentially difficult and divisive, exactly the sort of issues that politicians would prefer to avoid. It is not that there is evidence of clear injustice in the health care system in Canada, but then neither do they have an assuredly just approach to health care rationing. The lesson from Oregon is that these sorts of public democratic deci-sions are essential for reasons of both justice and efficiency. This is a lesson Canada has yet to accept.[26]

Managed Competition

Let us now turn to the Clinton Administration proposal for health reform. During March and April of 1993 I served as a member of one of the working groups for Hillary Clinton's Health Reform Task Force. Specifically, I served on Working Group number 17, titled "Ethical Foundations of the New Health Care System." Why was there an "ethical foundations" working group at all? My reading is that this will be one of the distinctive features of health reform under the Clinton Administration. That is, the Clinton Administration has embraced the fundamental premise of the "Just Caring" project[27] and Oregon, namely, that the problem of health reform is fundamentally a moral problem and only secondarily an economic or organizational problem. Costs must certainly be contained, not primarily because there are huge inefficiencies in these escalating costs, but because escalating costs create escalating inequities throughout the system. Businesses at large, and insurance companies in particular, are strongly motivated to exclude from jobs and health insurance those individuals who can be prospectively identified as likely having the greatest health needs. This may be good business (because it protects profit margins), but it is bad ethics. Health reform that failed to address these kinds of gross inequities in our health care system would not be worthy of being called "reform."

The specific charge that was given to our working group was to articulate the "moral vision" that was to guide health reform. There were a total of fourteen "principles" that our working group articulated that seemed to capture the moral considerations most relevant to just health reforms. These principles will compose the preamble to the actual legislation submitted to Congress and will also introduce several other documents that will be made public later. These principles are intended to be one means of engaging the broader public in the debates about the direction of health reform.

Here are some of the main features of the Clinton proposal that have relevance to the objectives of this essay. First, a critical defining feature is that a very comprehensive package of health benefits will be guaranteed to all Americans. The moral objective here is to eliminate the two-tiered health system we currently have. There will be no Medicaid program for the poor, though it is likely the long-term care portion of Medicaid will remain, since only modest long-term care reform is likely to be incorporated in the Clinton reform proposals.

Second, the vast majority of Americans will be receiving their health care through vertically integrated comprehensive managed care plans, now referred to as "Accountable Health Plans" (AHPs). These plans, in turn, will be supervised by an entity known now as a "Consumer Health Alliance," which will be both a purchasing agent for consumers and a strict quality-assurance mechanism. It may also have some health planning responsibilities. For most states one of these alliances will cover the state.

Third, risk rating of individuals by these managed-care plans will not be permitted. That is, consumers may join any health plan in their area, and discrimination on the basis of prior or prospective health risks, or on the basis of socioeconomic status, will not be permitted.

Fourth, the federal government will establish strict and detailed quality-assurance criteria that AHPs must meet, with special attention given to the quality of care provided to special populations whose health needs have been underserved in the past.

Fifth, to control costs there will be global budgets established at the federal level, the state level, and the level of AHPs. This means that AHPs will be required to deliver that very comprehensive health package within the limits of the budget they have, determined mostly by the size of their enrollment. It is at this point that the "Just Caring" project has the most to offer a health reform effort.

Finally, though this is an effort at *national* health reform, the Clinton administration will grant considerable flexibility to the states regarding *how* they achieve the goals of health reform outlined above. But the states will be strictly accountable for protecting equity (comprehensive benefits package must be guaranteed to all), protecting quality, and containing costs. By way of illustration, states can choose, if they wish, not to have AHPs, but to adopt a variant of a Canadian-style single-payer system.

The Princeton health economist Uwe Reinhardt is quoted in *The Wall Street Journal* (April 22, 1993) as saying, "The whole idea of managed competition is to delegate these painful decisions [about resource allocation for very expensive, marginally beneficial life-prolonging medical care] into the dark corners of the HMO. . . This is a smart way of delegating painful decisions from the government to the private sector." Now Reinhardt is correct in saying that this is something that could happen to AHPs operating under global budgets. And if this were to happen, then this would be seriously unjust because, as I have argued earlier in this essay, invisible rationing violates a core element of our shared conception of justice, what John Rawls refers to as the "publicity condition."

The term *rationing* triggers negative reactions in the minds of most Americans. Part of this has to do with a suspicion that rationing cannot be done fairly, that there will always be those who game the system and thereby escape the sacrifices that are expected of everyone else. What will prevent these suspicions from being realized within AHPs? There are three things that are crucial.

First, a lot will depend upon the moral integrity of physicians and their commitment to fair treatment for all their patients. Physicians are the primary allocators of access to health care. No one can obtain any significant health services without the cooperation of physicians. If there are rationing protocols within an AHP that make explicit the sorts of noncostworthy marginally beneficial health services that should be denied to all members of that AHP, then it is the moral responsibility of physicians to implement those protocols honestly and fairly. If they are tempted to game the system in favor of the patient before them now (in the name of compassion), then they need to be reminded that in a closed system with a fixed budget they are effectively denying those resources to other patients *who are their patients also,* who have health needs that make a stronger and more just claim to those resources—and these other patients are as deserving of compassion as the patient before them.

Second, physicians will not be disloyal to the interests of the patient before them or lacking in compassion if the rationing protocols within that AHP are a product of a public moral conversation that has occurred among the members of that AHP. That is, if the members of that AHP have imposed these rationing/cost-containment protocols upon their future selves because they have made the judgment that there are other health needs that have greater priority for the limited resources available to that AHP, then the patient before this physician is among those who have endorsed these limits *for himself.* Further, the likelihood is that the patient has already benefitted from a more rational deployment of limited health resources, which is then another moral consideration that speaks against cooperating with this patient to circumvent the rationing protocols.

We must face the likelihood that rationing protocols will vary from one AHP to another, raising concerns of equity. But there are broad principles of health care justice that must not be violated by any rationing protocol in any AHP. Thus, there would be no moral justification for a rationing protocol that denied ICU care specifically to AIDS patients with less than a 10 percent chance of surviving the current hospital stay; it would, however, be morally permissible for the members of an AHP to agree that anyone with any terminal illness who needed ICU care and who had less than a 10 percent chance of surviving this ICU stay would be denied access to an ICU. Any one of us is likely to come under the scope of this rationing protocol in the future, and none of us can now game the system by agreeing to this protocol, since we are all likely ignorant of our future in this matter, and all of us can agree that there are much better uses for those terminal ICU care dollars—all of which would motivate each of us to agree freely and autonomously to such a protocol.

There is a vast gray area in the choice of rationing/cost-containment protocols. A number of differing protocols may be "just enough" so long as they are freely and democratically chosen by the members of a given AHP. Thus, it is easy to imagine that some AHPs will choose to save money by denying bypass surgery to patients with single-vessel coronary disease and less than 70 percent occlusion. That saves forty thousand dollars per case, and 20 percent of the bypass surgery we now do in the United States falls in this category. This is marginally beneficial care, though some AHPs may provide these anyway and cut costs elsewhere.

There are lots of possible trade-offs. What is morally critical to protect fairness is that we observe scrupulously the lessons we should learn from Oregon in these matters. Specifically, we must avoid piecemeal, uncoordinated rationing.

Trade-offs must be made in ways that are systematic, deliberate, public, account-able, and a product of informed democratic deliberation within the AHP. All who are going to be affected by these rationing protocols must have a fair opportunity to participate in the shaping of those protocols so we can honestly say that they are self-imposed. Individuals should not have the option of avoiding the risks and bur-dens associated with cost containment.

On this last point there may be some concern that individuals could game the system by switching AHPs at critical moments. But there will be little real op-portunity for this since essentially the same comprehensive package of health ben-efits will be guaranteed to all. Though the details of rationing protocols may vary from plan to plan, there will also be enough overlap to assure that injustices are not permitted. Unlike Canada, the U.S. will likely provide some opportunity for individuals to purchase "topping out" insurance, though what will be purchased are either marginally beneficial, noncostworthy services or services in the domain of beneficence. Either way, there is not an obvious violation of considerations of justice, so long as there is not public subsidizing of such purchases and so long as no one within the system is denied a health service to which they have a just claim.

Canada or Clinton?

It is difficult to compare the two leading alternatives to health care reform. Needless to say, careful moral judgment in these matters is dependent on empiri-cal detail. We have ample such detail with respect to the Canadian health care sys-tem, but the Clinton administration proposal is still lacking in important detail at this writing. Further, the Clinton proposal will be subjected to all manner of con-gressional compromise and negotiation, the result of which may be a policy prod-uct that at best is a very marginal improvement over our current health care system. If that were to be the case, then the result might be open to serious moral criticism from the perspective of nonideal justice. As things are now, I will argue that the Clinton proposal has at least 90 percent of the moral advantages of a single-payer system; and, more importantly, it actually has the potential to be morally superior. It also has some substantial *potential* flaws that will be remedied only by taking se-riously the lessons I draw from Oregon. Specifically, there is the risk that rationing would remain an invisible and unaccountable process, as it is now, which is to say that it would violate the "publicity condition," which Rawls has emphasized as a core element of justice in liberal democratic societies.[28]

Notes

1. Michael Walzer introduced the phrase "spheres of justice" to suggest that there are areas of our social/political life that require relatively distinct conceptions of justice. He would endorse the idea that health care is one such distinct sphere, as would I. (See his

Spheres of Justice: A Defense of Pluralism and Equality [New York: Basic Books, 1983], pp. 84–94). But Walzer is reacting against grand theories of justice, such as the one offered by John Rawls in *A Theory of Justice*. I would argue that Rawls's conception of justice is not as antithetical to Walzer's spheres of justice as Walzer seems to believe, especially if we remind ourselves that the subject of Rawls's conception is "the basic structure of society," not each and every socioeconomic transaction that occurs. (On this, see John Rawls, *Political Liberalism* [New York: Columbia University Press, 1993], lecture 7, "The Basic Structure as Subject," pp. 257–88). Further, I would contend that our conception of health care justice does need to be linked to a larger conception of justice, if, for no other reason, health care competes as a social good with other social goods for societal resources. If there were no encompassing framework for adjudicating such conflicts morally, then we would risk substantial injustices in the allocation of social goods. (Some, such as Daniel Callahan, would argue that an imperious health care sector has already done just this. See his *What Kind of Life: The Limits of Medical Progress* [New York: Simon and Schuster, 1990], pp. 17–30.) Still, my larger point will be that an encompassing conception of justice can do only very limited moral work for us in addressing the very specific problems of justice peculiar to health care. I elaborate on this claim in my earlier essay "Just Health Care (II): Is Equality Too Much?" *Theoretical Medicine,* vol. 10 (Oct. 1989), pp. 301–10

2. See D. Himmelstein et al., "The Vanishing Health Care Safety Net: New Data on Uninsured Americans," *International Journal of Health Services,* vol. 22 (1992), pp. 381, 387; S. Marquis and S. Long, "Uninsured Children and National Health Reform," *Journal of the American Medical Association,* vol. 268 (1992), p. 3473; L. Gostin, "Foreword: Health Care Reform in the United States—The Presidential Task Force," *American Journal of Law and Medicine,* vol. 19 (1993), pp. 2–3; S. Woolhandler and D. Himmelstein, "Reverse Targeting of Preventive Care Due to Lack of Health Insurance," *Journal of the American Medical Association,* vol. 259 (1988), p. 2872; H. R. Burstin et al., "Socioeconomic Status and Risk for Substandard Medical Care," *Journal of the American Medical Association,* vol. 268 (1992), pp. 2383, 2387; T. Brennan, "An Ethical Perspective on Health Care Insurance Reform," *American Journal of Law and Medicine,* vol. 19 (1993), pp. 38–43; L. Gostin and A. Widiss, "What's Wrong with the ERISA Vacuum? Employers' Freedom to Limit Health Care Coverage Provided by Risk Retention Plans," *Journal of the American Medical Association,* vol. 269 (1993), pp. 2527–32; Council on Ethical and Judicial Affairs, American Medical Association, "Caring for the Poor," *Journal of the American Medical Association,* vol. 269 (1993), pp. 2533–37.

3. See J. Merrill and A. B. Cohen, "The Emperor's New Clothes: Unraveling the Myths about Rationing," *Inquiry,* vol. 24 (Summer 1987), pp. 105–9.

4. L. D. Brown, "The National Politics of Oregon's Rationing Plan," *Health Affairs,* vol. 10 (Summer 1991), p. 30.

5. Brown, "National Politics," 49–50.

6. Brown, "National Politics," 50.

7. M. Garland, "Health Care in Common: Setting Priorities in Oregon," *Hastings Center Report,* vol. 20 (Sept.–Oct. 1990), pp. 16–18; M. Garland, "Justice, Politics, and

Community: Expanding Access and Rationing Health Services in Oregon," *Law, Medicine, and Health Care*, vol. 20 (Spring–Summer 1992), pp. 67–81; D. Eddy, "Rationing by Patient Choice," *Journal of the American Medical Association*, vol. 265 (1991), pp. 105–8; D. Eddy, "Oregon's Methods: Did Cost-Effectiveness Analysis Fail?" *Journal of the American Medical Association*, vol. 266 (1991), pp. 2135–41.

8. Oregon Health Services Commission, *Prioritization of Health Services: A Report to the Governor and Legislature*, 1991.

9. J. Kitzhaber, "Rationing Health Care: The Oregon Model," *Center Report* (The Center for Public Policy and Contemporary Issues, University of Denver, vol. 2 (Winter 1990), pp. 3–4.

10. For some of the details of the Coby Howard case and the history that surrounded it see D. Fox and H. Leichter, "Rationing Care in Oregon: The New Accountability," *Health Affairs*, vol. 10, no. 2 (Summer 1991), pp. 14–17.

11. N. Daniels, "Is the Oregon Rationing Plan Fair?" *Journal of the American Medical Association*, vol. 265 (1991), p. 2232.

12. See J. Hadley et al., "Comparison of Uninsured and Privately Insured Hospital Patients: Condition on Admission, Resource Use, and Outcome," *Journal of the American Medical Association*, vol. 265 (1991), pp. 274–78; N. Lurie et al., "Termination from Medi-Cal—Does it Affect Health?" *New England Journal of Medicine*, vol. 311 (1984), pp. 480–84.

13. For examples of how such invisible rationing is effected in Great Britain in the dialysis program see H. Aaron and W. Schwartz, *The Painful Prescription: Rationing Health Care* (Washington, D.C.: Brookings Institution, 1984), p. 35.

14. Kitzhaber, "Rationing Health Care," p. 4.

15. See N. Daniels, *Just Health Care* (Cambridge: Cambridge University Press, 1985); D. Callahan, *Setting Limits: Medical Goals in an Aging Society* (New York: Simon and Schuster, 1987); D. Callahan, *What Kind of Life: The Limits of Medical Progress* (New York: Simon and Schuster, 1990); R. Veatch, *The Foundations of Justice: Why the Retarded and the Rest of Us Have Claims to Equality* (Oxford: Oxford University Press, 1986); T. Brennan, *Just Doctoring: Medical Ethics in the Liberal State* (Berkeley and Los Angeles: University of California Press, 1991); E. Emanuel, *The Ends of Human Life: Medical Ethics in a Liberal Polity* (Cambridge: Harvard University Press, 1991); Leonard M. Fleck, "Pricing Human Life: The Moral Costs of Medical Progress," *Centennial Review*, vol. 34 (Spring 1990), pp. 227–54.

16. Callahan, *What Kind of Life*, esp. chap. 2, "On the Ragged Edge: Needs, Endless Needs."

17. The exact wording of this principle is: "Allocations for health care must be part of a broader allocation policy which recognizes that health care only be maintained if investments in a number of related areas are balanced" (Kitzhaber, "Rationing Health Care," p. 4).

18. This is the central point for which I argue in my essay "Just Health Care Rationing: A Democratic Decisionmaking Approach," *University of Pennsylvania Law Review,* vol. 140 (May 1992), pp. 1597–1636. This is a symposium issue on the topic "The Law and Policy of Health Care Rationing: Models and Accountability." See also Garland, "Justice, Politics, and Community."

19. Daniels, "Is the Oregon Rationing Plan Fair?" p. 2232.

20. See L. M. Fleck, "The Oregon Medicaid Experiment: Is It Just Enough?" *Business and Professional Ethics Journal,* vol. 9 (Fall 1990), pp. 201–17.

21. H. Aaron, "The Oregon Experiment," in *Rationing America's Medical Care: The Oregon Plan and Beyond,* ed. Martin Strosberg et al. (Washington, D.C.: Brookings Institution, 1992), pp. 107–11.

22. Raisa Deber notes that "there are few incentives for system-wide efficiency in the Canadian model." By restricting themselves to macrocontrol mechanisms, such as global budgets, the provincial governments protect a very broad measure of clinical autonomy for physicians. But there are costs in terms of fairness and efficiency; and I would argue that clinical autonomy that is not systematically informed by considerations of fairness and efficiency loses much of its moral and professional lustre. See R. Deber, "Canadian Medicare: Can It Work in the United States? Will It Survive in Canada?" *American Journal of Law and Medicine,* vol. 19 (1993), p. 85.

23. For one summary of many of the objections of representatives of disability groups, see A. Capron, "Oregon's Disability: Principles or Politics," *Hastings Center Report,* vol. 22 (Nov.–Dec. 1992), pp. 18–20. See also the companion article by P. Menzel, "Oregon's Denial: Disabilities and Quality of Life," *Hastings Center Report,* vol. 22 (Nov.–Dec. 1992), pp. 21–25.

24. D. Hadorn, "The Oregon Priority-Setting Exercise: Quality of Life and Public Policy," *Hastings Center Report,* vol. 21 (May–June 1991), special suppl., pp. S11–16.

25. This is clearly the position that is being taken by Lawrence Brown (see note 4, above). See also Kevin Grumbach et al. "Liberal Benefits, Conservative Spending: The Physicians for a National Health Program Proposal," *Journal of the American Medical Association,* vol. 265 (1991), pp. 2549–54.

26. Over the past ten years there has been enormous discussion of the Canadian health care system. A very readable recent volume is *Looking North for Health: What We Can Learn from Canada's Health Care System,* ed. Arnold Bennett and Orvill Adams (San Francisco: Jossey-Bass, 1992). Among Canadian health economists the most important person to read is Robert G. Evans for purposes of cross-border comparisons. See his "Controlling Health Expenditures: The Canadian Reality," *New England Journal of Medicine,* vol. 320 (1989), pp. 571–74; see also R. G. Evans et al., "The 20-Year Experiment: Accounting For, Explaining and Evaluating Health Care Cost Containment in Canada and the United States," *Annual Review of Public Health,* vol. 12 (1991), pp. 481–514; also "Illusions of Necessity: Evading Responsibility for Choice in Health Care," *Journal of Health Politics, Policy, and Law,* vol. 10 (1985), pp. 439–55.

27. For a detailed description of the "Just Caring" project, as well as its intellectual rationale, see L. M. Fleck, "Just Caring: An Experiment in Health Policy Formation," in *Improving Access to Health Care: What Can the States Do?* ed. J. Goodeeris and A. Hogan (Kalamazoo: Upjohn Institute, 1992), pp. 233–62.

28. Rawls, *Political Liberalism,* pp. 66–71; more generally, lecture 6, "The Idea of Public Reason,"pp. 212–54.

13

Future of Long-Term Care

Robert L. Kane

In the United States the elderly have done disproportionately well with regard to social programs. Beginning from a greatly disadvantaged situation in the early 1960s, when they were literally priced out of the health insurance market, they have been able to buy their way back through a program of universally covered services under Medicare. This program is financed by a combination of payroll taxes and general revenues. Its most recent extension to cover the costs of so-called catastrophic care has both reconfirmed the program's commitment to covering essentially acute services and introduced for the first time a financing scheme that requires the potential beneficiary population to cover the costs of additional services by a combination of premiums and a tax specifically on themselves.

The elderly by the 1980s were in an ironic bind. Compared to the situation two decades earlier, they were much better off. Their health-insurance coverage was better than that for many others in the population.[1] Their economic situation had improved from their being among the most disadvantaged to the point where their poverty rate now approximated the national average. The pattern of social spending during the intervening two decades had certainly favored the elderly, but, from another perspective, they still faced many of the same problems despite these advances. Their out-of-pocket expenditures for health care as a proportion of their income was at least as much as it had been when Medicare began. Any assistance with the terrible burdens of long-term care came at the cost of penury as part of a degrading welfare system.

Medicare was modeled after the predominant health insurance programs of its era and carries all their stigmata. It has become a vehicle to encourage the growth of technologically sophisticated acute medicine. Ironically, when a special commission was appointed as a prelude to the passage of the catastrophic coverage bill to identify the catastrophic health costs still faced by the elderly, they were not prepared for what they uncovered. Over and over again, they heard testimony that the major catastrophe for older persons is long-term care. The financial costs of this tragedy are high, not so much the unit costs as the aggregate costs, because once begun it is usually a lifelong burden. Moreover, the personal costs are doubly high. Not only do the diseases that precipitate long-term care rob the victims of physical vigor, they often sap the very intellectual fiber that distinguishes humans from other creatures. Dementing illnesses are thus especially cruel. Long-term care also means continuous need for personal services, most of which continue to be provided by family, often at a high financial and personal cost.

Callahan's Proposal

In his anxiety to slow the rising costs of medical care, largely attributable to increasing use of expensive technology, Daniel Callahan has developed a simplistic approach to rationing based on age.[2] He has constructed an elaborate rationale for this approach, which relies on a sense that the elderly, having had a chance at life's opportunities, have an obligation to step aside. It seems to matter little whether they have benefited from these opportunities or have been the object of misfortune; they have had their shot.

The strength in his approach is at once its weakness. Age is a simple criterion to apply because it is simple in its concept. The basic tenets of gerontology speak to the increasing variation in a variety of performance measures with increasing age. Thus age is intended by Callahan to demark not some state of irreversible decline but rather a getting-off point, where aged persons have had enough of what society can offer.

However, Callahan is not ready to pull the plug on the elderly. He would deny them technologically sophisticated, and hence expensive, care but would allow them a generous portion of supportive services. Herein lies one of several paradoxes in his arguments. He would not restrict long-term care but would ration acute services to the elderly. 'Long-term care' is an admittedly amorphous concept lacking a precise, universal definition. A useful one, which paraphrases the tack taken by the federal government in defining eligibility for benefits, is the following: Long-term care is a set of health, personal care, and social services delivered over a sustained period of time to persons who have lost or never acquired some degree of functional capacity.

At the heart of the concept of long-term care is the idea of providing a range of services that will assist the dependent person to maintain his or her function as long as possible. Functioning is, in essence, the lingua franca of long-term care. It is the basis for determining eligibility for service and for assessing its effectiveness.

A closer examination of functioning reveals that it is made up of three components, each of which is necessary, and no one of which by itself is sufficient. A central aspect to functioning is the provision of adequate care. The first goal to improve function of an old or young person is to identify and remedy the remediable. Providing care, however compassionate, for a problem that can be eliminated by proper treatment is neither laudable nor efficient.

Having treated the treatable, one must then attend to the social and psychological (as well as the physical) environment of the client. Creating an environment in which autonomy is encouraged, even at the cost of some risk taking, is essential. The final component of function is motivation. Here again accurate information and a repudiation of age-based stereotypes are critical to improving the result. Transmitted pessimism can be a self-fulfilling prophesy.

The close link between treatment and function and the centrality of function to the core of long-term care expose one of the paradoxical aspects of Callahan's approach. If he encourages better long-term care, then he must champion improved function. But that requires better care, including access to the treatment modalities that are effective for this population. Surely there are instances where an ounce of treatment is worth a pound of maintenance.

Callahan himself acknowledges the importance of function and its superiority as a tool for rationing. However, such a use opens the opportunity for professional judgment and hence corruption. Age is a much simpler device, which can be wielded by inexpert directors. It is simply not very appropriate. Neatness cannot be allowed to supplant accuracy as a criterion for policy.

The other force motivating Callahan's push for age-based rationing is the pressure of demographics. The forecasts of larger numbers of older persons sends shivers through the spines of any who are planning health care in the future. Increasing age is associated with greater use of health care services, and age-specific extrapolations imposed on demographic forecasts conjure up a picture of medical bankruptcy.

However, these straight-line extrapolations ignore several lessons. First, there is no basis for assuming that the current patterns of disability will prevail. Moreover, if one were really interested in reducing those patterns, the best strategy would be to ration care not for the elderly but for the middle aged, whose survival will produce this larger group of disabled. We are not about to propose this course for obvious reasons of self-interest. Nonetheless, there is good reason to believe that the growing numbers of older persons may not consist entirely of disabled persons. The proportion of the very well elderly seems to be increasing at least as quickly as that of the disabled elderly.

Moreover, there is reason to believe that the attitudes of future generations will be shaped by the demographics. Just as our retirement policies became more generous when there was a demographic press to open new jobs to the large cohorts of the baby boom entering the work force, so too can policies to retain workers respond to a shrinking of the labor force. Similarly, our attitudes towards death and disability are very likely to change with circumstances.

There is an inherent danger in accepting today's view of the world as permanent, even to the point of applying current rates of a phenomenon to future scenarios. Think for a minute of how things have changed since Bismarck introduced age sixty-five as the age of eligibility for social insurance in Germany in 1872. At that time the average age at death was about fifty-three. Much has changed since then; little of it was expected. The forecasts then were quite inaccurate, and there is every chance that today's will be just as bad.

None of this means that we should avoid planning or assume a Pollyannaish attitude about the proportion of our national resources going into health care. There is already a growing pressure for better ways to assess the effectiveness of care. Care of the elderly should not be spared such scrutiny, but their age cannot serve as a simple lever to exclude them from eligibility for efficacious services.

Thus, we find ourselves with a strange bedfellow. Callahan is at least indirectly a supporter of greater investments in long-term care. However, his motivations seem misplaced. He would deprive even the functional elderly of their opportunity for benefit from medical technology but willingly expend enormous efforts on palliative care, even on those with no evidence of benefit. We may, of course, agree with his call for greater investment in long-term care while rejecting the limits he would place on acute care.

Issues for the Future

Funding is one of four important issues that will greatly affect the future of long-term care: the others are organization, quality, and personnel. Most of the current attention has gone into discussions of how to pay for such care, with active interest in the relative roles of the public and private sectors. At the same time, there is a modest movement toward redefining the role and components of such care. The third issue is the growing concern about developing meaningful ways to measure the quality of long-term care. In a sense, the three are interdependent: issues of quality should drive discussions of organization, and the form of care should affect its quality. One way of defining a role for both public and private support may lie in setting forth different areas of responsibility for coverage. The fourth issue deals with caregiving, both formal and informal. Essentially, it is a women's issue.

Long-Term Care Insurance. I strongly endorse the concept of universal coverage for long-term care (LTC). I believe that, after all the rhetoric has subsided, the most efficient way to provide such care will be through a publicly financed LTC universal-insurance approach. In other settings, my wife and I have used the Canadian program as a model for this country.[3] Although it may not be possible to import the Canadian system wholesale into the United States, it does provide an important lesson about the economic feasibility of providing care to all under a single program. (See the chapter by Fleck elsewhere in this volume for a description of the Canadian system.)

There is, however, a strong belief in the U.S. about the inherent value of the private sector and the power of the marketplace. Unlike Canadians, Americans are reluctant to see older persons leaving a legacy if public dollars are supporting their care. We have bought the concept of two separate sets of books: one public and one private. We have ignored total costs to focus on public costs.

The pressure to sell private LTC insurance seems inevitably to lead to one of two actions. Either one makes the coverage under Medicaid very bad in order to create a sufficient difference with privately paid care to form an incentive, or private insurance is sold as asset protection rather than as LTC coverage. In essence, it allows one to leave an inheritance. (Some suggest that children should buy it for their parents to protect their legacy.) It helps prevent the stigma of welfare, but this stigma seems to be subsiding, at least among the middle class.

It is unlikely that Americans will give up this fixation with private funding. Therefore, the American solution will likely be a compromise, containing both a public and private role. It does not seem likely that insurance per se will do the trick.

Because covering everything for everyone is too expensive, politicians have been looking for some way to make publicly supported LTC more affordable. Clearly one answer is to expect the patient to pay part of the bill. Two basic approaches to covering long-term care on a universal basis have been put forward: front-end coverage and back-end coverage. The former would provide payment for all or part of LTC for a fixed period of time (say six months) for all who needed it. After that point, individuals or their families would be responsible for paying for the care. (Provisions for the very poor, those offered under the current Medicaid programs, would still pertain). This approach, which was adopted by the Pepper commission,[4] has the political appeal of offering something to everyone who needs LTC. The disadvantage lies in its failure to provide substantial support for those who incur large LTC bills, primarily those who have long stays in nursing homes. Back-end coverage would better serve these people. It would provide coverage after a certain period had elapsed (perhaps a year). Again, the individual or his/her family would be expected to cover the costs for the initial period. The many persons who use nursing homes for shorter periods would receive no benefits, but those with the greatest costs would be better served.

Both approaches, but especially the latter, offer a clear role for private insurance. Back-end coverage leaves only a limited risk from covering a fixed period of exposure. Unless some form of universal coverage is put in place, the proportion of the population buying LTC insurance will likely remain small. Few see LTC as a real risk until close to the time they need it. By then the cost of coverage approaches the cost of care.

Restructuring. The answer to the LTC crisis for both organization and financing may come from a move to uncouple the two components of the nursing home; this has been the touchstone of LTC for some time.[5] This institution combines, as its name implies, care and shelter. The marriage has not been a happy one. With a pedigree that is a cross between a hospital and an almshouse, it has been accused of providing neither good care nor a decent living environment. Lately, new approaches have been springing up that use various forms of what has been termed "assisted living." Essentially, these are usually some form of residential care with varying degrees of formal care brought in as needed. The key element

in these arrangements is that the client is central. Their privacy and dignity are preserved as much as possible by enhancing their autonomy and control.

This model of uncoupling residence and care may hold an important answer for the future of LTC. It may also provide an answer to how to fund needed
care through a positive blend of public and private support. If the components
were separated, it may be feasible to talk about providing a floor of services that
would be available to everyone, regardless of income or assets. These services
would be available to anyone who needed them, such need being determined by
an assessment of the individual's capacity for performing those tasks essential to
functioning independently. The service package can be debated, but it would include those services needed to maintain a functional life, including such things as
nursing and homemaking (presumably superimposed on a substrate of primary
medical care already covered for the elderly). The housing component would
remain a privately paid issue. Thus, those in a nursing home would be expected
to pay for their room and board costs. But those wishing, and able to afford,
more commodious living conditions could buy (or rent) them and have services
brought to them as needed. In some cases, limitations on the provision of such
services would be needed. Those needing heavy care may have to move into con-
gregate housing for economies of scale. Those living far away may not be as well
served. Those with no money would need additional government support to
cover housing and food costs.

Such an approach would get away from the current notions of a nursing
home and allow people to purchase a lifestyle that gave them as much dignity
and independence as they wanted and could afford. It would also eliminate the
conflict in managerial philosophy often described as the medical versus social
models. People should be able to get the best of both. Rather than being viewed
as a patient complying with the rules of an institution, the client would be seen
primarily as a person living in a situation where care is offered. Clients have the
right to determine what care is actually provided, even who is permitted to enter
their rooms.

As a final inducement, the ability to buy better housing might prove a more
attractive inducement to purchase LTC insurance or to save than would the simple fear of becoming a welfare pauper.

Caregivers. The impending crisis lies in caregiving. The entry of women into
the labor market means that there will be fewer informal, unpaid supporters available to care for older persons. Women's greatly increased job opportunities will
make it harder to attract them to the menial jobs that form the backbone of LTC,
just as it is now hard to entice them into nursing. Market forces will likely force
some changes in pay scales for these jobs and will increase the use of technology to
substitute for people wherever possible.

The great revolution in LTC will likely come from improvements in information technology. Better monitoring and information organization will allow

more efficient use of personnel and encourage better decisions, but there will continue to be a heavy need for people. LTC is essentially a personal service.

Although many predict the demise of the American family and the loss of informal support, there is no evidence to support this contention. Family care remains the backbone of LTC and is likely to continue as such for some time. A greater challenge comes from how to find the caregivers to replace the informal caring when family are not available.

Quality. Quality of care remains a critical, if elusive, goal for long-term care. As we consider steps for resource allocation, we might first address the question of whether we are spending our current funds most wisely. There is at once a growing demand for more creativity and more accountability. It may be possible to reduce the regulatory burden, increase the meaningful accountability, and make the incentives within the system more rational.

Before we can talk about how to package it or how to buy it cheaper, we need a better understanding of what we are really buying. Quality of care is traditionally addressed in terms of three aspects: structure, process, and outcomes. *Structure* refers to the setting in which care is provided. It includes both the people providing the care and the physical environment. The qualifications of the health care professionals, the numbers and types of staff members per client, the existence of committees, and the way records are kept would all be elements of structure. Likewise, the physical structure of the facility, especially its invulnerability to fire, the width of its corridors, the presence of a sprinkler system, and the square footage per patient would be considered part of the structural concerns.

The *process* of care addresses the extent to which care is provided according to predetermined rules. One can create criteria for how to make a bed, what medications to administer for a given diagnosis, how to talk to a patient, or any other aspect of care. The key to useful process criteria is the strength of the association between doing things a particular way and achieving the results desired. In LTC there is little hard evidence to support such associations. The danger is that insistence on process will simply reinforce dogma and thwart creativity and innovation.

LTC is an area where it seems to make more sense to look directly at the outcomes of care, recognizing that there may be many different routes to the goals, several of which may not even have been discovered yet. Given the relatively low technical sophistication of LTC and the heavy reliance on motivation and compassion, it seems sensible to focus on whether the job achieves the ends expected and leaves as much room as possible for alternative ways to achieve the desired ends.

There are several reasons for looking to *outcomes* as the way to assess and assure quality.

1. Outcomes encourage creativity by avoiding domination by current professional orthodoxies or powerful constituencies. The process of creating regu-

lations is frequently influenced by a particular professional group that, with a high stake in the area, dominates the procedure to insist that only sanctioned individuals be allowed to perform the task, often in the absence of any persuasive evidence that such restrictions are associated with better results.

2. Outcomes permit flexibility in the modality of care. Because they do not dictate how care is provided, they allow for a choice among alternative modes of delivering care.

3. Outcomes permit comparisons of effectiveness across modalities of care. Likewise, the absence of a dictated route of care permits comparisons of the results from different approaches, but appropriate adjustments must be made to allow for possible differences in the characteristics of the clients that use the different care modalities.

4. Outcomes permit more flexible responses to different levels of performance and thus avoid the "all-or-none" difficulties of many sanctions. Rather than simply judging that care has passed a threshold of satisfactory performance, we can express outcomes in terms of the proportion of expected results actually achieved. The rewards and penalties can be thus proportionately titrated.

At the same time outcomes have some limitations.

1. Outcomes require a single point of accountability; all the actors—facility operators, agencies, staff, physicians, patients, and family—contribute to them. Under this approach the role of the provider includes motivating others.

2. Outcomes are largely influenced by the patient's status at the beginning of treatment; therefore, they must be used in a context of case-mix adjustment. The easiest and most direct way to address this issue is to use the ratio of achieved outcomes to expected outcomes as the measure of success. Henceforth in this discussion "outcomes" is used to mean that ratio of achieved to expected.

Outcomes should be used as the basis for quality assurance in long-term care. The outcome approach can be used in several ways.

1. There is already growing national interest in increasing the emphasis on outcomes in regulatory activities. Outcome measures can be substituted for most of the current structure and process measures. It is appropriate to continue regulation in areas such as life safety (e.g., concerns about sprinkler systems and wide corridors). Concomitant with an outcomes emphasis would be the reduction of regulatory burden. It is important to recognize, however, that it is *not* appropriate to dictate structure, process, and outcome at the same time. Such a policy removes all degrees of freedom and stifles creativity at the very point at which we want to encourage it. Under an outcome-regulated ap-

proach, providers whose clients do better than expected are rewarded, with less concern and less worry about the style of their caregiving, whereas those whose clients do relatively poorly are investigated more closely.

2. Outcomes can be incorporated into the payment structure to tie closer together the payment and the effects of care. Payments, either in the form of bonuses and penalties, or as a more fundamental part of the payment structure, can be used to reward and penalize good and bad outcomes, respectively. (For example, an outcome approach might use a factor reflecting the overall achieved/expected ratio for a client as a multiplier against the costs of care to develop a total price paid for that period of time; or one might use a similar ratio to weight the amount of money going to a given provider from a fixed pool of dollars committed to such care.) Such an approach must be viewed carefully within the context of our present case-mix reimbursement scheme for nursing homes, because the latter indirectly rewards deterioration in function. An outcome approach to payment is compatible with a case-mix approach that is used on admission only.

3. An outcome approach can be incorporated into the basic caring process. Ironically, despite its name, long-term care is mostly approached a day at a time. Little thought is given to how the patient fares over time. By structuring the information base used in assessing clients and developing care plans, the emphasis on outcomes can become a proactive force to guide care. The data from an assessment can be used to predict how a patient will do. Data from a series of observations of like patients can be used to create statistical models that can establish a level of expected outcomes. In the best situation, the information used to assess outcomes will come from the clinical records and will be the same information used to drive care. Using available computer technology it is feasible today to collect such data, translate them into care plans, and aggregate them for quality assurance at minimal additional cost. The computer allows such information to be displayed in graphic form. It is feasible to show both the client's progress over time and what that course might have looked like if he or she had received good care. The difference represents the extent to which the care actually rendered achieved better or worse results than might have been expected and provides direct feedback to the care providers to show just what difference their caring meant. The great advantage of such a scheme is its potential both to provide a better information base to plan care and to reinforce the creative use of such information to achieve improvements in function. Much of the current efforts going into more traditional regulatory activities might be redirected to this effort, with assessors used to validate the assessment and to focus more intense efforts on the miscreants.

   We have generally good consensus on the components of outcomes and less good consensus about how to combine these elements into a single score to indicate the level of success at a point in time. While it is desirable to use a variety of components to describe how well a client is doing, it is necessary to find a way to summarize the overall result. The gerontologic literature is quite consistent in citing the following as outcomes: physiologic function (e.g., blood pressure control, lack of decubiti), functional status (usually some measure of activity of daily living), pain and discomfort, cognition (intellectual activity), affect (emotional activity), social participation (based on preferences, not just busyness), social relations (at least a single person who can act as a confidant), and satisfaction (with care and living environment). To these must be added more global outcomes such as death and admission to hospital.

The usual practice is simply to add together the individual scores to create a composite total. But such an approach implies that each component is equally valuable, when that may not be the case at all.

There is already work available with nursing-home patients to show that these factors can be predicted with sufficient accuracy to be used in a regulatory model.[6] There is similar work to show that there is reasonable consensus across a wide variety of constituencies about the relative weights to be placed on them for different kinds of clients (e.g., different levels of physical and cognitive function at baseline).[7]

The outcomes approach offers significant assistance with a recurrent problem in regulation; namely, the development of standards. Standards reflect the expected rate at which the individual criteria for good care are met. Most commonly, such standards are set by a group of experts determining what seems reasonable. This approach is referred to as "generating nominal standards of care." Using outcomes may avoid many of the difficulties associated with relying on nominal standards. Rather than arguing about what is a reasonable expectation, the actual level of performance across providers of care can be used as the norm, and expectations derived from the actual outcomes can be associated with real care given by those felt to represent a reasonable level of practice. Under this arrangement, providers would be comparing their achievements to each other's past records, allowing for the possibility that everyone can do better.

Technology for Quality Assurance

Ideally, one would like to see a measurement approach that

- can cover the spectrum of performance,
- is easy and rapid to administer,
- is sensitive to meaningful change in performance,
- is stable within the same client over time,
- performs consistently in different hands, and
- cannot be manipulated to meet the needs of either the provider or the client.

The solution to this challenge is to create an assessment approach designed to maximize these elements. To cover a broad spectrum and still be relatively quickly administered, an instrument should be designed in a branching format. The user first focuses on the area along the continuum where the client is most likely to function and then expands that part of the scale to measure meaningful levels of performance. Branching can also ensure that the assessment is comprehensive but not burdensome. By using key questions to screen an area, the interviewer can ascertain whether there is a point on obtaining more detailed information in each relevant domain. Where the initial response is negative, the interviewer can go on the next branch point.

Reliability is more likely to be achieved when the items are expressed in a standardized fashion tied closely to explicit behaviors. Whenever possible, performance is preferred over reports of behavior. One cannot expect to totally avoid the gaming of an assessment. If the client knows that poor performance is needed to ensure eligibility, he may be motivated to achieve the requisite low level. One can use some test of ripeness bias, such as measures of social desirability, but they will not prevent gaming the system or detect all cheating.

Redundancy of effort in collecting information can be dramatically reduced by using computerized technology. Properly mobilized, computers can provide the structure needed to assure a comprehensive assessment with no duplication of effort. Because they are interactive, they can carry out much of the desired branching and can even use simple algorithms to clarify areas of ambiguity and retest areas where some unreliability is suspected. Similar algorithms can look for inconsistency as at least a screen for cheating.

Data stored on computers can be aggregated to look at performance across clients by provider (e.g., physician, nursing home, or agency). Data on a client can be traced across time to look at changes in function, and this, in turn, can be aggregated.

The next important step in the progression is to move away from a focus on a single point of care to link the related elements of care. In an ideal system, the information on a client would be linked to permit changes in status to be traced for that individual as he or she moves from treatment to treatment. Thus, hospital admission and discharge information, long-term care information, and primary care information would be merged into a common record. This means not a record in the sense we think of for a clinical record but a computer-linked record, which allows one to trace the client's movements and status. Finally, it would be very desirable to have data on the process of care as well as on the outcomes. This combination would allow better analyses of just what elements of care made a difference for which kinds of clients.

Such an approach to assuring quality is not a figment of imagination. It is within our grasp if we are prepared to invest in data systems and to commit ourselves to collecting standardized information. It requires a shift in some of our fundamental paradigms from thinking about whether we did the right thing to deciding if it made any difference after all.

It is essential to remember that an outcome-based philosophy requires two basic changes in thinking, both of which are difficult for clinicians:

1. Thinking in the aggregate, using averages instead of examining each case; outcomes don't work well for individual cases because there is always a chance that something will go wrong, and life does not provide a control group.
2. Attributing responsibility to the whole enterprise rather than pointing the finger of blame at some individual; a pattern of poor outcomes will mandate a closer inspection of the process of care, but outcomes per se are a collective responsibility.

Conclusion

Devoting attention to improving long-term care offers us an opportunity to rethink just what we seek to accomplish is maintaining and improving the quality of life for dependent persons. Especially as we face the mounting costs of care, with few indications that the expenditures have produced a commensurate reduction in pain, suffering, and death, we are motivated to reexamine our priorities. It is reasonable to question all the efforts at providing technologically sophisticated care to persons with poor prognoses. It is equally reasonable to challenge the intense efforts that go into making decisions about sustaining life at the point when life has little meaning, while avoiding careful examination of the daily assaults on the personhood of those consigned to long-term care. It is high time we thought not only about what we can afford but also about whether we are getting our money's worth from what we are already paying.

Notes

1. R. A. Hayward, et al., "Inequities in Health Services among Insured Americans: Do Working-age Adults Have Less Access to Medical Care Than the Elderly?" *New England Journal of Medicine,* vol. 318 (1988), pp. 1507–12.

2. D. Callahan, *Setting Limits* (New York: Simon and Schuster, 1987).

3. R. L. Kane and R. A. Kane, *A Will and a Way: What Americans Can Learn about Long-Term Care from Canada* (New York: Columbia University Press, 1985).

4. The Pepper Commission. *A Call for Action: The Pepper Commission U.S. Bipartisan Commission on Comprehensive Health Care* (Washington, D.C.: Government Printing Office, 1990).

5. R. L. Kane and R. A. Kane, "A Nursing Home in Your Future?" *New England Journal of Medicine,* vol. 324 (1991), pp. 627–29.

6. R. L. Kane et al., "Predicting the Outcomes of Nursing-Home Patients," *Gerontologist,* vol. 23 (1983), pp. 200–206.

7. R. L. Kane, R. M. Bell, and S. Z. Riegler, "Value Preferences for Nursing-Home Outcomes," *Gerontologist,* vol. 26 (1986), pp. 303–8.

14

Taking the Next Steps:
Devising a Good Lifespan for the Elderly

Daniel Callahan

It is both an honor and an intimidating burden to have so many interesting, probing papers written in response to my book. The honor is obvious: authors write books in order that their views will be read and taken seriously. That has wonderfully happened in my case. Yet there has also been something particularly intimidating about the responses. Their very richness and depth make it just about impossible to respond to them individually. At the same time, some of them seem to have misunderstood my argument or to have read it in a way that changes its meaning and impact. I could spend a tiresome amount of space simply saying, to this or that respondent, no, that's not what I said, or no, that's not what I meant when I said what I said. Authors of course are notorious for responding that way when criticized (we seem less prone to blame our supporters when they get us wrong). I will not do that in any specific way in this case.

I will get only one broad point off my chest, however, as a general response to what seems a common misunderstanding. I tried, in *Setting Limits,* to develop a nuanced and qualified case for two main contentions. First, we need to work together as a society to develop a fresh understanding of old age in the company of medical progress; the contemporary effort to "modernize mortality" is fatally flawed, particularly because of its harmful effects on the meaning of old age. Second, in trying to think through the health policy problems and implications of a growing proportion of elderly, we will need both to establish a stronger priority for caring over curing and consider the possibility that we will eventually need to establish an age limit on some forms of expensive, life-extending technological cure.

I meant for these two contentions to work in tandem, suggesting that even if we were not faced with economic pressures, we should in any case consider limits because of their possible intrinsic value for the elderly and because they encourage us to pursue a sensible outlook on the process of aging. Moreover, I significantly qualified my discussion of an eventual age limit by specifying the need—before that happens and as a *necessary* condition for its acceptability—to in fact come to a richer understanding of old age and to have in place a better, more balanced health care system for the elderly than now exists, one much stronger in its provision of long-term and home care and of other benefits that improve the daily quality of life of the elderly. For whatever reason, many of my critics have neglected to notice that important stipulation and qualification (or they seem to minimize its importance in my thinking), just as they have passed over in silence my further stipulation that I was thinking about policy twenty to thirty years in the future, not now. I am intent upon persuading a younger generation to begin thinking differently about health care and to be prepared to impose *upon themselves* when they become old limits that are not at present needed or feasible for the present group of the elderly. To ignore all those qualifications is to criticize a book I did not write and to assault a viewpoint I do not hold.

With that much said, let me move on to three issues raised by my book that I think will remain central in the years ahead, as the health care problems of an increasingly large number and proportion of elderly become ever more pronounced: (1) the use of categorical standards, particularly chronological age, to set limits on health care; (2) the meaning of old age and its place in allocation decisions; and (3) the development of health care policy in a pluralistic society. I begin with the question of the use of age as a categorical standard because it was clearly the issue that attracted the most attention and was found either the most wanting (the more kindly critics) or the most obnoxious. It is not hard to understand why. In suggesting the use of age as a standard, I was challenging the most central belief (may I call it a dogma?) of the contemporary effort to improve the status and image of the elderly: that the elderly are a heterogeneous group, proof against stereotyping, and that only their individual traits and needs should count for moral, social, or policy purposes. I am indeed challenging that belief.

Setting Limits: Individual or Categorical Standards?

I will not repeat here all of the demographic and economic reasons why a limit of some kind on health care for the elderly, some form of rationing, will be increasingly necessary over the coming decades. Fewer and fewer seem to challenge that proposition. Yet there can never be any happy way to limit health care resources. Whatever we give to one person is something potentially taken from another, at least if we are to work with relatively fixed budgets. We cannot meet all individual medical needs simultaneously any longer. Medical progress in the presence of budget restraints makes that certain. All of our rationing choices will be unpleasant. When we talk, then, about the imposed choices of rationing, the only fair standard can be a *comparative* one. The question cannot only be, What will we give up if, say, we use age as a rationing standard? The answer to that one is easy: a great deal. Instead, the question should be, How would the use of age as a standard of limiting health care compare with other unpleasant methods of limitation? We need to pit the methods of rationing against each other, not against the ideal world of unlimited resources in which we all wish we lived.

If we must limit health care, what are the choices available to us? We have, I suggest, only two general approaches available to us: individual or categorical decisions (though each admits of variations, to which I will return). The first approach I will consider is that of individual decision making. By that I mean the making of rationing decisions based on the condition of an individual patient and determined by the physician charged with the care of the patient. On the basis of the most common formulation of this position, we can decide, that is, that we will try to limit the provision of health care by withholding useless or only marginally useful treatment, giving the patient only that treatment that will genuinely be of benefit to the patient; and we will leave the determination of what counts as such care to the individual judgment of the attending physician in consultation with the patient and his family. Under such a system, physicians can of course be exhorted to use expensive resources carefully and thoughtfully and be educated about the most cost-effective ways of treating patients. In the end, however, the final choice is left to individual physician judgment, based on those personal standards that the physician believes most medically appropriate and morally acceptable. Inevitably, one would expect highly subjective quality of life judgments to come into play in individual decision making.

However attractive, I do not believe that an attempt to ration or limit care by this method is either conceptually coherent, professionally acceptable, or economically effective. It is conceptually incoherent because it makes the assumption that the choice of the efficacious, cost-effective treatment for each individual patient will add up, in the aggregate, to affordable health care in general. This is reminiscent of an "invisible hand" argument. Yet our emerging problem is not just that of eliminating useless or wasteful treatment but of eventually limiting even efficacious treatment because of its high cost. It may well turn out in that case that what is best for each and every individual is not necessarily a societally affordable health care system in the aggregate. This will be particularly true when, on the frontier of aging or individual need, more and more expensive, albeit efficacious, treatments are developed. An artificial heart may someday be an indicated and efficacious treatment for many individuals; that does not mean we will be able to afford to add them to the Medicare entitlement program. There is, in short, no necessary correlation between individually effective and socially affordable treatment.

Individual decision making should also be understood as being professionally unacceptable. If the purpose of a therapeutic decision is to advance the welfare of the patient, and only that, then there is no problem. It is consistent with that long-standing tradition of medical ethics that places individual patient welfare at its center. But if the ultimate purpose of the decision making is the societal goal of rationing care, then the physician is being placed in an untenable position, that of a clear conflict of interest.

Is the physician meant to serve the economic needs of society or the health needs of his or her patient? If the former, then the physicians will be sacrificing the traditional ethic; if the latter, then the goal of rationing is likely to be sacrificed. Of course the best of all possible worlds is one magically superintended by the "invisible hand" mentioned above; that is, the best decision for each patient turns out, with perfect coincidence, to be exactly what society can afford for health care. There is no reason to believe we live in that world, or that we ever will. The inherently unlimited nature of medical need guarantees that we will not. Even if we could overcome that problem, we would be left with another hazard, that of physician bias or capricious behavior with patients. There is by no means a consensus among physicians how best to treat each patient, much less consensus on how much should be spent on each patient. A rationing system that left the patient to the mercies of that situation would be to invite some unjust, prejudiced decisions and also to eliminate both visibility and accountability in the making of decisions.

The final reason why rationing should not be left to individual physician discretion is that it will almost certainly prove to be economically unworkable in that form. We have a considerable body of experience over the past twenty years of efforts to get physicians to behave in more cost-effective says. Despite those efforts, almost every form of cost containment has failed; none has had any but the most modest success. In great part that has been because physicians have been unwilling or unable to radically change their behavior. They have been intimidated by malpractice fears, subtly coerced by patient demands, economically seduced by incentives to provide expensive treatment, and lured forward by the need for "quality" care and the use of state-of-the-art diagnostic and therapeutic technology.

The availability of constantly improved technology—steadily raising the standard of what counts as acceptable care to a still-higher level—means that physicians are tethered to medical progress. They can ignore the latest and the best only at their professional and moral hazard. Note that I do not invoke here an argument from cupidity, that doctors simply want to make money and that is why cost containment has failed. Doubtless that is some small part of the truth. But the larger part is that we have a health care system that provides numerous incentives, apart from personal gain, to provide expensive treatment and to resist limits of any kind. Both the moral and the technological logic of contemporary medicine works in favor of more, not less, treatment, in favor of unlimited, not limited, treatment. There is the powerful ethic (partially religious in its roots) of preserving and extending life, an ethic that says that, when in doubt, it is better to treat than not to treat. However attractive for reasons of tradition, I conclude that a dependence upon individual case-by-case decisions to effect the rationing and limitation of health care expenditures simply cannot be effective or just. We must then look in another direction.

The second approach I will call "categorical," the use of objective and public standards applied uniformly to all similar cases. Two types of categorical choices can be distinguished, one that I will call "*flexible* categorical," the other "*fixed* categorical." By "flexible" I mean the establishment of clear and firm standards for treatment, and the limitation of treatment, but a delegation to the individual physician of the determination of whether a patient does or does not meet the standards and whether exceptions to them should be made for some patients. I take it that, for example, standards for admission to ICUs often fall into this category; there are official standards, but it is left to individual physicians to apply them.

The advantage of categorical standards that are flexible is, of course, that they allow for the possibility of recognizing individual patient differences and taking account of them. Their obvious disadvantage is that, if interpreted too liberally and loosely, they may not achieve their purpose, that of rationing and limiting care. There is also another potential problem. If the most difficult rationing decisions are likely to be those that require the denial of potentially *effective* treatment, then flexible standards will become even more problematic. They will invite more "exceptions" and evasions of a kind likely, in the aggregate, to defeat their general rationing purpose.

I mention the possibility of categorical standards that are *flexible* because they will strike many as the ideal compromise situation. They would seem to provide a middle ground between rigid and impersonal standards, on the one hand, and uncontrolled individual physician discretion, on the other. They are certainly worth considering, particularly if the right balance between firmness and flexibility could be determined. Their most likely general use, often commended, would come in devising ways of assessing likely treatment outcomes and then specifying treatment acceptability based on that assessment. One could, for instance, specify that a patient would not be eligible for reimbursement for a particular treatment unless, based on solid evidence, there was a high prospective likelihood that the patient would benefit from the treatment and that the benefit would be of long duration. Standards of this kind have been devised, for instance, for organ transplantation, and have been proposed for other forms of treatment.

We should, however, hesitate before enthusiastically embracing that approach. It can in fact be exceedingly difficult to devise good predictive criteria of treatment outcome, and the need to do so across a wide spectrum of treatments (necessary for broad rationing) would be a daunting one. Nonetheless, I do not want to deny that some forms of outcome assessment may be devised, and many efforts are underway to do just that. Assuming that the technical problems might be overcome, we are then left with the application problem. Once we have some practice guidelines, do we leave it to individual physician discretion to determine whether to use a particular regimen or therapy—to decide whether and to what extent the patient fits the standards and whether exceptions are in order—or do we demand that the physician uniformly and rigidly apply the guidelines? If we choose the former, then we open the way to abuse, evasion, or systematic ambiguity, and rationing plans that simply fail in practice. If, by contrast, we opt for the latter, we seem committed to rigidity and an unacceptable ignoring of individual differences.

There is no wholly happy or clean way out of this dilemma. If we feel we can afford a form of rationing that may not work, or not work well, we can use flexible categorical standards, adjusting them technically from time to time, and applying various pressures and sanctions to physicians who seem to regularly, or casually, bend the standards with their patients. But if we feel we *must* make rationing work, then we will be forced in the direction of more rigid standards. They will have to be rigid in the conditions under which some forms of treatment are to be reimbursed and rigid in allowing the physician little if any discretion in interpreting the treatment guidelines; that is, we will be led to *fixed* categorical standards.

I believe we will sooner or later need such fixed standards. What would be their advantage? By erecting an immovable barrier, they would be effective in setting limits. They would not have the inevitably permeable and porous quality that are likely with flexible barriers. They would be public standards, known to all and applicable to all. That would have the advantage of removing any suspicion of biased, capricious private standards that would be the case with hidden, individual case-by-case physician and patient standards. Their public nature would allow accountability. We could determine with relative ease whether they were being observed, and we could penalize those who failed to abide by them. They would be fair standards, in the sense that they would apply to everyone. If established by legislative bodies, they would be democratically established standards, open to public debate, to change based on experience, and could be reflective of community values and determination. That is hardly possible with private standards established out of the public eye by physicians (including patients and families) at the bedside.

The Meaning of Old Age and Its Place in Allocation Decisions

Would such *fixed* categorical standards be discriminatory? Would they be ageist? I must leave to legal scholars the question of what counts, legally, as unacceptable or unconstitutional discrimination. I will only note that the Medicare program itself is age-discriminatory, requiring that one be sixty-five to be eligible for its benefits. Since it is, moreover, the only entitlement program that does not require a financial need determination for eligibility, it is an exceptional program, conferring upon one age group—the elderly—a benefit conferred on no other age group. To claim (1) that it would be an act of discrimination against the elderly to use age as a limiting *standard* for a program itself based on age discrimination; and also to claim (2) that a *limitation* of an entitlement program that is itself already far more generous than any program available to any other group in the entire population would be unfairly discriminatory to the beneficiaries of that group—well, I find that a strange idea of discrimination. It is a wonderful example both of the old principle that to those who have shall be given and of why the well off become better off: give one group a special program not given to others, then claim that any restriction on that program is a special and odious form of discrimination against them.

Might we not, however, concede that the Medicare program itself is indeed a special, even age-based and thus age-discriminatory, program and yet balk at the idea of using age as a fixed standard for denying care once in that program? Indeed we might, but at the price of a double standard, and a suspicious one at that: the making of a uniquely open-ended claim on society. Would not the use of an age limit also imply that there was something special about a person's chronological age? Yes, it would. It would be to say that, once a person had reached a certain age—that is, had weathered a full, though not necessarily, finished life—it would not be unreasonable or unfair to say that enough was enough on eligibility to a public entitlement. We are not morally required as a society to make an *unlimited* commitment to provide every elderly person with *whatever* individual curative medicine is devised by technological progress at *whatever* the cost to extend the life of that person from old age to advanced old age. We are only required to provide a reasonable level of care. We may differ on what counts as "reasonable," but I can not imagine how any such standard could encompass unlimited care *regardless* of cost or societal burden. What kind of elderly person would make a claim of that kind?

The ultimate issue here is not the simple provision of health care for the elderly. We might be able to provide a reasonably decent level of care by current standards if we were willing to accept the present level of technology and intensity of care and not insist on constant progress or improvement. That is the *source* of the problem I am trying to address: the desire for more and better technology. To reverse that trend would mean, for instance, vigorously resisting the powerful impetus to extend high-technology procedures to the elderly, now conspicuously visible in dialysis, organ transplants, and coronary bypass surgery, for instance. I am simply contending that, if we choose to support such aggressive medical progress, then we cannot simultaneously promise the elderly an unlimited entitlement to its benefits. I take that to be an unreasonable promise. We do not know what that progress may turn up, and we have no assurance whatsoever that its benefits will of necessity be affordable. How can we responsibly say to the elderly, or any other age group for that matter: no matter what medical progress creates, or what it costs, we will give it to you.

This is only to say that we can no longer afford a highly individualistic policy if, at the same time, we insist upon the unlimited pursuit of technological progress to meet individual needs. We should instead begin devising policy with some more general view of the common good of all age groups in view. In the provision of health care to the elderly, my approach would be to see if we could achieve a public consensus on what counts as a reasonable level of health care for the elderly and reasonable limits on that care. Instead of working with individual needs and interests, I propose we work with the idea of trying to help the elderly as a group avoid a premature death and achieve a decently long, full life span. While individual elderly may want more, and could even benefit from more, we will have done our duty to them in our public-entitlement programs if we could get them through a full life span, by which I mean the late seventies or early eighties. We should simultaneously work to greatly improve long-term and home care for the frail elderly and make a variety of other needed changes to improve the daily life of the elderly.

The ultimate goal would be a coherent entitlement program for the elderly, one that better achieved a balance among the various needs of the elderly (correcting the present bias toward acute care) and one that made certain that the elderly, as an age group, would not take a disproportionate share of resources, those needed by other age groups for their welfare. Compared with the present Medicare program, some individuals might suffer and be worse off, those who might benefit from some future technological benefit that might extend their lives into the late eighties and nineties. But I am convinced the elderly *as a group* would be better off, as would other age groups as well.

No society that worked to improve the overall welfare of the elderly, that tried to help them avoid a premature death, that provided good long-term and home-care programs, could be accused of discriminating against the elderly if it set some limits on its entitlements to expensive forms of high-technology medical care. To adopt such a policy would only be to acknowledge that we cannot do everything, that it will be impossible to burn our economic candle at both ends, trying to provide basic social and nursing services while at the same time chasing endless technological progress to extend life. The price of having the former is to radically curtail the latter.

I apply the same reasoning, analogously, to other age groups. Instead of asking how we can meet each and every curative need for each and every individual— a hopeless quest—we should instead ask what kinds of policies would most generally benefit different age groups. We should aim to find a good balance between caring and curative needs and seek programs that would be in principle affordable. There is a well-known and desperate need at present for better health care for children, not to mention the need for improvement in a whole range of educational and social services for children. It would be much more sensible and helpful in the long-run to provide improved prenatal care for mothers, and better access to immunization, health promotion programs, and primary care for children, than to invest in improved high-technology neonatal programs. Toward that end, it would not be an act of discrimination against children to set a policy that limited neonatal intensive care to those babies with a very high certainty of benefit—for example, by use of a weight limit, or by the use of firm outcome assessment predictors, before allowing a child in a neonatal intensive care unit—while working simultaneously to improve the full range of other needed services. We would, analogously, do much better in the long run to reduce heart disease in adults by health promotion programs and better diets than by working to improve the outcome of expensive heart transplants.

We are, in any event, too intimidated by charges of "ageism." If "ageism" means the unfair stereotyping of the elderly, a discrimination against the elderly based solely on age, then what I am proposing will not qualify for that charge. It is, for one thing, not stereotyping to say that, as a group (and one with a special entitlement program), the elderly incur health care costs considerably greater than other age groups and that those costs will increase in the years ahead. That is a fair generalization (and not unfair simply because *some* elderly will be healthy all of their lives and die inexpensively in their sleep). The responsible establishment of policy requires that we attend to that generalization; it matters in allocation decisions.

Of course what I am proposing is a form of discrimination against the elderly, but the question is whether it is justifiable. I have given my reasons for thinking that it would be: the value and dignity of the elderly is not denied, and limits are proposed not because the elderly are not worth the money but because some effective way must be found to take account of other health and societal claims as well. To refuse to discriminate against the elderly would, in effect, allow their needs to dominate all others, a form of de facto discrimination against other age groups. To agree that we will need to set some limits on health care for the elderly (as many are now willing to do), but to want to do so in a way that does not discriminate against them, is to ask for little more than a way of squaring the circle. What matters is whether the reasons for discrimination are moral and just and whether, by the time we are ready to discriminate, we have done as well as is justly and human possible for the elderly *in a situation of scarce resources.*

I want to mention another reason to be concerned by too heavy a focus on anti-ageism as a basis for a philosophy of elderly health care. I have come to think that the campaign against ageism is one that, for all of its many political strengths, may inadvertently be robbing old age of the possibility of any deep, common cultural meaning. Why should that be the case? By its heavy emphasis on the heterogeneity of the elderly rather than on their common and general features, the anti-ageism movement has minimized those characteristics of aging that have always been needed to make sense of old age as part of the life cycle and in the biographical life of the individual. Those traits include a recognition that the elderly must pass social leadership over to the young, that the social significance of old age lies in its capacity for generativity and for transmitting on of the culture to a younger age group, and that old age is a time to collect and complete the self, not to pretend that meaning can be had only in more life (a losing cause if ever there was one).

An anti-ageist philosophy, worried mainly about prejudice toward the old, has too little room for the other side of the coin: finding a way to think about what it means to grow old as part of our human condition, a general problem and one that can never properly be grasped by a reductionistic individuality stressing the diversity of the elderly. When that kind of individualism is combined with a no less individualistic medicine—invariably oriented toward cure because, among other things, it reduces our dependence on each other—the result can be oppressive. It is a medicine slow to accept our human fate, which is aging and death. Not only do we need, then, to generalize about the elderly in order to establish sensible policy toward them; if we do not generalize, recognizing only individuals, we will fail to find for the elderly a meaningful place in our society.

Devising Health Care in a Pluralistic Society

Fair and reasonable standards for the allocation of health care resources for the elderly will require substantive societal agreement on at least three points: the social significance of old age, the place of old age in the life cycle, and what would count as a discharge of our reasonable public obligations to the elderly. Yet any proposal for substantive agreement on much of anything in our pluralistic society is often greeted with suspicion, if not hostility. "Thin theories of the good"— agreement on mainly procedural goods—are the most popular these days, in great part because many believe that they are the best we can do in a pluralistic society and the most we *should* do in order best to preserve freedom and cultural diversity. That is probably one reason why anti-ageism as a philosophy of old age is so attractive: it commits us to very little about the common features of old age but does supposedly allow us to combat all forms of discrimination against the elderly. Yet, as I tried to suggest above, it is too thin for meaningful policy purposes.

Could we come to agree on a substantive standard? We will not know until we make the effort. I tried in *Setting Limits* to work with the idea of a "natural life span" as a way of establishing some reasonable limits to publicly supported health care for the elderly. I was attempting to capture with that notion the idea of a full life, one marked by the achievement of many, if not all, of the ordinary goals of a life. If the health care system could get us up through a full life, I argued, it would have done well by us and would inflict no injustice if it set some limits to its duties thereafter. I did not invent the idea of a "full life." I was instead working with some ordinary observations of life, especially the common reaction to the death of an elderly person, very different from the death of a child or young person. In our culture and every other one I have heard of, the death of an elderly person at the end of a long life is not considered a tragedy but is understood as a sad, but eventually inevitable, part of life. All cultures, moreover, have some concept of a 'full' life, that is, one marked by achievement of the ordinary range of life goals—work, family, love, and so on. I want to build on this common notion as a basis for public policy, making the goal of policy the avoidance of premature death and getting everyone to the point where they would, on the whole, have lived out a "full life."

Many rejected this proposal—and the mode of thinking behind it—altogether. Is it not the case, they responded, that each elderly person is different, that they do not have identical life plans and goals, and that chronological age does not tell us where they are in either their biological or biographical life? I understand that perfectly well; but it is, in fact, irrelevant to my proposal that the elderly vary as individuals. It is the fact that they are varied *elderly* that should count for policy purposes. The elderly are different from each other, but not *totally* different. If they have lived until the late seventies or early eighties, it is most likely that most of them will have lived out most of the ordinary possibilities and opportunities of life. For policy purposes, especially for the allocation of resources, it is reasonable to attempt to meet the *general* needs of an age group, not the individual, idiosyncratic needs.

Hence, my conclusion: it is a *reasonable* goal to attempt to help each elderly person live a long, full life, one, in general, long enough to accomplish the ordinary range of life's possibilities; and it is unreasonable to tailor public policy to the wide range and inexhaustible variety of individual needs, especially the need (or desire) to live an unlimited life regardless of the burdens it places upon one's fellow citizens. It is reasonable, in short, to ask the public to help one live out a long life, and eighty is a long life. But it is not reasonable to make the demand one person I once debated felt entitled to: an artificial heart at great public expense at ninety-five in order to live to be one hundred if that is what one's personal life goals aspire to.

Here we see the importance of the need to generalize about the elderly—rather than treat them as heterogeneous individuals—as a necessary condition for fair public policy. An age limit would be, in one sense, unfair to some, those whose life for whatever reason was nowhere near in their own eyes to being a "full" life. But if the goal of the policy in general was to enable the elderly as a group to (*a*) avoid premature death and have the opportunity to live out the seventies and (*b*) to provide the elderly with decent long-term and home care regardless of age, it would be a decent policy. Not only would it aspire to an age that exceeds the present average life expectancy (seventy-five), but it would also provide a richer range of benefits than is now available up to, and beyond that age (eliminating only life-extending high-technology medicine beyond the late seventies or early eighties). At the least it could be considered a good trade-off. It would, in that sense, be a fair policy to the elderly as a group. To demand that policy orient itself to individual life goals is to demand what no society should have to provide: captivity to individualistic, open-ended aspirations. We have a personal right to such aspirations, but we can not demand that our fellow citizens provide the money for us to pursue them. We can only ask of them that we be given a decent, basic opportunity, one that will allow us to achieve most, even if not all, of our individual purposes.

This approach does presuppose that we can, if we try, come to some social consensus on the main ingredients of a full life and set some generally reasonable age by which we agree that for most people most of its parts will be in place. It also presupposes, in the case of the idea of a " full" life, that there already exist in the culture and its traditions the elements necessary to fashion such a consensus. Will there be easy agreement on that consensus? No. Will there be some people who will not accept the agreement achieved by others? Yes. But must there be a perfect consensus in order to establish a fair policy? No. Our political system is designed to accommodate itself to less than perfect consensus; and it is always possible for those who dissent to re-open the public debate and change the consensus.

In setting an age limit for health care entitlement purposes, we can, that is, attempt to use the same kind of political process we use for other social decisions, the same one we used for fixing 65 as the beginning age for Medicare, 16 for gaining a driver's license, 21 for drinking, and 35 to be President. Each of those numbers is, to some degree, arbitrary; but each represents a more or less successful effort to enact some generalization about age into actual policy. Each such generalization embodies some picture of the human good into a policy formulation. It does not deny individual differences, but it does imply the capacity to come to some agreement about what is on the whole good for people.

Why is there such a strong presumption among many that any effort to capture some notion of a general good of people, one rooted in chronological age, is so hazardous? My answer: because we have too easily capitulated to the idea that only individual good really counts morally and because it is thought impossible (and hazardous also) to fashion a conception of, and shape a consensus on, a social good that builds on general human characteristics. Yet there is a great hazard in avoiding the effort to devise a consensus on some social goods, especially (we should now know) medical goods. We are held hostage to individual demands and needs, the very nature of which in the medical arena is to be open ended, in principle subject to no limits of any kind. An attempt to build a fair policy in the face of that obstacle is doomed in the absence of any willingness to work with general characteristics and reasonable group standards. That is one reason why efforts to develop a minimally adequate standard of care for all age groups have failed; the very range of elasticity of medical demands and needs effectively thwart such efforts.

For this very reason also, there cannot be a successful effort to devise a fair standard of entitlement for individual elderly people based upon their individuality. The combination of their individual differences and a steady need-expanding medical progress will always defeat such efforts; no coherent, consistent policy can be devised. In devising health policy for the elderly, then, we can see with great clarity the impossibility of developing policy in the absence of some rich conception of the good of the elderly as a group and the inevitable failure of a policy approach that would focus on a combination of individual needs and procedural justice. That approach is falling apart before our eyes. One way or another, we will be forced back to some supposedly old-fashioned questions, even if we may come up with some more modern answers. What is a " good life" for the elderly? What should a " good society" seek for the elderly? What meaning is to be found in old age as the completion of the life cycle? How can we learn to live with the fact we are mortal creatures? How can we learn to live with resource limits in our old age? Those remain the important questions.

Contributors

Robert J. Barnet, M.D., is Clinical Professor of Medicine in the School of Medicine, University of Nevada, Reno.

Howard Brody, M.D., Ph.D., is Professor of Family Practice and Director of the Center for Ethics, Humanities and Life Sciences at Michigan State University.

James M. Buchanan, Ph.D., is Advisory General Director of the Center for Study of Public Choice, Harris University Professor at George Mason University and Nobel Laureate in Economics, 1986.

Daniel Callahan, Ph.D., is Director of The Hasting Center, Briarcliff Manor, New York.

Thomas R. Cole, Ph.D., is Professor and Graduate Program Director in the Institute for the Medical Humanities, University of Texas Medical Branch, Galveston.

Janet A. Coy, M.A., P.T., is Assistant Professor of Physical Therapy Education in the College of Health Related Professions, State University of New York Health Sciences Center at Syracuse.

Leonard M. Fleck, Ph.D., is Associate Professor in the Department of Philosophy and the Center for Ethics, Humanities and Life Sciences, Michigan State University.

Chris Hackler, Ph.D., is Director of the Division of Medical Humanities at the University of Arkansas for Medical Sciences.

John R. Hardwig, Ph.D., is Professor and Chair of the Department of Philosophy and Professor of Medical Ethics in the James H. Quillen College of Medicine, East Tennessee State University.

Nancy S. Jecker, Ph.D., is Associate Professor in the Department of Medical History and Ethics, School of Medicine, University of Washington.

Robert L. Kane, M.D., M.P.H., holds the Minnesota Chair in Long Term Care and Aging, Institute for Health Services Research, and is former Dean of the School of Public Health, University of Minnesota.

Robert A. Pearlman, M.D., M.P.H., is Associate Professor of Medicine and Health Services, Division of Gerontology and Geriatric Medicine, University of Washington.

Stephen G. Post, Ph.D., is Associate Professor in the Center for Biomedical Ethics, School of Medicine, Case Western Reserve University.

Reinhard Priester, J.D., is a Research Associate at the Center for Biomedical Ethics, University of Minnesota.

Jonathan Schonsheck, Ph.D., is Professor of Philosophy at LeMoyne College.

Sharon E. Sytsma, Ph.D., is Assistant Professor in the Department of Philosophy, Northern Illinois University.

Index

Aaron, Henry, 94, 134, 186
Abel-Smith, B., 130
"Accountable Health Plans," 191–194
Achenbaum, W. A., 21
Adams, John, 23
Advance directives, 5
AFDC, *see* Aid to Families with Dependent Children
AGE, *see* Americans for Generational Equity
Ageism, 26, 27, 39, 40, 93, 125
Agency for Health Care Policy and Research, 4
Aging, 27; meaning of, 12, 76, 85, 87, 108; "modernization" of, 79, 85; of population, 11, 73, 121; philosophical conception of, 76–87; policy, 20
Aid to Families with Dependent Children, 99
AIDS, 152
Alienation, 25
Allocation, of resources, 82, 95, 103
Alzheimer's disease, 43, 46–48
AMA, *see* American Medical Association
Patient's Bill of Rights (American Hospital Association), 156
American Medical Association, 151; Code of Medical Ethics, 133; House of Delegates, 133; Principles of Medical Ethics, 156, 159–160
Americans for Generational Equity, 19
Autonomy, 45, 50, 52, 93, 98, 110, 150–151, 184, 162, 201, 204; patient, 44, 149, 155–156; principle of, 184; professional, 1, 147–149, 160, 163

Baby-boom generation, 11, 19
Barer, M. L., 10,

Barth, Karl, 39, 40
Bartling, William, 96
Bell, Nora K., 83–84
Beneficence, 102, 125, 132, 147, 156, 194
Binstock, Robert H., 37
Birth rate, 11
Bismarck, Otto von, 201
Bobbitt, P., 95
Bodily integrity, 163
Botelho, Richard, 164
Bradley, Senator Bill, 29
Brain death, 116
Brock, Dan W., 85
Brody, Howard, 13
Brody, Baruch, 93–96
Brown, Lawrence, 178, 179
Butler, R. N., 39

Calabresi, G., 95
Callahan, Daniel, 12, 13, 21–25, 37–38, 71–74, 76, 78, 80, 84–89, 94, 97–98, 101–103, 107–108, 111–112, 115–117, 119–120, 151, 200–202
Canadian health care system, 9, 146, 151, 187–190
Capital formation, 65
Catholic Health Association, 150
Charity ethic, 149
Childress, James F., 37
Christianity, 37
Chronic care, 107–108; *see also* Long-term care
Churchill, Larry, 86–88, 124, 150
Cicero, 26
Clark, Philip, 164
Clinical judgment, 103, 187

Clinical protocols, 187; clinical/economic protocols, 103
Clinton Administration, 191
Clinton, Hillary, 191
Clinton health care proposal, 194
Codes of ethics, 156; see also American Medical Association
Cole, Thomas, 12
Common good, 219
Communitarianism, 6, 12, 22, 39, 184
Community, 76, 159; roles of, 170; sense of, 158, 164
Comparative standard, for evaluating rationing choices, 214
Compassion, 170
Competence, 116; mild impairment of, 116–117
Confidentiality, 156
Consequentialism, 71
Consumer sovereignty, 58, 60, 147–149, 161, 164
Coronary bypass surgery, 219
Cost, -containment, 10, 22, 94, 101, 103, 147, 148, 155, 180, 192, 216; -sharing, 157–158; -shifting, 2, 4, 6, 148, 189
Covenant, 12, 37–38; intergenerational, 34
Coy, Janet, 13
Cruzan, Nancy, 187
Crystal, Stephen, 33

Daniels, Norman, 22, 24, 25, 38, 51, 85, 87, 94, 97–98, 102–103, 123–125, 149, 153, 163
Danis, Marion, 150
Death, attitudes toward, 123; meaning and significance of, 23, 27, 76; philosophical conception of 76, 78–79, 81, 84, 86–87
Defensive medicine, 3
Dementia, 11, 46, 116
Department of Health and Human Services, 4
Dialysis, 94, 96, 123, 131, 219
Discrimination, 126, 128, 182, 221

Distribution, of resources, 23; of social goods, 29
Distributive justice, 89; see also Justice
Duties, of aged, 38; to identifiable individuals, 96, 100; intergenerational, 24; special, 126–127; of young, 38; see also Obligations

Ecclesiastes, 26
Economic value, end-uses of, 57–58
Eddy, David, 153
Efficiency, 62, 99, 155, 162
Emergency care, 116, 131
Engelhardt, H. T. 135
Equal access, principle of, 136
Equal entitlement, 136
Equal opportunity, 24, 34, 125, 149, 188
Equal regard, 35
Equal worth, 136
Equality, 125, 170; as a goal in basic health care, 138; of opportunity, 125, 188; of persons, 122; principle of, 136
"Equitable access," 177
Erikson, Erik, 29
"Ethical individualism," see Individualism
Ethics committees, 44
Etzioni, Amitai, 34
Evans, R. G., 10

Fair access, 152, 162–163
Fairness, 137, 159, 181, 193; within families, 50; between generations, 12
Family practitioners, 173
Family law, 52–53
Family, 43–54
Fee-for-service, 157
Feminism, 35
Fidelity, 147
Fleck, Leonard, 10, 13, 202
Flexner Report, 160
Freedom, 35, 135, 158; of choice, 9, 161
Fried, Charles, 100
Full life, 219, 222–223

Function, 149, 200–201, 208
Futile treatment, 36, 134

General medical care, 116
Generational equity, 12, 19–20, 29, 34
Generational conflict, 33
Geriatric medical care, 80
Germany, health care system of, 8, 151, 162, 201
Gerontological Society of America, 33
Gerontology, 200
Global budgets, 187, 189, 190, 192
"Good life," 224
"Good society," 224

Hadorn, D., 188
Hardwig, John, 12
Hawaii, health care system of, 8, 151
Health, as a form of secular salvation, 28
Health care, individual-centered view of, 151; community-centered view of, 151, 173; quality of, 154, 162, 192, 205–207; as force for social unity, 159; as a social good, 93; policy, 214; resources, 132, 137; values, 145, 177
Health care expenditures, 88, 177; for business, 3; as percentage of US GDP, 1; as percentage of Canadian GNP, 189; total for people sixty-five and over, 21
Health care reform, 4–11, 154, 182, 191
Health care services, basic, 131, 138; nonbasic, 132–133, 137; employer-financed, 151; right of access to, 170; universal access to, 147, 154, 156
Health education, 131
Health insurance, 157; catastrophic coverage, 199; mandated employment-based coverage, 7; national, 7, 8, 174; nursing home coverage, 11; play-or-pay system, 7; private, 6, 8; risk pooling, 6; risk rating, 7, 191; single-payer system, 188; universal coverage, 6, 154
Health maintenance organizations, 5, 124; see also Managed care

Health Professions Education Act of 1963, 149
Health Reform Task Force, 191
Hebrews, ancient, 37
Heteronomy, 50
High-technology medicine, 129, 130, 180, 190
Hill-Burton Program, 149
Hippocratic tradition, 150
Home care, 103, 173, 223
Howard, Coby, 180–184

ICU, 134–135
Incompetence, 44–45
Individualism, 39, 146–147, 150–151, 221
Informed consent, 155
Institute of Medicine, 154

Jecker, Nancy S., 13, 80, 86
Jefferson, Thomas, 23, 25
Jonsen, A., 127
Judaism, 37
"Just Caring," 191
Justice, 24, 34, 95, 127–138, 156, 170, 174, 182, 186, 192; nonideal, 186, 194; the original position, 126; social, 6, 78; veil of ignorance, 22, 63–65, 93; see also Generational equity and Distributive justice

Kane, Robert, 12
Kant, Immanuel, 50
Kilner, J., 126
Kitzhaber, J., 179
Kohli, Martin, 25
Koop, C. Everett, 36

Laissez-faire, 67
Law, 101
Levels of care, 116
Lexicographic preferences, 60–65
Liberalism, 28, 110

Libertarianism, 96
Life course, 24–25; life cycle, 26, 224; *see also* "Natural life span"
Life-expectancy, 37
Life-extending treatment, 22, 74, 77, 80, 83, 85, 112, 117–118; decision to forego, 13
Life history, 127
Life plan, 24, 109, 112
Life, stages of, 23, 26
Life story, 107
Life, value of, 93, 122
Long term care, 11, 23, 88, 98, 103, 116–117, 199, 200–203, 223; financial burdens of, 47; insurance for, 202–203

Managed care, 5, 124, 147–148, 157, 161, 188, 192
Managed competition, 188
Massachusetts, 151
May, William F., 38
Meaning, 76
Means-testing, 9
Medicaid, 4, 6–8, 10, 81, 99, 129, 149–150, 154, 163, 173, 178, 180–181, 186
Medicare, 2, 8, 11, 19, 36, 98, 126, 131, 148–149, 162, 171, 199, 215, 218, 224
Medicine, goals of, 87, 115, 123
Mehlman, Maxwell, 94
Mercy killing, 35
Middle Ages, 38
Midwives, 173
Minnesota, 151
Mitchell, George, 169
Moody, Harry R., 28, 123–124
Moral assessment of policy alternatives, 71–72, 83
Moral community, 12, 27–28
Moral conversation, 109, 193
Moral inquiry, 109
Moral principles, 71
Moral psychology, 86
Morone, James, 148

Morreim, Haavi, 95
Magnetic Resonance Imaging, 180, 190

Narcissism, 38
National Leadership Commission on Health Care, 151
"Natural life span," 22, 23, 74, 77, 83, 98, 111–112, 116–117, 119–120, 123, 125, 222; *see also* Full life
Natural talents, 112
Negotiated fee schedules, 189
Neoconservativism, 110
New York, 151
New York Times, 169
Norway, 146, 151, 159
Nurse practitioners, 173

Obligations, of benevolence, 132; of charity, 132; intergenerational, 34; patient, 52; social, 102; special, 49
Old age, as biological limit, 23; meaning of, 22, 26–28, 214, 218, 221; productivity in, 29; virtues and obligations of, 22
Oregon health care reform plan, 10, 134, 151, 178–179, 185–188, 190
Organ transplants, 219
Outcomes assessment, 217, 220

Palliative care, 23, 79, 96, 107, 108, 116, 131, 155
Paternalism, 96, 155
Patient advocacy, 147–148, 156–157
Patient education, 3
Patient-centered ethics, 48
Pauly, Mark, 155
Pearlman, Robert A., 13
"Life Plan Peer Network," 13, 109–112
Pepper Commission, 151, 203
Persistent Vegetative State, patients in, 116, 132
Pharmacists, 173
Physicians for a National Health Program, 169

Pifer, Alan, 29
Post, Stephen, 12
Poverty, 149, 199
Powell, Anthony, 27
Premature death, 77, 99, 219–220
Prenatal care, 181
Preston, Samuel H., 33
Preventive health care, 3, 129
Primary care, 131
Primary goods, 110
Priorities, 75
Privacy, 204
Proxy decision makers, 44, 48, 54
Proxy decisions, 43–44, 48–50, 52–54
Prudence, 39
"Prudential Lifespan Account," 23–24
Public policy, 71, 177
PVS, see Persistent Vegetative State, patients in

Quality of life, 13, 116, 118, 134, 179, 187–188
Quality-adjusted life years, 122, 188
Quietism, 72
Quinlan, Karen Ann, 101

Rational choice, 58
Rationing, 88, 134, 178, 214; by ability to pay, 184; ad hoc, 115; age-based, 12–13, 35, 80, 97, 99, 103, 108, 100, 111, 115, 118, 121, 124–125, 128, 218, 223; categorical standards for, 216–218; of high-technology services, 130, 137; and identifiable individuals, 101; invisible, 94, 190; of life-extending treatment for premature infants, 180; of lifesaving treatment, 94; medical-benefit standard, 134–138; "patient-centered," 129, 135, 138; protocols, 192–193; for, 216–218; moral relevance of identifiable individuals to, 101
Rawls, John, 22, 95, 109–110, 126, 170, 192, 194

Reagan, Ronald, 21
Reciprocity, 38
Redistribution of resources, 39
Reinhardt, Uwe, 192
Resentment, 127
Resources, social, 75, 100, 224
Respect, for patients, 155; for persons, 122, 124
Responsibility, financial, 157; personal 157–158
Rie, M. A., 135
Rights, 40, 125; to information, 155; to privacy, 156; to property, 132
Rosenthal, A. M., 169

Safety net, 151
Scarcity, 57, 75, 78–79, 81; absolute, 93, 181; relative, 93
Schonsheck, Jonathan, 13
Schwartz, W. B., 94, 134
Self-interest, 39
Self-respect, 109–112
Simmons, Leo W., 37
Smith, David, 171
Social advocacy, 159
Social justice, see Justice
Social resource allocation policy proposal, 74–75, 78, 85–86, 88; effect on women, 84–85
Social Security, 20, 30, 36
Social solidarity, 158–159
Social worth criteria, 134
Socialized medicine, 7
Spitter, M., 123
Suicide, 35
Supererogation, 138
Supportive care, 98
System-gaming, 187, 193–194
Systma, Sharon, 13, 101

Technological determinism, 58
The Wall Street Journal, 192
Tolerable death, 81, 124
Tradition, 40

United States, Congress, 179; federal budget deficit, 6; health care policy, 145; health care expenditures as percentage of GDP, 1; percentage of population over 65, 20; percentage of population uninsured, 4
United Kingdom, National Health Service, 159
Utilitarianism, 126
Utility, 58–59, 71

Values, 145; community, 150, 179; essential, 162–163; instrumental, 163–164

Values framework, 146, 164
Veatch, Robert, 145
Virtue, 24, 38, 39
Vitalism, 115, 118–119

Walzer, Michael, 171
Washington, D.C., 110
Welfare state, 19, 29
Wisdom, 28
Wolinsky, Frederic, 160